We dedicate this book to the memory of our friend
and colleague Alan Parker, and to Vicky, Dominic
and Freya.

**Organisation and Management
in the Public Sector**

Organisation and Management in the Public Sector

Alan Lawton · Aidan G. Rose

Pitman Publishing
128 Long Acre, London WC2E 9AN

A Division of Longman Group UK Limited

First published in 1991

British Library Cataloguing in Publication Data
Lawton, A.
  Organisation and management in the public sector.
  1. Public Sector. Management
  I. Title II. Rose, A. G.
  350

ISBN 0 273 032747

Printed in Great Britain by The Bath Press, Avon

Contents

List of figures

List of tables

Preface

The student on a course studying public sector organisations is faced with a bewildering range of literature. In recent years the volume of books, articles, journals and papers that feature on reading lists seems to have grown exponentially. In adding to this we seek to provide a book which, firstly, introduces the reader to the theoretical literature on organisations, and secondly, applies that literature to the modern British public sector. The book is intended for teachers and students on undergraduate degree courses, BTEC/Higher National programmes, and on professional courses such as the Institute of Chartered Secretaries and Administrators (ICSA).

Chapter 1 examines the development of the modern public sector and explores some of the features which distinguish the public sector from the private sector. It also introduces the concept of public sector management.

Chapter 2 explores a number of values and concepts that are of particular importance in the public sector, in particular, the distinction between policy and administration, and the notion of accountability.

Chapter 3 examines the idea of bureaucracy, its features and how it has been used in modern public sector organisations. The literature on the dysfunctions of bureaucracy is also considered.

In Chapter 4 we look at formal approaches to organisations. The chapter includes discussion of the work of the classical school of management, and systems and contingency theories of organisations, and goes on to examine the formal expression of organisational structures in terms of organisational charts.

Following this, Chapter 5 examines the informal side of organisations, the importance of the individual, groups, culture and discretion.

Chapter 6 discusses power and conflict. Theories of power within society are examined alongside power within organisations. Power in the context of decision making is analysed as is the notion of conflict characterising organisations.

Chapter 7 examines the leadership factor, theories of leadership and what is expected of a leader in the public sector.

In Chapter 8 theories of motivation are linked to psychological explanations of individual behaviour examined in Chapter 5.

Chapter 9 looks at planning and decision making. It examines prescriptions as to how organisations should plan and decide and also looks at how they behave in practice.

Chapter 10 is concerned with resourcing the public sector. It includes three case studies on central government, local government, and the National Health Service.

Chapter 11 brings together a number of themes which can collectively be called the 'new agenda' for the public sector. It examines the idea of how organisations respond to change in theory and returns to the theme of public management that was introduced in the first chapter.

Chapter 12 examines how public sector organisations have responded to the new agenda through the commitment to a number of themes such as consumerism. It also looks at the proposition that a new orientation has taken place within public sector organisations.

Chapter 13 examines some current themes which seem likely to be of continuing importance in the 1990s. It also raises doubts concerning the scope of, and commitment to, the changes that we examine in Chapters 11 and 12.

At the end of the book we provide two sections that, we hope, will be of particular help to the reader. Firstly, in Appendix A we provide a guide for further study. This is intended to supplement the guides to further reading provided at the end of each chapter by listing potential sources of information which are likely to help the reader regarding current and future developments. Secondly, Appendix B offers some exercises which will enable the reader to apply the material covered in the book.

We owe a debt to numerous people. In particular we wish to mention students on public administration courses at Teesside Polytechnic between 1982 and 1988; those at Newcastle-upon-Tyne Polytechnic since 1987; and those at the Polytechnic of Wales since 1988. A number of colleagues at those institutions have also provided valuable assistance and comment on drafts: they include Paul Crompton, Eileen Gill, Paul Griffiths, Paul McGregor (now at the Northern Development Company) and Anthea West. We have also benefited from the assistance of some first-class librarians, including Austin McCarthy, and the staff in the Government Publications Centre at Newcastle-upon-Tyne Polytechnic. We are also indebted to the many anonymous civil servants and local government officers who have provided useful material. Although we could not have completed the book without the help of all these people, as well as the assistance and persistence of Penelope Woolf at Pitman Publishing, we remain responsible for any inaccuracies, errors and omissions.

Finally we wish to thank Gillian who suffered our disruptions for longer than she ought to have done.

Chapter 1
The public sector

Introduction

This book is about organisation and management in public sector organisations. It is about how such organisations are structured, what people do in them, why people do what they do and how all of these things have changed over the years. How do we find out about such organisations? Approaches to the study of public administration reflect different academic disciplines including economics, sociology, psychology and politics. Any examination of organisation theory and its application will make extensive use of a variety of academic disciplines. These different disciplines will offer differing and often competing ideas which need to be examined, analysed and criticised.

The study of public sector organisations is made all the more complex and thought-provoking because of the competition of ideas between different academic and political standpoints. Added to this is the input from those who actually practise administration or management, giving us a 'real world' perspective. This essential input often gives us insider accounts of a world which, in a system where much work of government is conducted away from the public gaze, we are not normally privileged to see. Diaries and essays, such as Richard Crossman's political diaries (1979) or the work of Sir Geoffrey Vickers (1965), have made substantial contributions to the literature on public sector organisations. However, the reader must be prepared to treat some insider accounts with a certain amount of scepticism. Authors may be bitter because of personal experience, they may be members of a sectional interest group, or may simply be biased or malicious. Perhaps it is better to ask a few simple questions about anything that is written: Who wrote it? What is their background? Why did they write it? What did they seek to achieve? Who published it and why?

In recent years there has been a vigorous and often heated debate about how public administration courses should be taught. One school of thought has maintained that courses should place a strong emphasis on scholarship, academic training and a liberal education. Thus, many degree level courses in public administration begin with a year studying the disciplines of the social and political sciences, typically politics, economics, sociology, psychology and research methodology. This is then followed by courses in administrative structures, organisation theory and policy making which integrate and apply much of the literature from the disciplines introduced in the first year.

The alternative approach is to suggest that courses should equip the student with the skills and techniques of administration. Such courses would stress communication skills, problem solving and the mastery of techniques such as cost-benefit analysis and project planning. The major proponent of such an approach has been the Business and Technician Education Council which set out detailed guidelines for public administration courses based on providing the student with the knowledge and skills to make a contribution to the world of work.

Within the former approach, the study of public sector organisations has been underpinned by a concern with a number of approaches. Firstly, as Butcher (1984) points out, it has been approached through the study of public institutions such as the civil service, the National Health Service and local government. The concern has been with how they are structured and what people do in these organisations. This method, known as the public administration approach, was dominated by respect for the importance of the Westminster model of government and the role of administrative and constitutional law. Though few texts reflect this approach today, Greenwood and Wilson (1989) provide a review of many of the major issues. We assume that the reader has a basic knowledge of the structures of the institutions we discuss in this book.

Secondly, the study of public sector organisations has focused on the structure of organisations, how people behave in them, what motivates employees in these organisations and so on. It is this approach that we examine in the early chapters of this book.

Thirdly, such organisations have been studied from the perspective of decision making. Consideration is given to how public policies are made and put into action. This approach examines how policy is influenced, how decisions came to be made, how they are put into effect and how they are reviewed. The public policy approach is considered in such texts as Burch and Wood (1990), Hogwood (1987) and Hogwood and Gunn (1984).

Sources of information on public sector organisations are nothing if not diverse and the unfamiliar reader is likely to be bewildered by the range of sources available. In Appendix A we provide guidance on gathering information about current and future developments in and about public sector organisations.

Problems of definition

So far we have assumed that there is something called the public sector that is waiting to be studied. However, defining public sector organisations is not always easy. Certain organisations, for example government departments and local authorities, are obviously part of the public sector while others are not. We would not consider McDonalds or the local newsagent as part of the public sector. But the language that we use in describing the public sector sometimes only serves to confuse. We have public schools that are private schools and which are subsidised. In higher education we have a public sector (the polytechnics and the colleges) and a university sector both of whose principal source of finance is the public sector and are accountable to the Secretary of State for Education. The position in Wales further complicates matters as the polytechnics and colleges are accountable to the local authorities too. In the civil service we find administrators who now call themselves managers who are accountable to senior officials known as secretaries who may not know one end of a typewriter keyboard from the other.

The careless use of language can also serve to confuse. The term 'opting out' when used in relation to hospitals or schools misleadingly implies to many that there is the possibility of transfer from the public sector to the private sector. What is actually meant is opting out from an existing form of administration rather than a complete transfer from one sector to the other.

More importantly, there is a grey area where organisations may not obviously belong to one sector or another. For example, is an industry in the public sector if government owns 51 per cent of the shares and in the private sector if government owns 49 per cent of the shares? If a local authority provides 100 per cent funding for, say, a law centre, is it a public sector organisation or a voluntary body if it relies, in part, on voluntary workers? Is a committee consisting of civil servants and representatives from industry a public sector committee or not? The examples will continue to multiply as long as public sector organisations, however defined, continue to engage in partnership and joint ventures with the private sector.

It is clear that we are more concerned with certain organisations such as government departments, local authorities and the National Health Service. However, we do not seek to provide a hard-and-fast definition. Rather, we ask the reader to consider the influence of a number of themes that we consider in the book such as the impact of the political process and the role of politicians, public accountability, bureaucratic organisation, finance and so on.

The size of the public sector

Before the industrial revolution the family, a private sector organisation, was both a unit of production and of consumption. The family as a unit produced food, clothes and shelter prior to the consumption of those goods. The family provided social services such as care for the elderly and education. The mass move to the Victorian cities resulted in pressure for services to be provided on a collective basis. The period from the late nineteenth century until 1945 saw the state take on and develop new functions. From 1945 until the mid-1970s there was perceived by many to be a broad consensus that the overall balance between the public and private sectors was about right. Since the mid-1970s there has been a vigorous debate about the proper size and role of the public sector. In no small way we may have come full circle, with Mrs Thatcher urging families to care for the elderly instead of relying on the state to provide homes for the elderly.

The size, scope and operation of the public sector are at the heart of the debate about the success of the economy, the nature of community relations, the state of law and order and defence, the cultural climate and the freedom of the individual. If schools are unable to recruit teachers it may affect the quality of the workforce in the future. The values of the police officer may affect the relationship between minority groups and the penal system. Investment in the arts can serve to improve our broader cultural education. Remote bureaucracies may mean that individuals are unable to get access to services.

Writers concerned about the growth of the state have attempted to measure that growth. Different measures have been constructed including changes in revenues to government, changes in expenditure of government, the number of people employed by government, the extent of service provision and counts of the numbers of laws passed (see Taylor, 1983). While all measures are ultimately unsatisfactory, Schmidt concludes that 'The role of government in most advanced industrial democracies increased dramatically in the three decades following World War II'; and that: 'The major component of this expansion was growth in welfare expenditure' (Schmidt, 1983, p. 261).

Various explanations have been offered as to why this is the case. These include:

- the public sector expands in direct relation to the expansion in the economy as a whole;
- tax systems which rely on indirect taxation and insurance contributions encourage growth;
- politicians try to maximise votes and promise spending at election time, and frequent elections, therefore, encourage growth;
- bureaucrats have a vested self-interest in expanding the size of the agencies they work in;
- economies unable to maintain full employment tend to have large public sectors because of the need for income support programmes (see Schmidt, 1983).

Although it is not our intention or our purpose to engage in a critical examination of the growth of public sectors throughout the industrialised world, it is worth making a number of points which arise from the literature that will be examined in later chapters. Firstly, we cannot consider the public sector in isolation. We must view it in the context of the economic environment and economic performance of the country. As we shall see, the economic problems precipitated by the oil crises of the 1970s were to have a dramatic impact upon public sector management in the 1980s. Secondly, the nature and extent of the democratisation of the political system will be reflected in the organisation and extent of the public sector. Perceived inadequacies in the system of representative government have resulted in alternative forms of citizen representation such as the ombudsman, consumer councils and the customer evaluation of performance. Thirdly, the behaviour of politicians and officials can determine whether or not organisations grow. Politicians may promise higher levels of service provision in return for votes, and the internal structures and processes of public sector organisations may encourage officials to fight to increase their share of budgets rather than be interested in saving money.

Public and private organisations

The year 1979 saw the election of a Prime Minister and a government that was committed to 'rolling back the frontiers of the state'. This was to take a number of forms:

- reduce expenditure on the public services allowing income tax to be reduced;
- taking out of state control companies and industries that it was felt ought to be in the private sector;
- the sale of assets such as council houses;
- exposing services to competition.

There were both political and economic reasons for this commitment to limit the role of the state. The Conservative Party believes in the pursuit of individualism and the freedom of choice rather than state provision or collectivism. At the same time the increase in the number of people owning their own homes or shares would do the Party no harm at the ballot box. From an economic point of view, reducing the burden of state ownership would, it was felt, allow cuts in income tax. There was also the belief that exposing nationalised industries or local authorities to the competitive marketplace would increase their efficiency. The culture of the private sector would, it was felt, lead to a more efficient and effective public sector. As we shall see later, this belief translates into attempts to introduce the practices and techniques of private sector managers into the public sector. To what extent, though, is the public sector like the private sector? Opinion seems to be divided between those who argue that the public sector is unique and operates under different conditions than the private sector. More recently this conventional wisdom has been questioned, with writers stressing similarities and arguing that increasingly any differences between the two sectors are becoming blurred.

The public sector is unique

There is a range of arguments that are put forward to indicate the uniqueness of the public sector:

- public sector organisations are not exposed to the competitive world of the market and hence have no incentives to reduce costs or operate efficiently;
- objectives are usually ill-defined and expressed in vague terms such as serving the public, maintaining law and order, reducing inequality, removing poverty or improving health;
- strategic planning is more difficult because of the short-term considerations of politicians;
- the public sector organisation is susceptible to greater and more open accountability with politicians, pressure groups, taxpayers and voters all having an interest in the performance of the public sector;
- the functions of the public sector are limited by statute;
- the public sector is funded by taxation and not by charging for its services;

- certain goods have to be provided by the state. Defence, law and order and street lighting are enjoyed collectively and are, in theory, equally available to all. The provision of such 'public goods' cannot be left to the vagaries of the market.

The public and private sectors are converging

Critics of the above view hold that increasingly such distinctions are becoming blurred and we should recognise the similarities:

- increasingly the public sector charges for some of its services, for example, through increased prescription charges or charges for leisure facilities;
- the private sector also operates within a political environment as decisions made by politicians to – for example – keep interest rates high will have a profound effect upon the very existence of some firms faced with high borrowing costs and reduced sales;
- the activities of the private sector are also constrained by statute as firms are regulated over unfair trading practices, health and safety at work or environmental pollution;
- public and private partnerships have developed over urban redevelopment where groups such as *Business in the Community* have promoted private sector involvement at local levels.

Thus, it is often difficult to distinguish clearly between the two sectors and it may be more fruitful to examine organisational differences in terms of size, decision-making processes, structure and management style rather than concentrate upon which sector the organisation is in (see Howells, 1981).

A management study of the service offered by government departments to the public undertaken by the Cabinet Office also included research in private sector organisations. It concluded that:

> Comparison with the private sector has to be treated with caution. In the private sector there is a direct relationship between commercial success – as measured by profitability and market share – and the standard of customer service. The public sector position is more complicated and in many instances distinctly different. In general the reasons for providing a service in the first place, the nature of that service and the manner in which it is delivered, are not dictated by markets. In these circumstances the balance between public expectations and the level of service to be provided is decided on the basis of political judgements about economic and social priorities. All that said, those who execute public service functions have a professional responsibility to do so to the highest standards of service possible, within the given level of resources, and this is what civil servants want to achieve. (Cabinet Office, 1988, para 1.5, p. 2.)

Such sentiments could be applied to any part of the public sector and the issues that the quote raises are issues that we address throughout this book.

From public administration to public management

In recent years many writers and practitioners have considered the changes in the organisation and the management of public services and have sought to reflect those changes by using the term 'public management'. Evidence of this can be seen by the change in the name of organisations such as the Institute of Health Service Administrators to the Institute of Health Service Managers. Many courses taught at polytechnics, colleges and universities which were referred to by titles such as Public Administration, Public Sector Studies or Public Policy Studies, now find that the word management is creeping into the title. Whether this reflects profound changes in the syllabus or is a marketing ploy is open to debate.

The impetus to the adoption of the word 'management' was aided by the publication in 1982 of a book that was to become the bible for the flourishing Master's in Business Administration courses. A term was to enter the language of both business people and public sector officials alike. We refer to Peters and Waterman's *In Search of Excellence* (1982). The authors examined a number of companies, including Boeing, IBM and McDonalds, which they identified as excellent and suggested that excellent companies had a number of characteristics. It is worth looking at these characteristics in full, as the public sector strives to be 'excellent'.

1. *A bias for action.* The effective organisation gets on with the job, unlike the position in government where the official analyses, consults but does not take a decision unless forced to do so. Organisations must become more flexible and be quick to experiment. They must get away from the traditional patterns of formal communication and rigid and fixed organisational structures that stifle action.

2. *Get close to the customer.* The successful organisation hears what the customer is saying and responds to customer requirements. If not they would go out of business. Most public sector organisations have never faced the possibility of going out of business. Local authorities, for example, have been monopoly providers of services and have never been challenged. Too often in the public sector bureaucracy tends to look inwards and upwards rather than outwards to the customer.

3. *Autonomy and entrepreneurship.* Individuals should be encouraged to take responsibility and show initiative rather than merely follow routine and allow themselves to be governed by the rulebook.

4. *Productivity through people.* Everybody within the company is encouraged to innovate to improve the service. It is based upon a culture where people have high expectations of each other. In the public sector the emphasis has been upon reducing costs rather than improving the quality of the service. Staff training has thus tended to suffer.

5. *Hands on, value drive.* Individuals within the organisation share a common set of values and are motivated by organisational goals. We know politicians have values and these will change over time. If public officials are to subscribe to the

values of the politician then can they serve another party in government? This would call for a dramatic cultural change. Perhaps an alternative would be to move away from traditional sources of value systems such as professionalism and towards a commonly agreed framework based on the customer and the local area. Too often in public sector organisations we find weary cynicism or conflict generated by departmentalism or professional jealousies.

6. *Stick to the knitting.* Organisations must identify what they are good at and stick to it. In the public sector, statutes require public sector organisations to provide specified activities, whereas private companies can withdraw from one activity and concentrate upon another. However, increasingly the public sector can choose how to provide services. One solution may be to retain central expertise in some area and contract other work out to the private sector.

7. *Simple form and lean staff.* The successful organisation is one that has a lean structure with few hierarchical tiers. This would contradict the traditional bureaucratic form with long hierarchies.

8. *Simultaneous tight–loose properties.* Core values are controlled at the centre but autonomy is located lower down the organisation to enable action based upon those values. A balance is there to be struck between central direction and local discretion.

Conclusion

At the heart of the Peters and Waterman analysis is the theme of organisational culture which stresses the importance of values. Peters and Waterman suggest a set of values that may challenge existing values in the public sector. If their prescription is the correct one then public sector organisations would have to sacrifice values such as neutrality, impartiality and detachment and reassess the concept of accountability and responsibility. It is to an account of these values that we now turn in Chapter 2.

Further reading

Greenwood and Wilson (1989) set the context of public administration in Britain in Chapter 1. Many of the issues concerning the differences and similarities between the public and private sectors are to be found in the collection of essays edited by Perry and Kraemer (1983). A commentary on the different approaches is to be found in Gunn (1987). A short synopsis of some of the issues is to be found in Dopson and Stewart (1990). Fuller treatment of the arguments surrounding the size of the public sector are to be found in Taylor (1983).

Chapter 2
Values and concepts

Introduction

The aim of this chapter is to introduce a number of concepts essential to the study of public sector organisations. In particular, we are concerned with the values of the administrator and with the impact of political values on the public sector. Implicit in such a distinction is that there is a division between politics and administration and that one activity is performed by politicians and the other by officials. We need to examine whether this demarcation exists in practice or whether the roles of politicians and officials are more complex than this contention implies.

Values in administration

It is important to understand the idea of values. Values can underpin the thinking of those involved in the provision of services and dictate the nature of what they provide, how they provide it and to whom they provide the services. It is expected that politicians will bring political values to the process. For example, Labour politicians have traditionally emphasised ideas such as the equal distribution of wealth, democracy and participation, while Conservative politicians have tended to emphasise ideas such as market freedom, enterprise and self-help. These will, of course, change from time to time and from place to place. Equally, we can identify administrative values which will be generated by administrative cultures and will also be subject to change.

Accountability can ensure legal and financial rectitude and expresses the need for public bodies to reflect the demands which society makes on it for honesty and freedom from corruption. In certain societies levels of political and administrative corruption exist and are often tolerated. As we shall see, British administration prides itself on its honesty and lack of corruption.

It is argued by Stanyer and Smith (1976, p. 31) that 'public services are generally provided under the imperative of equality; that is, public bodies are expected to treat everyone equally'. However, it is difficult to establish what this means on a case by case basis: they cite the example of payments of cash benefits where everyone should be treated on an equal basis. Other examples reveal that equality may not always be easy to define. For instance, over recent years it has become clear that different police forces have adopted different policies with regard to the possession of small quantities of cannabis for personal use – some caution offenders while others prosecute. Equally, health service statistics reveal that waiting lists for particular operations in some areas are considerably longer than in other areas. Thus because of the decentralisation of administration, people in similar circumstances in different areas can expect to receive a different service.

With the benefit of hindsight – and in the light of the debates of the 1980s – the term *equality* or making people equal or uniform might be better substituted for the term *equity*, a term which relates more closely to fairness in the application of rules. A problem arises with officers who are in a position to exercise discretion or make judgements in order to arrive at a decision. We have to consider what guidance these officers need in order to arrive at those decisions – should general rules be established or should they be allowed to use intuition?

Consider the example of the housing allocations officer who has to make a decision about the allocation of housing for three families, one black and two white, only one of which, in the opinion of social services, urgently needs long-term accommodation. There are two permanent allocations available. Let us assume that the allocations officer is prejudiced and actively dislikes black people and allocates the two white families. Clearly this is not the sort of conduct that society expects of our public servants. This requires us to consider how this problem can be countered. Perhaps the answer lies in the values of the organisation: if individuals who are able to exercise discretion identify with the values of the organisation rather than their personal motives then we will achieve not only organisational efficiency but also, in this extreme case, fairness and equity (see Simon, 1976, Ch. 10).

It is impossible to make broad generalisations because of the diversity of public sector organisations in terms of the number of decision-making or rule-making bodies and the range of activities carried out. Law is often specific to particular types of organisations, for example local government or the health service, and can only be applied to those bodies. Organisational rules are made by individual bodies and will, of course, vary from body to body: with more than 400 local authorities in England alone we can expect up to 400 different sets of rules about how to go about doing business. Organisations and groups in organisations develop their own cultures, norms and values and these will influence the eventual products or outputs of the organisation. The diversity of the public sector means that there will be extensive variations in practice and it is therefore impossible to formulate general rules. Values in the public sector can be seen, in part, as a function of the values of society in general such as they can be defined. However, it is possible to identify certain ideas that have underpinned administrative thinking in Britain.

Trust

A premise of the British system of government is the relationship between the official and the politician. As we shall see in a later section of this chapter, the convention is that of the official serving the politician and offering advice. In return the politician defends the official. For example, in central government the convention of ministerial responsibility protects the official from the public eye.

Another aspect of trust is that between the officials themselves. Heclo and Wildavsky's (1981) study of the Treasury suggests that Whitehall is one big village where everybody knows everybody else and trust is the currency with which the inhabitants of the village deal in.

Neutrality

The tradition is that of the official not taking sides but offering impartial advice. Personal beliefs are suspended in order that the official can deal with any political master. Later we discuss the impact of thinking about human relations which could lead us to question whether the idea of neutrality ever existed in practice.

Probity

The tradition is that of officials serving the public as guardians of the public purse, charged with acting in the public interest rather than reflecting private interests. In Britain the official is deemed to be relatively incorruptible compared to counterparts elsewhere in the world where corruption amongst officials is common. Occasionally, we have cause to question the level of probity. The Poulson scandal which affected both local and central government in the early 1970s, the Wardale enquiry in 1983 into allegations of misconduct in the Property Services Agency, and allegations of corruption in the sale of cemeteries by Westminster Council (see the *Guardian*, 17 February 1990) serve as examples.

Professional honour

Unwritten codes of conduct for public officials include virtues such as loyalty, impartiality and pride in a job well done. Cricketing metaphors are used in Whitehall circles so that an individual who has a 'safe pair of hands' is approved of, as is somebody who 'is a team player' and 'goes into bat for the department'.

In a classic statement of the professional ethic of the administrator, Wilding includes: '. . . two spoonfuls each of honesty, tenacity and obedience; and one spoonful of humility' as part of the ingredients that go to make up this ethic (1979, p. 185).

Permanence

A difference between our senior officials and those, for example, in the United States of America, is that our officials are non-elected and enter the organisation as a career. Thus there is a tradition of serving government rather than seeking short-term political gain.

Secrecy

It is impossible to leave our consideration of values without mentioning secrecy. In this age of Glasnost it is ironic that in Britain we have what is considered to be one of the most secretive systems of central government amongst Western democracies. It is dominated by the Official Secrets Act and the 'thirty-year rule' which prevents the release of certain government papers, such as minutes of Cabinet meetings, until at least thirty years have elapsed. Officials are constrained by the requirements of secrecy and the lack of openness of the organisation itself. Proponents of open government argue that as government becomes more open it will be more difficult to hide incompetence and error behind the cloak of secrecy. Government would thus become more accountable and the 'faceless bureaucrat' would become a thing of the past. In Sweden there is a right of public access, with certain constraints, to official documents. Similarly, in the United States of America, freedom of information legislation gives the individual the right to inspect certain files.

Local government is, in theory, more open since the Local Government (Access to Information) Act of 1985. The influence of the Prime Minister's Committee on Local Government Rules of Conduct (Redcliffe-Maud, 1974) and the Royal Commission on Standards of Conduct in Public Life (Salmon, 1976) led to local authorities refining procedures on conflict of interest, the receiving of gifts and hospitality from clients and so on (see Parker *et al.*, 1986).

Not only do we have to take account of the values of the individual official but also those of the organisation. Some organisations make explicit statements of their values. For example, Sandwell Metropolitan Borough Council is committed to the following values:

- The Council will always act legally.
- The Council will always act in a caring manner, and will be equally caring towards all of the people of Sandwell.
- The Council will be responsive to the needs, ideas and decisions of the people of Sandwell and will encourage their active participation.
- The Council will deliver its services in an effective and efficient manner and will ensure value for money. (Sandwell MBC 'Aims and Values'.)

Politics and the policy/administration dichotomy

As we noted in the previous chapter, a distinguishing feature of the public sector is the existence of the political dimension. Politicians will bring political demands to the process just as consumers make economic demands in the marketplace. These will reflect the values and policies of the politicians which we discussed in the previous section. For example, Labour politicians commonly emphasise the provision of welfare services and equity in the provision of those services, while Conservative politicians may place emphasis on law and order and the control of overall public expenditure as a political priority. As Peter Self has argued, one of the problems that the public sector faces is trying to limit demand for services where there is potentially infinite demand such as with health care:

> An imperative of business efficiency – some would say its first rule – is market *innovation*. New products must be developed which consumers want sufficiently to yield a profit. But in government the problem is more one of market *compression*. Administrative controllers must somehow weed out the surplus of political demands for expenditure as best they may'. (Self, 1977, p. 267.)

It should be noted that certain policy areas and activities are often exposed to close political scrutiny, for example schools or social services, while others – such as the security services – are relatively insulated from scrutiny by politicians.

In the section on accountability below we will discuss the significance of this layer in terms of the demands that politicians make. Then we will look at the potential conflict between the policies of politicians which reflect convictions and values and possibly enhance their electoral prospects, and the administrative and management mechanisms that exist to further rational and efficient government. We need first to consider the roles that politicians and administrators play. In doing so, we are concerned with what actually happens in practice rather than making any normative statements about what politicians and administrators should do.

Orthodox views of the way in which public sector bodies work tell us that it is the role of politicians to make policy. They will do this with the help and advice of officials and a knowledge of the views of their constituents and pressure groups. Although the constitutional position is that Parliament is a sovereign body, the literature on the subject informs us that, in practice, the powers of Parliament have declined over the last hundred years to a point where one writer on the subject, Philip Norton (1985), terms it as 'policy peripheral'. If Parliament is at the margins of policy making then we need to look further to establish the locus of decision making. The politicians who form the government of the day are assisted by a body of permanent officials – civil servants. We need to examine the relationship between the elected politicians and the appointed civil servants. To do this, it is helpful to look at a set of models developed by Aberach *et al*, (1981). Table 2.1 indicates the four basic images of administrators that the models identify. Image 1 administrators reflect the view that firstly there is a clear distinction between policy and administration, and secondly that it is established practice that politicians have exclusive control over the making of policy and that administrators have exclusive control over administration. Such a distinction may have been applicable at one time, but with the complexities of modern government this simplistic distinction no longer appertains. Politicians will often take a detailed interest in the implementation of policy, so in addition to setting the broad parameters for education or transport policy, ministers may pay particular attention to, for example, an application by a school to opt out of local authority control or an application for a by-pass round a rural village.

Table 2.1: Types of administrative actors

Image	Typology	Example
Image 1	Policy/administration dichotomy is an ideal and an empirical reality	Northcote Trevelyan blueprint for the civil service in the 1850s. Discredited view of contemporary patterns of policy making
Image 2	Career officials involved in policy, but restrict themselves to imparting relevant facts and knowledge	Orthodox description of minister–civil servant relations
Image 3	Any participation in policy making requires some level of political calculation and manipulation, but administrators eschew passionate commitment	Official identifies with policy but respects constitutional position
Image 4.1	Officials involved in defensive bureaucratic obstruction	'Yes Minister' civil servant
Image 4.2a	Officials involved in positive executive – bureaucratic government, have detailed policy knowledge. Pro-active policy commitment	Professionally qualified officials eg. social workers, planners, architects, housing professionals
Image 4.2b	Officials identify with fortunes of specific political party	Downing Street Policy Unit members; advisers, politicians, etc.

(Source: Adapted from Campbell and Guy Peters, 1988)

Image 2 concedes that administrators will be involved in policy, but argues that their role will be restricted to providing politicians with the relevant facts and information. While there may be administrators that conform to this image, there is ample evidence available to suggest that administrators may identify with policies either on an individual or departmental basis.

Image 3 proposes that administrators are required to make political calculations either when dealing with politicians or when putting policies into practice. For example, when civil servants are drafting answers to parliamentary questions or providing advice to ministers, they take into account the likely response that ministers will make to that advice. The Clive Ponting case, when he alleged that civil servants were drafting misleading parliamentary answers relating to the sinking of the *General Belgrano* in the Falklands War, brings this point out clearly (Ponting, 1985).

However, this may not be a complete description of reality. There is evidence to suggest that officials may be more active in the role that they play. This brings us to Image 4. This model has been developed by Campbell and Guy Peters (1988) to distinguish between different types of administrators all of whom are active in policy making.

Many politicians have been highly critical of the way in which civil servants can obstruct the will of politicians. Accounts by (usually left wing) politicians with ambitions to reform government illustrate how their policies were frustrated by the unofficial policies of their departments (see Benn, 1980). The familiar process of the frustration of the will of the politician as satirised in *Yes Minister!* and *Yes Prime Minister!* illustrates Image 4.1. This is essentially a situation where administrators will receive a proposal from a minister and proceed to engage in defensive obstruction in order to maintain their interests. They are not initiating but reacting in a way that will attempt to preserve the status quo and the interests of the bureaucracy. In the next chapter we examine related theories of bureaucracy.

Image 4.2a is one where administrators are pro-actively engaged in policy making. Here, the expertise of the official and the situation in which he finds himself will allow him to play a crucial role in the development and execution of policy. An extreme example of this will be the security services who, according to the accounts of journalists such as Duncan Campbell and former security officials such as Peter Wright (1987) and Colin Wallace, are unaccountable and therefore make policy without reference to politicians. In local government, professional officers will have substantial expertise in their area of policy. As such they will play an important role in the shaping of policy before it is presented to local politicians.

In recent years we have seen a proliferation of policy advisers being recruited to central government and local government to provide advice direct to politicians. The Image 4.2b administrator will identify with the fortunes of the politician or party whom he or she serves. These officials have often been appointed by politicians frustrated by the obstruction of the administrative machine as an attempt to gain control over the process of policy making and administration (see Carvel, 1984 for Ken Livingstone's prescriptions from a left-wing point of view and Hoskyns, 1984 for a view from the right).

The four images of administrative actors are helpful in analysing what role the actors are playing. It is important to understand that different images will apply at different times and that the same person may play several roles depending on the situation. What the model does tell us is that the simple distinction between policy and administration is unrealistic. Although most detailed decisions do not become political matters, politicians can and do become involved in small and detailed administrative matters. For example, local government councillors undertake site visits to examine the details of planning applications while administrators can and do shape policy decisions such as the deployment of military resources.

This serves to add to the complexity of our system of public administration. According to the orthodoxy, politics is a world normally inhabited by politicians with the values that they bring to the process typified by uncertainty, and indeterminacy, whereas administration is a world inhabited by the administrator typified by rationality, routine and stability. Experience tells us that the reality is not as simple as that, and that in practice the two worlds are closely integrated and the possibility of distinguishing the ends which politicians want to reach from the means to achieve those ends is a remote one (see Self, 1977, Chapter 5).

Accountability

Accountability is, of course, not exclusive to the public sector. Private sector organisations attach great importance to accountability as a method of examining how people discharge responsibility and the financial performance of the organisation. However, it has been argued that the concept of accountability takes on greater importance in the public sector for a number of reasons:

- Public sector organisations are the guardians of monies collected through taxation and policies approved through the democratic processes, and the public demand that those responsible for public monies and public policies present a public account of their activities.
- Because of the responsibilities entrusted to public servants, we expect high standards of conduct from them. These standards will cover the way in which they spend money, the way in which policy is determined and put into practice, and sometimes even the way in which they conduct their public lives.
- The goals of private sector organisations may be much more precise and more widely understood than those in the public sector. A characteristic of public sector organisations is that they often have multiple goals which may conflict with each other. For example, the prison system has as two of its main tasks: 'to keep in custody, with such degree of security as is appropriate, having regard to the nature of the individual prisoner and his offence, sentenced prisoners for the duration of their offence . . .' and 'to provide for prisoners as full a life as is consistent with the facts of custody, in particular making available the physical necessities of life; care for physical and mental health; advice and help with personal problems; work, education, training, physical exercise and recreation; and opportunity to practise their religion'. (Home Office, 1989b, p. 3.) There is potential for conflict between the first and second objective. The first is aimed at punishing the offender and protecting the rest of society from dangerous people, while the second is aimed at enhancing the quality of life for the offender with a view to effective rehabilitation.

Other reasons for understanding the concept of accountability are:

- The diversity of public sector organisations and the huge variations in the activities that they undertake mean that differing methods of accountability will apply in different situations. It is therefore difficult to generalise about the process of accountability in the public sector. The mechanisms of accountability in local authorities are different from those in central government, which in turn vary from those in the National Health Service. It is, however, possible to detect certain trends such as the increasing importance that is being attached to management accountability in all parts of the public sector.

- The scale of the public sector organisations, which are frequently large organisations with long chains of command, often present logistical problems in controlling the activities of those charged with putting policies into practice.

Accountability defined

Accountability is a process where a person or groups of people are required to present an account of their activities and the way in which they have or have not discharged their duties. They are required to present this account to a nominated person or agency. The way in which they present the account may be governed by a set of rules – written or unwritten – which may vary in sophistication. As we shall see, accountability is a complex phenomenon and operates in different ways in different circumstances.

To understand the concept of accountability we need to appreciate its different dimensions and the way in which these dimensions are applied to public sector organisations.

As members of the public, we *expect* our public servants, whether they are politicians or officials, to be accountable for the way in which they discharge the duties of their office. However, there are occasions when people are not held to account, or the scrutiny to which they are subjected is found wanting. For example, during recent years there has been much criticism about the lack of accountability of the security services such as MI5 which is responsible for internal security in this country. This is because Parliament has been unable effectively to scrutinise its work.

A Home Office scrutiny of the management and resourcing systems for the magistrates' courts pulled no punches:

> There is no coherent management system for the service. At the national level, the role of the Home Office is so uncertain, and its powers so limited, that it might be truer to say that there are 105 local services, each run by a committee of magistrates. But the local structure is just as confused, with 285 justices' clerks enjoying a semi-autonomous status, under committees which are fundamentally ill-suited to the task of management. It is impossible to locate clear management responsibility or accountability anywhere in the structure. (Home Office, 1989a, para 4.)

Accountability can be linked to the concept of responsibility. As Day and Klein remind us: 'One cannot be accountable to anyone, unless one also has responsibility

for doing something' (1987, p. 5). Simon et al. (1950) state that responsibility can be viewed in three ways:

- responsibility as legal authority – for example having responsibility for a job;
- responsibility as a moral obligation – the irresponsible parent may not fulfil his obligations to his children;
- responsibility as responsiveness to values – where a public servant is charged with carrying out the wishes of others with particular reference to the values that are held by those charging the servant with carrying out the function.

Taking the third of these approaches, accountability can be defined as 'those methods, procedures and forces that determine what values will be reflected in administrative decisions. Accountability is the enforcement of responsibility'. (Simon *et al*, 1950, p. 513.)

In other words, when studying public sector organisations, we are concerned about accountability as a method of achieving responsive government and administration. As we know, accountability works in different ways in different situations. However, we can develop our understanding of the concept by following a framework set out by Gray and Jenkins (1985). They maintain that in any accountability relationship there are two actors or sets of actors: the *steward* and the *accountees*. The steward entrusts an actor or a set of actors with responsibility for resources or responsibilities or both. Those charged with that responsibility are known as the accountees who, usually in return for a reward, will be required to present an account of the way in which they have discharged their responsibilities.

The nature of the account will depend on the *code of accountability*. The code, which is a set of guidelines for the conduct of stewardship, will vary from one situation to another. For example, accountants have a rigid code (Statements of Standard Accounting Practice) governing the way in which accounts are presented and financial information is used, while the code by which the public holds local government councillors to account is imprecise and subject to definition by individual electors. Indeed the evidence available to us through empirical studies shows that voters in local elections 'tell us very little indeed, if anything at all, about citizen preferences on specifically local matters' (Newton, 1976, p. 29) and that '80 per cent of voters at local elections vote in accord with their national party choice' (Miller, 1986, p. 172).

When an account is presented, the steward should have the power to pass judgement on the way in which the duties have been discharged. As we have pointed out above, accountability is normally seen as a positive exercise attempting to secure responsive administration, yet the process could ultimately result in the accountee being discharged of the responsibility.

Early forms of accountability concentrated on the way in which monies were spent and the question of whether the activities of organisations were within the law. There was concern about the misuse of public funds and bribery and thus rules were made to ensure the probity of organisations. Although, as we shall see, this concern has been a continuing one, the concept of accountability was to be refined.

Political Accountability

More recent forms of accountability have concentrated on the political dimension. This manifested itself, for example, in the method of accountability that we expect to find in central government. The senior civil servant in the department – the Permanent Secretary - would be accountable to his minister. The minister, as a member of the Cabinet, will be accountable to Parliament for the discharge of office. This is known as the doctrine of Ministerial Responsibility, one of the conventions upon which our system of central government depends. The model assumes that powers are vested in the appropriate minister, with civil servants taking decisions in the name of the minister.

Such a system of accountability may have been appropriate in a time when the scale of the public sector was much smaller than today. In the twentieth century the growth of the state has meant that this model of accountability is no longer sufficient. Large government departments will make thousands of operational decisions and it is unrealistic to assume that ministers can be held responsible for, for example, the loss of a benefit claim form.

Therefore we have a much more complex system of accountability which has a number of dimensions. Under the model of Ministerial Responsibility, civil servants have traditionally been protected from public scrutiny. However, in recent years the faces of senior civil servants have become increasingly more visible with appearances before the departmental select committees to answer questions on behalf of their ministers and appearances in front of the Committee of Public Accounts as accounting officers of their departments.

As we have mentioned above, the criteria by which local electors hold local government councillors accountable is imprecise. This is not to state that the process is a static one – indeed it is subject to change over time. The Thatcher governments have sought to make local authorities more accountable to their electorates through the implementation of the Community Charge or Poll Tax. Critics will respond that charge payers are not fully made aware of the different charges set by counties and districts, and that Poll Tax capping would not be necessary if enhanced local accountability was the overriding criterion for its implementation. No doubt there will be studies conducted which will seek to analyse whether the Poll Tax influences electoral behaviour. However, until then we can only speculate.

Managerial accountability

Perhaps the simplest way to distinguish between political accountability and managerial accountability is to see political accountability as involving an account being presented to an external and public audience while managerial accountability is concerned with the internal processes. This may involve a shift in the nature of the account from a potentially more global set of considerations to a more restricted set of considerations about how things are done with particular reference to organisational objectives and resource considerations. For example, the values that politicians possess have been superimposed on the process, the overall priorities set, and policy decisions made. The process moves on to issues such as how the policy should be put into practice, how this can be done within the available resources, and how the implementation of the policy is to be reviewed.

Managerial accountability is concerned with issues such as cost effectiveness, efficiency, budgetary control, monitoring performance and effectiveness. Systems of accountable management may be introduced to delegate responsibility to those nearest the point of service delivery, for example area office managers. This takes place on the assumption that those close to the point of delivery are best able to make decisions about service delivery. It involves making decisions including, for example, delegating powers such as viring money from one budget heading to another, promotion of staff, making of local rules and so on, further down the hierarchy.

It is unrealistic to pretend that policies are simply passed over to administrators who unproblematically put them into practice in strict accordance with the wishes of the politician. Instead the public sector contains large departments and agencies which play an important role in shaping the policies that are delivered at the end of the day. It is important that these agencies and the individuals and groups that make them up are held accountable for the tasks for which they are responsible.

As we have already noted, people working in public sector organisations are not neutral and do not blindly follow the wishes of their managers and political masters. The idea that administrators leave their political views, moral codes and values at home each morning is a view which is widely discredited. Instead, as human behaviourists argue, people and groups in organisations develop their own goals which may be incompatible with the goals of the organisation.

With the growth of the size of the public sector, there have been demands for greater managerial accountability in public sector organisations. This derives from the concern that in periods of budgetary growth new money allowed new activities to be undertaken without any questioning of whether existing activities were being performed as efficiently as possible or, indeed, if they were any longer necessary. In relation to the civil service, the Fulton Report (1968) argued that the service suffered from a lack of managerial accountability, with little awareness of the need to question activities or justify expenditure. Since Fulton, government has responded with a number of initiatives with varying degrees of success. These initiatives, which include Programme Analysis and Review (1970–1979), the Management Information System for Ministers (1980 and ongoing with different names in different departments), the Financial Management Initiative (1982 and ongoing), and most recently, the Next Steps (1988 and ongoing) are considered in detail in Chapter 10.

There is an inevitable tension between the demands for political accountability where control is exercised from the top down, often with layers of administration exercising supervisory functions, and managerial accountability where decisions are often delegated down the hierarchy as close as possible to the point of delivery.

Decentralisation of decision making conflicts with the traditional requirement for control through hierarchical chains of command.

Added to this, managerial accountability may involve decisions based on assumptions about so-called rational management techniques based on a scientific study of work which may come into conflict with the demands of political accountability which involve the incorporation of values, party political considerations, convictions and prejudices which lack any rational foundation. For example, one of the most sensitive planning decisions in recent years has been the proposed location of the rail route from London to the Channel Tunnel. Rational techniques developed to aid decision making, in particular, cost-benefit analysis, have advanced the case for certain routes. However, the environmental impact of noise, redevelopment and disturbance to local communities has led to mobilisation of interest groups campaigning against proposed routes. Members of Parliament, with constituencies in the affected areas, sensitive to the wishes of their local constituents (and their majorities in Parliament) have been articulate in their objections to proposed routes.

A further problem needs to be considered when we look at nationalised industries. If the public sector engages in commercial operations such as producing motor cars or steel, there is a tension between the demands for public accountability and the needs for commercial confidentiality. If a state-owned car company is to compete on equal terms with car companies in the private sector, it will need to adopt the same principles of commercial confidentiality as its rivals. It will therefore wish to keep secret information on, for example, new product design and investment programmes if its competitors are not to gain an advantage. On the other hand, if government is subsidising the operation for economic or social reasons, politicians may demand an account of the performance of the company (see Curwen, 1986).

Accountability to the law

The actions of public sector organisations are subject to challenge in the courts of law. Many critics of our system of public administration believe that its actions are not subject to sufficient scrutiny and that the public need greater safeguards against the actions of the administration.

Since the end of World War II we have seen the development of judicial reviews of the decisions of government bodies. Central to this is the doctrine of *ultra vires* which limits the powers of public bodies to that which the law empowers them to do. Here the decisions of local authorities, ministers and so on, can be challenged in the courts on the grounds that, for example, they have exceeded their powers.

Accountability to the consumer or client

As stated above, the doctrine of Ministerial Responsibility has been shown to be an unsatisfactory mechanism to question detailed administrative decisions. In response to demands for a more accountable administration, there has been a development in machinery through which individuals who feel aggrieved at the decisions of the administration can attempt to gain redress. In many cases there is the opportunity to appeal against an administrative decision to a tribunal. This opportunity exists if, for example, a planning application is refused or where an application for a social security benefit is denied.

During the 1960s there was sustained pressure for a mechanism which would allow members of the public with grievances relating to administrative decisions to pursue those complaints through ombudsmen. This was because of the sheer volume of administrative decisions taken by public sector organisations and the unsuitability of Parliament as a mechanism for resolving those disputes. This pressure resulted in the creation of the Parliamentary Commissioner for Administration in 1967 and the Commissioners for Local Administration in 1974 who were given limited sets of powers to investigate complaints made by the public of maladministration by central and local government respectively. Similar machinery exists for the National Health Service.

Throughout the 1980s, public sector organisations have been under attack for being unresponsive to the needs of consumers. Many critics have argued that such organisations have grown in size to serve their own interests rather than concentrating on financial control and meeting the needs of those to whom they are supposed to be providing a service. This criticism has led many organisations to reconsider the way in which they organise and deliver the services they provide in order to be more accountable and responsive to their customers. Local authorities may be more responsive by adopting clear methods for the receipt and investigation of complaints by local people. Public housing organisations may become more responsive to tenants by ensuring more effective delivery of the service with decentralised local offices in easy reach of tenants or, to use the current language, customers. They can also make contracts with customers which include undertakings to complete repairs within a stated period or develop consultative networks to establish the needs and wants of customers and respond to them.

Professional accountability

The public sector employs many types of professionals for their expertise in specific areas of work. Professionals spend many years studying for qualifications in, for example, accountancy, law, architecture, engineering or social work. Sociologists have argued that this process of professional training together with the fact that they spend much of their working lives surrounded by people with similar qualifications means that they will absorb the values of the profession and see their reference group as their peers rather than their political masters. This may lead to distortions in policy, particularly in local government where professionals tend to assume dominant positions and can exercise considerable influence. It is quite possible that the wishes of political masters may be for one set of policy preferences while the professional group tend to prefer another. The resolution of this conflict may be in favour of the trends of the profession rather than those policies of the politicians – particularly when professional advancement and career development may be decided by fellow professionals in the broad professional community rather than by local politicians.

There are areas of work in the public sector from which politicians may not wish to exercise direct political control. For example, areas where professionals make scientific judgement about a particular issue such as safe levels of radiation for the public. Politicians may decline to question or comment on the appropriateness of such levels as this is seen as a matter of scientific rather than political judgement. Supporters of this view will maintain that there are matters which should be left to those who have the appropriate qualifications (an argument used to support the clinical judgement of doctors) whilst critics argue that such judgements involve moral judgements which should be subject to public accountability. For example, decisions on whether to deploy resources in the direction of one form of medical care rather than another should be subjected to political accountability.

An alternative view is advanced by health economists who have argued that the allocation of National Health Service resources should be determined by the rational criteria that economists use to allocate resources elsewhere. Hence the concept of the quality adjusted life year, the idea being to allocate health resources in such a way as to maximise the number of years that a patient will live with an adjustment for the actual quality of those years.

Accountability summarised

As we have seen, accountability is a complex phenomenon. In public sector organisations it is not restricted to hierarchical accountability to politicians at either the local or national level. Accountability of public sector organisations has a number of dimensions:

- political accountability;
- managerial accountability;
- legal accountability;
- consumer accountability;
- professional accountability.

We have considered the operation of the process of accountability and the evidence available to us suggests that the issue is nothing if not complex. It is important to recall that the mechanisms of accountability may not provide for full and effective scrutiny of the actions of public sector organisations. For example, if professionals see their fellow professionals as points of reference for accountability then this may be at the expense of public accountability. Efficient and prompt delivery of services may occur at the expense of detailed and time-consuming scrutiny by political masters. Also, there remain parts of the public sector over which there exists little or no accountability. We are well aware of the arguments of the critics of the secret services who argue that it lacks any effective accountability. Similarly, critics of recent initiatives, such as the creation of urban development corporations, have argued that these have assumed wide-ranging powers in relation to planning with the ability to make decisions without reference to the interests of the local communities and thus serve the interests of those who seek to develop property rather than those of long-standing residents of the area.

Accountability is thus an ongoing issue in the public sector. As we have seen, mechanisms of accountability change over time and reflect cultural, political and social demands. This will continue to be the case as accountability will be only one of many considerations in the organisation and management of the public sector.

Conclusion

In this chapter we have introduced a number of concepts which are ongoing themes in the public sector in Britain. So far we have made no attempt to draw any conclusions as to whether the public sector is intrinsically different from the private sector; we have merely pointed to those themes which will be referred to and developed in later chapters. We acknowledge that accountability is a concern for most large organisations irrespective of whether they are in the public or private sectors. Equally, many organisations will experience the problem of making a distinction between policy making and administration and how and who is involved in these activities. Further, all organisations will have cultures and sets of values which influence the way they work and relate to the outside world. At this stage we are merely setting the ground for debate. Later chapters will consider how people behave in public sector organisations and cope with recent developments in the organisation and operation in those organisations, which will assist the reader to draw more informed conclusions.

Further reading

Day and Klein (1987) provide a very useful review of accountability in five public services. Gray and Jenkins (1985) discuss the mechanics of the process in detail and its application in central government. Metcalfe and Richards (1987) provide the same. Accountability is a consistent theme in Savage and Robins (1990) and Flynn (1990). On secrecy, see Jones *et al.* (1990). Hennessey (1989b) reassesses the need for a professional ethic in the civil service and attempts to indicate what such an ethic might consist of. Wass (1983) examines the traditional values of the civil servant in modern times.

Chapter 3
Bureaucracy: idea and operation

Introduction

In this chapter we will examine what is meant by the term 'bureaucracy' and the way in which the concept is used in the public sector. As we shall see, bureaucracy is an idea which has made a major contribution to the structure and functioning of public sector organisations in the twentieth century. Therefore we need to understand the principles which underpin the idea of bureaucracy. In addition to this, we need to understand how it has operated in practice and to consider criticisms of the idea and alternative ways of organising public sector organisations.

Bureaucracy has been defined in many ways (see Albrow, 1970, or Smith, 1988). Albrow identified three major concepts of bureaucracy. Firstly, bureaucracy can be conceptualised as a form of government which could be distinguished from other forms such as monarchy or democracy. Under such a system, bureaucrats are employees of the state. Secondly, bureaucracy can be seen as a system of administrative efficiency. As Jackson (1982) observes, this approach sees bureaucracies as complex organisations with hierarchies which can be found in both the public and private sectors. Finally, the word is commonly used as a pejorative term of abuse by the public when they come up against red tape and obstruction in the British system of public administration. People use the term to refer to an inefficient system of public administration that misuses public money.

Although there is no agreed definition of the term, when studying public sector organisations, the term is more properly used to refer to a particular method of determining how organisations are structured and the methods by which the tasks of the organisation are achieved.

Origins of the term

For students of public sector organisations, the study of bureaucracy inevitably starts with Max Weber (1864–1920), a German sociologist, who saw it as a method of rational organisation. Weber was an academic whose concern was to examine organisations and offer a detached analysis. He was concerned about the nature of authority systems in organisations and why people followed orders without coercion. If those in a subordinate position follow orders of those in a superior position they are conferring legitimacy on the authority system.

He identified three types of legitimate authority systems:

1. **Charismatic authority** – 'resting on the devotion to specific and exceptional sanctity, heroism or exemplary character of an individual person.'
2. **Traditional authority** – 'resting on an established belief in the sanctity of immemorial traditions and the legitimacy of status of those exercising authority.'
3. **Rational/legal authority** – 'resting on the belief in the "legality" of patterns of normative rules and the right of those elevated to authority under such rules to issue commands.' (All quotes from Weber, 1971, p. 15.)

These three classifications are known as 'ideal types'. This is not to imply that they are ideals to which organisations should aspire. Rather, Weber states that we are unlikely to find them existing in the real world; instead he merely formulated the three concepts 'in the sharpest possible form'. He constructed them hypothetically for the purpose of comparison.

Under a system of rational/legal authority, 'obedience is owed to the legally established impersonal order' or in other words to a legal system where orders are issued and obeyed because of the authority that the office holder has. Bureaucracy is the purest form of the rational/legal authority system.

What are the features of bureaucratic administration?

Beetham summarises Weber's basic features of a bureaucratic system as:

hierarchy: each official has a clearly defined competence within a hierarchical division of labour, and is answerable for its performance to a superior;
continuity: the office constitutes a full-time salaried occupation, with a career structure which offers the prospect of regular advancement;
impersonality: the work is conducted according to prescribed rules, without arbitrariness or favouritism, and a written record is kept of each transaction;
expertise: officials are selected according to merit, are trained for their function, and control access to the knowledge stored in the files. (Beetham, 1987, pp. 11-12.)

Who are the bureaucrats?

In Box 1 we can see an extract from Weber which identifies the main criteria against which bureaucrats are appointed. As Beetham points out, at its simplest, administration can be understood as 'the coordination and execution of policy', and a system of administration as 'an arrangement of offices concerned with translating policy into directives to be executed at the front line of the organisation (shop floor, coal face, battlefield etc.)' (Beetham, 1987, p. 13.)

Box 1: Weber's criteria for the appointment of bureaucrats

1. They are personally free and subject to authority only with respect to their impersonal official obligations
2. They are organised in a clearly defined hierarchy of offices.
3. Each office has a clearly defined sphere of competence in the legal sense.
4. The office is filled by a free contractual relationship.
5. Candidates are selected on the basis of technical qualifications. In the most rational cases, this is tested by examination or guaranteed by diplomas certifying technical training, or both. They are appointed, not elected.
6. They are remunerated by fixed salaries in money, for the most part with a right to pension. . . .The salary scale is primarily graded according to rank in the hierarchy. . .
7. The office is treated as the sole, or at least the primary, occupation of the incumbent.
8. It constitutes a career. There is a system of 'promotion' according to seniority or to achievement or both. Promotion is dependent on the judgement of superiors.
9. The official works entirely separated from ownership of the means of administration and without appropriation of his position.
10. He is subject to strict and systematic discipline and control in the conduct of the office. (From Weber, 1971, pp. 21–2).

Therefore, not everyone involved in a bureaucratic organisation is a bureaucrat. We need to distinguish the administrative staff from the corporate group that employs them. For example, in a local authority, the administrative staff could be a bureaucracy whilst the corporate group that employs them – the council – is certainly not. They are normally part time, elected and involved, at least notionally, in policy making. We also need to distinguish between those who are charged with the process of administration and exercise authority within the organisation and those who assist that process. Whereas typists are essential to the administrative process, they are not bureaucrats as they do not exercise authority in the Weberian sense (Beetham, 1987, pp. 11–12). Thus it does not necessarily follow that those at the top and bottom of organisations are bureaucrats. In local government, approximately one-third of the labour force are manual workers, one-third are teachers or fire-fighters, which leaves one-third as non-manual workers (see Fowler, 1988a, p. 13). Therefore if we follow this approach to defining bureaucracy, we are only concerned with a part of the organisation.

We now need to examine why Weber attached so much importance to the idea of bureaucracy. He argued that bureaucracy was potentially superior to systems based on charismatic authority or traditional authority. Smith cites Weber's claims for the bureaucratic system. Weber argued that it is technically:

> capable of attaining the highest degree of efficiency and is in this sense formally the most rational known means of carrying out imperative control over human beings. It is superior to any other form in precision, in stability, in the stringency

of its discipline and its reliability. It thus makes possible a particularly high degree of calculability of results . . . It is the scope of its operation, and is formally capable of application to all kinds of administrative task. (Weber, cited by Smith, 1988, p. 4).

In other words, bureaucracy has the potential to be 'more efficient (with respect to the goals of the formal hierarchy) than are alternative forms of organisation . . .' (March and Simon, 1971, p. 30). It must be recognised at this point that this potential may not be realised and that so-called dysfunctions which undermine the efficiency and operation of the organisation may manifest themselves.

Crucial to the success of the bureaucratic form is the existence of formal rules. Hood summarises the features of a rule structure that would conform to the wishes of the 'rule and rote' school of thought:

- the rules are known by all;
- the purpose of the rules is clear and based on a valid theory of cause and effect;
- rules are consistent with each other;
- it is clear when rules are to apply;
- the scope for subjective interpretation is limited;
- where rules involve the categorisation, they are robust and unambiguous. (Hood, 1986, pp. 21–2.)

Is bureaucracy suitable for public sector organisations?

Weber's ideal type may appear attractive to those seeking to organise public administration. As Brown and Steel put it: 'Clients of large (and particularly public) organisations expect fair, and therefore uniform, treatment which can best be secured by a system of centralised authority implemented according to rules.' (Brown and Steel, 1979, p. 160).

Parts of the public sector, such as the benefits service, the Inland Revenue and the immigration service, can be expected to conform to this set of criteria since the public have every right to expect that different people in similar circumstances will be treated in a similar way. Yet, as Brown and Steel (1979, p. 162) note, even in these cases, there is a substantial amount of discretion involved in the way the service is run. As they go on to point out, there are many areas of the public service where the Weberian ideal type is hard to find. For example, in the National Health Service, government scientific establishments, or social service departments of local government, the professionals (be they practising doctors, scientists or social workers) will exercise a considerable degree of influence in the decisions that are made rather than being controlled by some hierarchy above them.

Because bureaucrats, at least in theory, work without arbitrariness or favouritism, they are able to deal with successive governments of different political beliefs. Indeed it is the detachment of the public servant that is cited as a virtue of the civil service by Sisson – himself a former civil servant:

The most serious responsibility of the administrator is to lay aside his preferences in favour of an objective assessment of the situation, not in terms of anything he may hold to be good, but in terms of the game as it is played in Whitehall. (Sisson, 1959, p. 152).

Are public sector organisations bureaucracies?

So far we have worked on the assumption that public sector organisations in Britain do in many cases approximate to the ideal type. In order to verify this assumption, we need to look at the evidence. We know from the very idea of an ideal type such as Weber's rational/legal ideal type, that it will never be found to exist in reality. We can, however, examine how closely certain public sector organisations approximate to the theoretical construct.

In his study of Birmingham City Council (1980) Haynes argues that local government has long been organised along the lines of classical bureacratic design. This has happened for very good reasons. Classical bureaucratic design has allowed local government to cope with the increase in the number of tasks and the growth of the complexity of the system. It also assisted the local authorities to provide impartial and accountable administration (Haynes, 1980, p. 10). As evidence of this, Haynes cites the creation of strong functional specialisation (or departmentalism); the principle of vertical hierarchy for control, authority and communication; the emphasis on rights, duties, technical qualifications; and the rigid grading structures and standardised procedures (Haynes, 1980, p. 12). He argues that the pressures to continue managing the plethora of legislation and provide services took priority over organisational reforms. Indeed, it was not until the late 1960s that organisational reform came on the agenda. As we shall see later, considerable changes have taken place during the last twenty years in the way that local government is organised.

The civil service of the mid-eighteenth century was characterised by a spoils system of nepotism and jobbery. Hennessy's major work on the service (1989a) documents the ongoing emphasis placed on the need for efficiency. The Northcote–Trevelyan Report on the civil service (1854) recommended a system of administration based on a clear division of work, entry to the service through competitive examinations, and promotion on the basis of merit. These recommendations were adopted in the period up to the end of the century by a service that was steadily accumulating a wider range of functions. During the twentieth century, the service has grown from a relatively small service to an employer of over 700,000 people in the late 1970s. Even today, despite the Thatcher cuts in the service, it remains a major employer with about 570,000 employees. We still have to ask the question: is the Civil Service a bureaucracy in the Weberian sense?

In his analysis of the systems of administration in four countries, Page argues that British and French senior civil servants can 'relatively accurately be described as career officials' (Page, 1985, p. 33). Members of the French 'grand corps' have much in common with our senior officials. However, Mrs Thatcher has made significant interventions in the appointments of a number of Permanent Secretaries in an attempt to create a service which will serve her more effectively. Ridley (1983) suggests that this selection takes place on a non-party political basis – the criteria is the ability to be forceful in policy implementation. Recruits to the service are selected through a process of competitive examination though there are major criticisms of the method of selection of the so-called 'high-fliers' which tends to favour those from particular educational backgrounds.

The ideal type places an emphasis on control in order to ensure that the wishes of those at the top of the hierarchy are carried out by those at the bottom of the hierarchy. This is not always the case in practice. Many workers at comparatively low positions in the hierarchy in public sector organisations will be relatively isolated from direct supervision. Lispky (1979) cites the examples of teachers, policemen and social workers who, because of the nature of the work, have the opportunity to exercise considerable personal initiative in the exercise of their duties. However, it is important to note that such work is subject to increasing control from above: teachers through the imposition of the national curriculum and performance appraisal; policemen through technological advances, including the two-way radio; and social workers through organisational responses to cases such as the Cleveland child abuse crisis and the Jasmine Beckford case in the 1980s.

Bureaucracy assessed

A cursory examination of many modern public sector organisations may lead one to conclude that they often approximate to the Weberian ideal type. Not only in Britain either. Ministries in West Germany are structured on an hierarchical basis and rigid departmentalism, and task allocation exists (Peters, 1990). However, we need to remember that Weber stressed that the rational/legal bureaucracy was only potentially the most efficient form of administration. He did concede that this would not necessarily be the case. Much of the writing on public sector organisations has been written with the ghost of Weber in the background. Watson argues that every organisation is faced with a basic paradox:

the means used by the controlling management of the organisation to achieve whatever goals they choose or are required to pursue in an efficient way (i.e. at the lowest feasible cost – short and long term) do not necessarily facilitate the effective achievement of these goals since these 'means' involve human beings who have goals of their own, which may not be congruent with those of the people managing them (1987, p. 174).

In other words, we are introducing an organisation's most dynamic variable: people. People will identify with an organisation's objectives to varying degrees, some will be loyal to the nth degree, others will identify very closely with the success of the organisation. Still others may be motivated by economic reward alone and seek personal satisfaction elsewhere, for example from family and friends.

Because of this paradox, many writers have examined the so-called dysfunctions of bureaucracy and the possibility that in addition to the intended consequences of rational and efficient administration, bureaucracies produce unintended consequences which may conflict with the goals of those in authority and inhibit the efficient and effective operation of the organisation.

At this point it is appropriate to examine a number of classical studies of organisations which illustrate examples of these unintended consequences. Although by their very nature these case studies relate to specific organisations at particular points in time, it is possible to look at other organisations and identify the same or similar traits and patterns of behaviour. These studies show the following dysfunctions:

- rules can become ends in themselves;
- problems of close supervision and vicious circles;
- rules can be adapted to increase the effectiveness of the organisation;
- the dictatorship of the official.

Rules can become ends in themselves

All organisations have certain objectives that those in positions of authority choose or are required to achieve. A system of rules is thus intended as a means to achieve those objectives. These rules are set by those in authority as a method of achieving control over the organisation and achieving reliable and uniform behaviour by those holding office in the organisation. Merton's study (1940) shows how rules become internalised by those working for the organisation and therefore it becomes possible for people to lose sight of the objectives behind the rules. A particular feature is rigidity of behaviour. The consequences are that demands for reliability are satisfied, individual cases are decided by the use of simple categories and that there are increased difficulties in dealing with clients.

The problems of close supervision and vicious circles

A study of a gypsum plant by Alvin Gouldner (1954) revealed that if workers are perceived by supervisors to have a lack of motivation then one response is to supervise their work more closely. This response by the supervisor raises two possible problems. Firstly, if workers are motivated they may do the job better without close supervision. Secondly, workers associate close supervision with strictness and punishment. Gouldner observes:

> . . . close supervision enmeshed management in a vicious circle: the supervisor perceived the worker as unmotivated; he then carefully watched and directed him; this aroused the worker's ire and accentuated his apathy, and now the supervisor was back where he began. Close supervision did not solve his

problem. In fact, it might make the worker's performance in the super's absence, even less reliable than it had been. (Gouldner, 1954, pp. 160–1)

The effect is that impersonal rules are formulated in order to reduce the tensions which are brought about by subordination and control, but the result (illustrated in Figure 3.1) is that the rules serve to perpetuate the tensions they are designed to eliminate by reinforcing the low motivation of the workers.

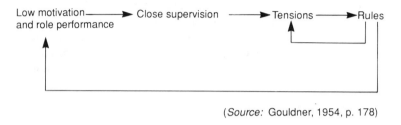

(*Source:* Gouldner, 1954, p. 178)

Figure 3.1 The vicious circle of close supervision and rules.

Following Gouldner, Michel Crozier's (1964) study of two parts of the French public service reveals the development of impersonal rules which prescribe behaviour to be followed for all possible circumstances. For example, promotion from one level in the hierarchy to another is by open competitive examination. Therefore, a person's personal attributes and career achievements are not taken into consideration. Similarly, when a person moves within a level in the hierarchy, this is governed by the seniority principle again without reference to other factors. The result of this is that there is no scope for individuals to exercise initiative – all workers are protected from their superiors and subordinates by a set of rules imposed from outside.

Crozier also cites further means by which the exercise of discretionary power is reduced. For example, decision making tends to be centralised. The power to make decisions or rules or to change or interpret rules moves further and further away from the point where the rules are carried out. The consequence of this is that the organisation becomes increasingly rigid, that innovation is stifled and that those making decisions – those at the top of the organisation – concentrate on ensuring internal issues such as fairness and the elimination of favouritism rather than adjusting the organisation to fit better with its environment. The very people with the knowledge and facts at their fingertips, those at the operational level, are excluded from the decision- and rule-making process.

Crozier's study reveals that the goals of the organisation are displaced by the goals of the various groups at different levels of the hierarchy. Each group wishes to protect itself against other groups in the organisation. Each group will assert its own uniqueness and importance to the organisation as a whole. Also, those with expertise in a particular area will have power because their task cannot be subjected to detailed prescription and regulation. This can lead, paradoxically, to a situation where the tighter the regulation of the organisation, the greater the independence and power of the experts because, as Crozier argues, in a bureaucratic organisation 'power increases in direct ratio to its rarity' (1964, p. 192).

Following from this analysis, Crozier argues that the system of vicious circle of displacement of goals identified by Merton and Gouldner which was outlined above can be elaborated. The displacement of goals leads to difficulties in dealing with customers, poor communication with the outside world, lower productivity and difficulty in completing the tasks of the organisation. Those seeking to control the organisation use impersonal rules, close supervision and centralisation which lead to increased frustration at all levels because decisions are not discussed. The consequence of this is that those at the top of the hierarchy then move decision making further up the hierarchy, which only serves to aggravate the problems that they seek to solve. The problem is compounded by the fact that those lower in the hierarchy seek rules to govern relationships between subordinates and superiors in order to protect themselves from arbitrary or unpredictable decisions by the manager.

Rules can be adapted to increase the effectiveness of the organisation

Until now the criticisms of bureaucratic organisations have illustrated how systems of control can break down and reduce the effectiveness of the organisation. Although we are still concerned with the importance of control in the organisation, the point that Blau (1963) makes is that rules can be adapted to increase the effectiveness of the organisation. He conducted a study of two American public sector organisations – a law enforcement organisation and a careers service – which illustrate this point. In the law enforcement agency a major rule of the organisation was that all bribes must be reported and acted on. However, the group who were likely to be offered bribes had developed an informal rule that nobody reports the offering of a bribe. The rule was enforced by the groups through the threat of ostracism from the group if a bribe was reported. This led to increased organisational effectiveness because, firstly, it eliminated the need for time to be taken up in reporting the bribe and the subsequent investigation that would take place, and secondly, the officer then gained the upper hand in the investigation because the 'client', unaware of the informal rule, would co-operate with the officer conscious of the ramifications if the bribe was reported.

In his study of the careers service, Blau observed that senior management sought to introduce a culture of competition amongst officers charged with the task of placing people in jobs. The procedure was to compare the performance of each officer. Blau found that the statistical evaluation of performance interfered with operating efficiency and there was an organisational need for mechanisms to combat competition. This was done in one section by developing co-operative norms (1963, pp. 80-1).

We are all aware that trade unions can impose a sanction known as 'working to rule' in order to stifle the effectiveness of the organisation. The lesson we learn from Blau is that organisations involve people and that if they are motivated towards the objectives of the organisation, they can increase the effectiveness of the organisation.

The dictatorship of the official

Weber understood the possibility that the actions of the bureaucracy could be in conflict with the democratic process:

> The pure interest of the bureaucracy in power, however, is efficacious far beyond those areas where purely functional interests make for secrecy. The concept of the 'official secret' is the specific invention of the bureaucracy, and nothing is so fanatically defended by the bureaucracy as this attitude which cannot be substantially justified beyond these specifically qualified areas. In facing a parliament, the bureaucracy, out of a sure power instinct, fights every attempt of the parliament to gain knowledge by means of its own experts or from interest groups . . . Bureaucracy naturally welcomes a poorly informed and hence powerless parliament. (Cited in Hennessy, 1989a, p. 347.)

The fear of an overpowerful bureaucracy is thus not a new one. It has been a concern for politicians such as Tony Benn who points to the power of the civil service to manage and absorb the Labour Party's policies (see for example Benn, 1980). Brian Sedgemore (1980), a former civil servant and Labour politician, points to the difficulties that politicians face in breaking out from the established values and thinking of government departments. Thompson argues that the two systems that find themselves working so closely together have sharply conflicting value systems. Democracy emphasises equality, participation and individuality while efficiency of bureaucracy is based on hierarchy, specialisation and impersonality (Thompson, 1983, p. 235). In later chapters we will consider strategies which have been mounted to resolve this conflict.

The New Right critique of bureaucracy

One of the most important critiques of bureaucracy, primarily because of the political currency that it enjoyed on both sides of the Atlantic in the 1980s, is the critique offered by authors on the New Right. Many of these writers sought to apply economic thinking to public sector organisations. Therefore just as business people can be seen as profit maximisers, politicians can be seen as vote maximisers and bureaucrats as bureau maximisers.

In particular, Niskanen (1971, 1973) argues that bureaucrats have a personal interest in the growth of the bureau as they have a vested interest in large budgets and rewards in terms of salary, status, public reputation and so on. This is compounded by a system in the United States which provided weak Congressional control over state spending, thus allowing high budgets to go through. He argues that these budgets may be up to twice the size of a comparable budget prepared by a private sector organisation operating in a competitive environment. Although it is debatable to what extent this argument applies in Britain, the acceptability of Niskanen's thesis by Mrs Thatcher's government has led to active consideration of alternatives to bureaucracy.

Niskanen advances alternative forms of service provision in an Institute of Economic Affairs (1973) paper. Firstly, he points to bureaucratic alternatives such as competitive bureaucracy. Under this system, bureaux would compete to provide services and in doing so they would drive prices down and reduce the over-supply which monopoly providers of services are allegedly guilty of. Also, incentives could be offered to maximise the profit of a bureau. These could take the form of reward systems such as performance-related pay and deferred prizes for managers who reduce costs. The introduction of performance-related pay in the civil service and incentives for National Health Service managers demonstrate the influence of these ideas.

Secondly, Niskanen points to market alternatives such as the provision of services by non-governmental agencies financed by per-unit subsidies or vouchers for, for example, education, or private supply of services such as tele-communications.

Thirdly, he argues that there are political alternatives such as the regular re-allocation of posts on committees which review the work of bureaux. The intended effect of this could be to stop politicians 'going native' or identifying with the service providers and high levels of service provision. Also, a two-thirds voting rule could be introduced to prevent legislatures passing high budgets on a simple majority, or the taxation system could be made more progressive so that those in low-income groups who demand high levels of service provision would be less inclined to articulate their demands.

Conclusion

The concept of bureaucracy has been fundamental to thinking about how public sector organisations have been structured. Its advocates argue that bureaucracy is an appropriate form of organisation for the performance of certain tasks where dependability and reliability are of the essence. However, it cannot be universally adopted with unquestioning enthusiasm. The literature on bureaucratic dysfunctions reveals that it produces unintended consequences and may not be the most efficient form of administration. Bureaucracy is not a neutral machine for the transmission of politicians' policies into practice. This is not to deny the influence of bureaucracy. To quote Peter Self: 'The Weberian model of a hierarchical, rule-dominated administration still has some validity for some parts of the system but not for others. Public administration has become a patchwork quilt of complex relationships and numerous decision points, on which new forms of politics are brought to bear.' (1977, p. 4.)

In recent years the bureaucratic form of organisation has come under challenge from all quarters, and by politicians who see it as inefficient and a barrier to the effective implementation of their policies. Added to this, there has been frequent public criticism that it is remote and disabling, and bureaucrats themselves have argued that it stifles their initiative. In later chapters we will examine the challenge to bureaucracy and how the public sector has developed new administrative structures to deliver public policies.

Further reading

Pugh's (1984) helpful collection of readings provides the reader with excerpts from the more significant work on the structure of organisations. Beetham's (1987) book *Bureaucracy* provides a useful introduction as does the more dated book of the same name by Albrow (1970). More specific public sector applications include Brian Smith (1988), Page (1985) and Haynes (1980). Eva Etzioni-Halevy (1985) provides a thorough review of the literature on the conflict between the political process and the bureaucratic process.

Chapter 4
The formal organisation

Introduction

The previous chapter was concerned with bureaucracy as a form of government. In the next two chapters we shall be examining a number of different perspectives on organisations. These perspectives fall under two main headings – the formal and the informal approaches to organisations. In this chapter we link the discussion of bureaucracy to the wider concern with formal organisations in general and examine the formal relations, structures and processes that exist within an organisation. In contrast to this, the informal approach to organisations concentrates upon the informal relations that exists between individuals and groups within an organisation.

Within the public sector we need to be aware of formal relations existing at different levels and we need to show how these organisations relate to each other. Thus, whilst we shall discuss the structures of local government we need to be aware that local government exists at different levels, i.e. county, district and parish or, in Wales, community councils each having both formal and informal relations with each other. We also need to be aware that local government exists within a wider network of quangos, agencies and voluntary organisations (see Rhodes, 1988). More importantly, local government exists within the context of central government domination. Within each level of government we may find competing tensions inherent in the relationships between the different sectors. Thus, for example, within local government there appears to be an increasing tendency to move towards a more decentralised service provision and organisational structure; at the next level of government the centre may be wishing to increase its control over what local government does. A second dimension that we need to be aware of is one of organisational change and the reasons for it. We can ask 'Why are new departments created?' or 'Why are old ones abolished?' and 'Why are new methods of working introduced?' We may like to think that such changes enable the organisation to be more efficient and effective in achieving its goals and yet it may well be that such changes arise as a result of trying to satisfy an individual's political ambitions or to undercut the ambitions of a rival. Organisational change may be the result of these kinds of issue rather than in response to some logic of organisational design.

Sir Patrick Nairne (*Guardian*, 2 August, 1988) suggests that political factors were of paramount importance when the DHSS was created in 1968. It seemed that a fuller role was required for the M.P. Richard Crossman and this had precedence over any organisational logic. Former head of the civil service Lord Armstrong comments that: 'There are some general principles of organisation, but the application of them is constantly interrupted by short-term political considerations. In my experience politicians have a contempt for good organisation.' (Quoted in Ponting, 1986, pp. 124.)

A third dimension that we also need to be aware of is the development of organisational structures over time. In local government this is not so much a problem because of the wholesale reorganisation of local government in 1974 which followed a more or less universal pattern in terms of new structures and new functions. A set of reasons was given for re-organisation in terms of linking an appropriate size to the functions to be performed in order to reap the benefits of the economies of scale. Similarly, successive re-organisations of the National Health Service have attempted to impose some form of uniform pattern on the structure.

It is more difficult in central government to trace a common pattern or rationale for the present structure of government departments. Each department has its own history, traditions and culture, and to impose a general framework to account for their development is not easy. The title of Chapman and Greenaway's history of government departments is *The Dynamics of Administrative Reform* (1980), and it captures the ebb and flow of central government changes. This is understandable when we consider differences in:

- **size** There are approximately 2400 civil servants in the Department of Education and Science and there were 96,000 in the old DHSS before its split into two separate departments in 1988.
- **functions** The Department of Education and Science is concerned with advice and monitoring, whereas much of the work of the Department of Social Security is dealing with clients.
- **organisation** Some departments, such as the Welsh, Scottish, or Northern Ireland Offices, are organised on a geographical basis while others such as the Treasury are primarily centred in Whitehall.
- **history** The Treasury can be traced back to the eleventh century whereas the Department of the Environment was created in 1970. It is important that we bear these differences in mind when we attempt to analyse the formal nature of public sector organisations.

The classical approaches

We have discussed the importance of Weber in understanding the workings of bureaucratic organisations. There are other classical studies that attempt to understand how organisations work.

Scientific management

As the heading suggests, this approach is concerned with the application of the methods and techniques of science to organisations. It is the belief that universal and general principles can be applied to every organisation. The approach suggests that organisations can be viewed as essentially the same and that there are few differences between organisations that cannot be overcome by the application of general principles. Two of the leading exponents of this approach to organisations were F.W. Taylor and H. Fayol. Unlike the academic approach of Weber, however, Taylor and Fayol were not content to just analyse organisations. Both were concerned to offer prescriptions as to how organisations should be run with a view to particular management ends.

Taylor was an engineer by training and his approach to understanding organisations reflected both his scientific background and the belief in science as the solution to society's problems that was so characteristic of the late nineteenth century. Taylor (1967) examined the traditional working methods of individual workers in a number of studies covering such simple tasks as bricklaying or shovelling materials. He believed that it was possible to apply scientific principles to each task which would replace the old rule-of-thumb method of working. He believed that the workforce should be selected on the same scientific basis. Such an approach would lead to a more efficient worker and hence to a more profitable organisation. He also believed that the worker was rational and would respond to financial incentives as a way of increasing productivity. Hence the payment by piece-rate for the individual worker. Taylor believed in the division of labour since tasks could be broken down into simple repetitive jobs. This would allow the individual to specialise in a particular job and the division of labour would lead to a clear distinction between management and the workforce. The modern versions of Taylorism are expressed in terms of job design and work study. Similarly, the concepts of the division of labour and organisation through specialisation still hold sway within many organisations.

Although Taylor was carrying out his research at the beginning of the century and despite the fact that his conclusions did not meet with the universal approval of either the workers or the management he left an important legacy which later theorists built upon:

- the application of universal scientific principles;
- specialisation;
- division of labour;
- clear hierarchies;
- ethos of management control.

Those familiar with either central or local government within Britain will, no doubt, recognise some of these features as characteristic of their own experiences:

- emphasis upon routine tasks;
- clearly defined tasks;

- clear hierarchical control.

The concern with the scientific approach to organisations was developed by Henri Fayol (1988) although the scientific discipline that he used was biology rather than engineering. He was apt to use biological metaphors to explain the workings of organisations. His principles of management were as follows:

1. The division of labour and the stress upon the advantages that such specialisation brings.
2. The stress upon authority.
3. The stress upon discipline and the penalties incurred when discipline broke down.
4. The concept of the unity of command – a dual-command system leads to dissension and chaos.
5. The unity of direction since, to use one of Fayol's biological metaphors, 'a body with two heads is a monster'.
6. The subordination of individual interests to those of the organisation as a whole.
7. The fair remuneration for the workforce. Like Taylor before him, Fayol believed in the motivating force of money.
8. The principle of centralisation. Centralisation, like the division of labour is, according to Fayol, a feature of the natural world.
9. A scalar chain or line of authority, both vertically and horizontally.
10. A concern with order. This is the idea that there is a place for everyone and everything.
11. Equity in the form of equitable treatment for the workers.
12. Initiative.
13. Stability of tenure.
14. 'Esprit de corps'. This is the notion that union is strength. The modern-day equivalent of this is the idea of an organisation having a corporate image such that all those within the organisation can respond to and identify with.

Fayol suggested that management is concerned with planning, with organisation, with command, co-ordination and control. Formal authority is important.

There is a sense in which scientific management is concerned with a way of thinking about organisations irrespective of the individual prescriptions of individual writers and researchers. It links into organisational structure insofar as structure is concerned with:

- specialisation;
- with standardisation of rules and procedures;
- standardisation of employment practices;
- formalisation of rules clearly specified;
- centralisation;
- a concern with configuration, i.e. is the chain of command long or short.

The advantage of this formal approach to organisations is that it shows how organisational objectives can be reached by:

1. Formally allocating people and resources. Individuals may feel happier if they have a clearly specified job within the organisation and know exactly where they fit into the workings of the organisation. It helps if we know where to go for formal approval of decisions, or know who is responsible for what. Accountability and responsibility can be clearly located.
2. Such an approach also clearly specifies operating procedures and mechanisms laid down in a formal manual for example. In local government the existence of Standing Orders, codes of conduct, and conditions of service clearly stipulate what can and cannot be done in certain circumstances. This is particularly important when we consider that much of the work of government is legal in nature involving the carrying out of statutory responsibilities.
3. It also indicates the decision-making procedures which show how and where decisions are made within organisations. Again the formal committee structure of local government indicates where authority is located. We shall see later, though, that in practice this may not always be where power is located.

A more recent organisational theorist illustrates the enduring qualities of these principles. According to Child (1977) the five major dimensions of an organisational structure consist of:

1. The allocation of tasks and responsibilities to individuals.
2. The designation of formal reporting relationships.
3. The grouping of individuals into units, units into departments and departments into larger units. It allows the compartmentalisation of tasks and jobs.
4. It shows where authority is located.
5. The structure can be designed to show channels of communication, interpretation and participation.

The mechanistic and the organic organisation

Burns and Stalker (1961) offer us a more sophisticated version of this approach by suggesting that we also need to take into account the context within which different types of organisations operate. They compare two different types of organisation, what they term the 'mechanistic' and the 'organic'. The mechanistic organisation is characterised by:

- a hierarchical system of control and communication;
- functionally specialised and precisely defined jobs;
- information flows up the organisation;
- decisions and instructions flow down the organisation;
- loyalty and obedience.

We can see the similarities here between the scientific approach to organisations and its similarity to bureaucracy that we looked at in the previous chapter.

However, in contrast to those who can see nothing good in this type of organisation, Burns and Stalker argue that this type of organisation may be appropriate to an organisation operating within a particular environment. If the organisation is in a stable environment then such formality may be no bad thing. The problem is that if the organisation is in an unstable environment then a different, more flexible, organisational structure is necessary. As we shall see later this is one of the reasons behind the call for changes in the civil service and local government in Britain. It is argued that the traditional bureaucratic mechanistic structure that has been operating for so long can no longer cope with the dynamic environment that we now live in.

Burns and Stalker contrast this type of organisation with the organic organisation, which is characterised by:

- jobs lose much of their formal definition;
- functions cannot be demarcated easily;
- interaction is lateral as well as vertical;
- the content of communications is information and advice rather than instructions – participation rather than control.

Burns and Stalker argue that this type of organisation is more likely to survive in an uncertain environment. Thus, using the distinction between mechanistic and organic organisations we can argue that insofar as we live in an uncertain world where political consensus is not guaranteed and economic stability is not assured then our public sector organisations ought to be moving more towards an organic, and away from, a mechanistic structure.

We can conclude this section then by picking out a number of criticisms of the scientific management approach to organisations.

1. It may prove difficult to co-ordinate the many specialised tasks and divisions that are required by the division of labour.
2. It may prove difficult because individuals may not be able to see the whole of the organisation since they are so wrapped up in their own specialised part of it.
3. The organisation may prove to be inflexible and unable to respond to changing circumstances.
4. It may be too bound by rules and not allow individuals to exercise discretion within their work.
5. It may lead to lack of motivation. Individuals may be seen as 'cogs in the machine' and one of the major criticisms of Taylor's approach was that he had a tendency to treat workers as automatons who would respond to financial incentives automatically.
6. Individuals lower down the organisation may be given little responsibility with few decisions delegated down the organisation to them.

Whatever the structure, an organisation needs people to make it work and hence the need to take into account the roles of individuals, their beliefs, values, motivations and how they interact with each other and with groups. This is examined in the next chapter and it forms the basis of the human relations approach to organisations. To what extent, however, can the principles that we have looked at so far help us in designing an organisational structure?

Organisational design

The concern of the writers that we have looked at in the preceding pages are with a number of organisational variables:

- specialisation of tasks;
- standardisation of rules, procedures and work practices;
- formalisation in terms of clear duties and responsibilities;
- centralisation and control;
- configuration in terms of the different levels within a hierarchical structure;
- communication and instruction;
- co-ordination of the different activities.

All organisations will have to address these issues and the way in which they do so will depend, to some extent, on what kind of environment they are working in – be it stable or unstable.

A second set of concerns is with the structuring of the organisation and the way in which it groups its activities. Mintzberg (1983) suggests that different criteria are available:

1. **Knowledge and skills** – a university may be divided into departments based upon knowledge in a subject area. We thus find Departments of Philosophy, Mathematics, Politics and so on. Hospitals are often composed of groupings based around particular medical skills such as physiotherapy or radiology. In central government we have, for example, the Central Statistical Office offering statistical expertise.
2. **Functions** – many organisations are divided into departments centred around the function that they perform such as personnel, finance, research and marketing. Local authorities are often composed of these kinds of functional departments.
3. **Time** – some organisations operate on a shift system so the structure is based around a particular shift. This is often the case with a continuous production plant, but we also find it in hospitals and also in the police force.
4. **Output** – some firms will have departments reflecting a particular product such as furniture, soft furnishings or kitchenware. This is less common in the public sector.
5. **Clients** – an organisation may be constructed around the clients. This would take the form of one department being responsible for all the services affecting a particular client group. A recurring theme in government re-organisation is whether or not to have, for example, a Ministry of Children, or a Department of Senior Citizens. Some local authorities have committees organised upon a

particular client group basis such as women, ethnic minorities, the disabled and so on.

6. **Place** – very simply the organisation is divided on a geographical basis. Thus we have the Welsh Office, Regional Health Authorities, and County Councils. The problem is, when re-organising in terms of place, to make sure that people's wishes are taken into consideration. The new county of Cleveland created after the local government re-organisation of 1974 has failed to create a sense of identity amongst its inhabitants and many still feel a sense of belonging to North Yorkshire.

The Haldane Report (1918) on the machinery of central government, which has since dominated thinking on the design of central government, examined a number of these criteria and recommended the distribution of government work on the basis of functions performed. Such a basis is fairly common throughout Western Europe. Most governments seem to have departments of defence, transport, education, the environment and so on. As we have indicated earlier, though, the dynamic of administrative reform seems to have been fairly arbitrary in terms of central government. Within the same department we might find more than one of these criteria in evidence. For example, the social services department within a local authority is a functional department. Its internal structuring, however, may be on a geographical basis in terms of area offices and on a client basis in terms of individual officials having a number of cases to deal with.

Thus, not only are there ambiguities in practice in terms of the organisational design of public sector organisations but they do not tell us very much about the power and status that attach to particular departments. The Treasury is only a small department in terms of the number of civil servants that work there but it has tremendous power as a result of its financial role at the heart of government.

Organisational charts

Almost all organisations of any size have organisational charts which show how an organisation may be expressed in formal terms. Such charts purport to indicate where control is located, the degree of centralisation, the division of labour, tasks, hierarchies and so on. Thus, in local government we often find charts modelled on the pattern indicated in the Bains Report (1972) on the management and structure of local authorities. The Report encouraged the idea that there is one ideal form of organisational structure which can be applied to all organisations. As we have already indicated the reform of local government in 1972 attempted to put some uniformity on to the pattern of local government in Britain. The Bains Report recognised the diversity of local authorities but suggested that certain basic structural features should be common to all authorities. Thus the structure of a district council may look like Figure 4.1.

Below the chief officers the rest of the department's staff will be arranged on the same hierarchical basis. The tradition within local government is to have a parallel structure for the councillors. The officers are arranged in terms of both functions

Figure 4.1 Structure of a district council.

dealing with housing or environmental health but also support services dealing with finance or personnel. However, the structure above does have a number of weaknesses:

- it tells us nothing about which departments or chief officers might be more important than others;
- such charts are fairly simple in nature and do not indicate the complexity of the organisation. Thus an organisation may need departmental or unit charts to show all the jobs and tasks that go on within an organisation;
- such a vertical representation tells us nothing about the relationships that go on between the centre and field offices. Thus an education department may be organised on an area basis so that the centre plays only a co-ordinating role. In the provision of services the field or area offices may be more important than the centre;
- it tells us nothing about where power is located. We have seen charts that describe the organisational chart of a police authority and yet miss off the lowly police constable. For the public this may be the most important part of the organisation;
- such charts also tell us nothing about decisions, channels of communication (it assumes these to be formal) and relationships (it assumes these to be hierarchical). In reality individuals will often by-pass these formal structures in order to get things done by contacting their opposite number in another department directly. Like the formal approach to organisations, such charts give us a picture of how an organisation works but it is only a partial picture and misses out on the crucial aspect of how people behave within organisations.

Most organisational charts reflect vertical relations. A more sophisticated approach is to adopt a matrix structure which also examines horizontal relations. Indeed the Bains Report advocated the use of programme teams which cut across the traditional departmental structure of local government. This would ensure communication and co-ordination horizontally as well as vertically. A matrix structure can indicate how relationships may be brought together across functional departments which in practice is how organisations are more likely to operate.

Thus, for example, in deciding to build a new school there will be other departments than just the education department involved. There will be a need for the technical support services, for new roads to be built for access, for liaison with police, social services and so on. To ensure co-ordination a project team may well be set up which draws upon the various departments.

	Education	Architects	Planning	Transport
Project A (New School)				
Project B (Extend Playing Fields)				

Figure 4.2 Matrix structure.

Likewise in central government the creation of task forces to deal with specific problems such as those associated with the inner city will cut across departmental boundaries. Here the structure is determined by the problem to be solved rather than by trying to fit a particular problem or project into a formal structure. It shows how in reality there is a need to communicate horizontally as well as vertically. Such an approach forces managers to communicate with one another and it helps break down rigid departmental boundaries. It does, however, sacrifice one of the classical principles of organisational structures – which is the unity of command.

Systems theory

Systems theory is a more modern perspective upon organisations and sees organisations as a system interacting with the environment within which they operate. The work of Burns and Stalker that we briefly introduced earlier is an example of an approach to organisations using the concept of a system. We can define a system as an organised unitary whole composed of interdependent parts or sub-systems and with boundaries separating it from its environment and other systems.

Systems theory borrows ideas from the physical sciences and economics and applies them to organisations. For example, we can characterise the human body as a system which is comprised of a number of sub-systems. The reproductive system, the digestive system, the thinking system all go to make up the overall system. Similarly, a motor car is a system which takes the driver and passengers from point A to point B. It is also made up of a number of sub-systems – the braking system, the heating system, the gearing system and so on. If one of these sub-systems does not work properly it will affect the working of the system as a whole and the motor car will not function to the best of its abilities.

Both the human body and the motor car interact with the environment. The motor car uses inputs such as petrol, oil and human effort and produces outputs such as movement, noise and other forms of pollution. The human body will use inputs such as food, oxygen and ideas and produce outputs such as activity and carbon dioxide. The concept is expressed diagrammatically in Figure 4.3.

Figure 4.3 Systems theory.

We can apply this thinking to organisations and look at how they interact with their environment and with other organisations. Thus we can talk of a local government system which is different from a central government system but nevertheless interacts with it.

Some sytems are considered to be closed and others are thought of as open. Thus, a mechanistic system is closed and an organic system is open to the environment. If we take local government as an open system we can see that inputs from the environment will include the following:

- *legal*, e.g changes in the law;
- *economic*, e.g. decrease in resources;
- *political*, e.g. attitudes of political parties;
- *demographic*, e.g. declining birth rate;
- *technological* e.g. new computer systems.

Local government then transforms these inputs into outputs in the form of the provision of services such as education or housing. Its ability to do this depends upon what goes on within the system itself, i.e. who has power, who makes decisions, who implements decisions and so on. Systems theory helps us to understand the role of organisational change and why organisations differ.

Organisations need to be adaptive to respond to the changing inputs and therefore the process of management and organisational structuring will need an environmental orientation. Of course, sometimes the boundaries between systems are not entirely clear. Do we define a system as one local authority or is it the system of local government as a whole? Is it the Training Agency or the whole system of training? Is it a prison or the whole criminal justice system? Perhaps these kinds of questions are best answered by knowing what we want to analyse. If we want to understand the functioning of a pay-roll system of a local authority we could see it as a system and the near environment will include the other departments of the local authority as well as the banks, building societies and other financial institutions. If we wish to examine the problem of recidivism amongst offenders, to look at the prisons alone would ignore the crucial roles played by the courts and the Home Office in the determination of sentences and the prison system we have.

The contingency approach

The perspective adopted by the 'contingency' theorists rejects the view that there is one best model for an organisational structure. Rather, such theorists suggest that for any particular organisation the most appropriate structure is that which best fits the particular organisation, depending upon the relationship between a number of variables. These variables will include size, technology, people, purposes and environment. Within an organisation, depending upon these variables, it may make sense to have different organisational structures. Thus a local government department offering central support services such as the Training Department may require a different structure than one which is decentralised and based around service provision. A number of studies based primarily upon private sector organisations have analysed the impact that these variables will have.

- Child (1977) has examined the relationship between size and the economic performance of the organisation.
- Perrow (1967) has examined the relationship between technology and structure.
- Woodward (1958) has looked at the relationship between technology and organisational performance in the manufacturing industry
- Lawrence and Lorsch (1967) analysed the internal structure of firms in the plastics, container and consumer food industries in terms of differentiation and integration. Differentiation refers to the different relationships, departments and goals that exist within an organisation and integration is the degree of co-ordination and co-operation between different departments with inter-departmental tasks. The matrix structure that we examined earlier would take account of these two variables.

Unlike systems theory, the contingency approach examines particular organisations. The theory argues that we cannot develop one universal scientific approach to create the perfect organisational structure, but rather we have to look at a number of variables and see how they interact with each other within particular organisations. Thus to reorganise central government, say, without taking into account the many different functions that the individual departments perform will not work. Any change has to be designed to fit the particular needs of particular departments. The problem is the difficulty of selecting the key variables and then analysing the relationships between them.

Organisational performance tends to be multi-faceted. Changing the technology in an organisation may have no impact unless there is a willingness on the part of staff to adapt to it or unless the operating processes take account of the increased speed of communications that new technology can allow. Which is more important and can we clearly identify the key variable? Similarly, there may be no control over the consequences of changing the different variables and there may be unforeseen consequences. We also need to take into account other variables, particularly when concentrating upon the public sector. Thus, Hinings *et al.* (1975) note the importance of political values and power. The contingency approach does, however, draw our attention to the fact that different structures may be necessary for the different activities that an organisation performs and takes account of the differing environment within which organisations operate.

Summary

The stable mechanistic organisation form is more appropriate when the following conditions hold:

- the environment is relatively stable;
- the goals are well defined and enduring;
- the technology is relatively uniform and stable;
- there are routine activities;
- decision making is programmable and co-ordination and control processes tend to make a tightly structured, hierarchical system possible.

The adaptive organic organisational form is more appropriate when the following are true:

- the environment is relatively uncertain and turbulent;
- the goals are diverse and changing;
- the technology is complex and dynamic;
- there are many non-routine activities in which creativity and responsiveness are important;
- the systems of communication and co-ordination are informal and non-hierarchical. (Kast and Rosenzweig, 1985, pp. 111–17).

Decentralisation

Finally we need to spend some time considering the role of decentralised administration in the public sector. At the time of writing this is of particular importance as more and more government activities are being provided at a more localised level. Such moves have taken a number of different forms:

- in the National Health Service clinician budgeting has been introduced so that doctors' responsibility for clinical practice will be matched by the responsibility for management and financial consequences of their decisions;
- in education the introduction of the Local Management of Schools will pass many of the decisions affecting individual schools to the school itself and away from the local education authority;
- there is a long history of decentralised management in the field of housing where local offices on council estates have their own budgets for minor repairs.

Decentralisation is usually examined from two perspectives:

1. The deconcentration of administration where an activity is located at a more local level as with field offices.

2. The decentralisation of the decision-making processes where power is given to those lower down the organisation.

In local government in particular we have seen substantial moves towards more decentralised forms of service provision in terms of area offices, or neighbourhood forums. (Stoker *et al.*, 1988). We have to ask what is being decentralised? Is it (a) structures; (b) physical location; (c) services; or is it really power over decision making?

We can contrast centralisation with decentralisation. The advantages of *centralisation* will include:

- easier implementation of a common policy for the organisation as a whole. A working party on government statistics has, thus, advocated the centralisation of central government statistical services (*Guardian*, July 26 1990);
- preventing sub-units becoming too independent;
- making for easier co-ordination;
- improving economies of scale and a reduction in overhead costs;
- greater use of specialisation;
- improving decision making which might otherwise be slower and a result of compromise because of differentiated authority;
- ensuring uniform and equitable treatment of clients.

The advantages of *decentralisation* are:

- it enables decisions to be made closer to the operational level of work;
- it encourages motivation and is good for morale;
- it allows responsiveness to the customer or the client;
- it will break down bureaucratic procedures;
- it will allow increased accountability since it will be more difficult to pass the buck up the organisation.

Decentralisation is thus seen as an alternative to the bureaucratic practices that we investigated in the previous chapter.

According to Hambleton and Hoggett (1984) decentralisation will allow:

- the improvement of services;
- greater accountability of services;
- easier distribution of services;
- increased political awareness by encouraging participation.

Decentralisation has supporters from all parts of the political spectrum. On the left it is believed that it will encourage political participation, and on the right it is believed that it will get the central state off the backs of individuals and allow greater individual choice. We can ask, though, to what extent does it allow individuals to have (a) control over day-to-day operational matters; (b) control/influence over strategic decisions; (c) control over finance?

Conclusion

There are a number of tensions inherent in organisational structures and the formal approach to organisations needs to recognise the tendency for different organisational principles to pull in different directions. These tensions are between:

● **Central control and decentralisation**

Although we have indicated the growing strength of the movement towards decentralisation we have to embrace this with caution. We used the example of the Local Management of Schools to indicate devolved decision making to the school itself. And yet, at the same time, central government has imposed the National Curriculum on the education system which seems to move in the opposite direction. Tensions also exist between:

● **Integration and differentiation**

Lawrence and Lorsch (1967), as we saw earlier, developed this tension in their contingency approach to organisations. In central government there are a number of mechanisms for co-ordination. There are also a number of inter-departmental committees based in the Cabinet and there is Cabinet itself to co-ordinate government policy. There are also co-ordinating departments such as the Treasury in central government and the Chief Executives Department in local authorities. Such co-ordinating mechanisms are required to counter the tendency of functional departments to pursue their own goals and interests even when in conflict with the interests of the organisation as a whole. Another area of tension is:

● **Continuity and adaptability**

We have indicated that organisations exist within a changing environment and they have to respond to this environment. At the same time they also need to ensure continuity. This is particularly important for public sector organisations where a change in the ruling political party may mean a change in policies and priorities. One of the advantages of the bureaucratic structure is that it can ensure continuity through the use of standard work practices and also provide some measure of stability. Other contributions to continuity will be the existence of professional norms and values that persist over time; the need to be responsible and accountable to Parliament; and the constraints placed upon radical change by legal requirements.

The picture that is emerging is of dynamic organisations existing within changing environments with the need to balance competing tendencies to survive. This picture is added to in the next chapter where we examine the informal relations that exist within organisations, and in Chapter 6 where we examine power.

Further reading

Most of the introductory texts to organisational theory will have a chapter on the classical, systems and contingency approaches to organisations. Mullins (1989) is particularly thorough. The selected readings in Pugh (1984) include excerpts from the classical texts. Mintzberg (1983) is especially good on organisational design. Haynes (1980) is extremely good on the local government context; likewise Pitt and Smith (1981) on government departments. A wealth of material on the history and organisational structures of central government can be found in Hennessey (1989a). Child (1977) examines the notion of organisational structure in depth. Hambleton and Hoggett (1984) raise many of the issues associated with decentralisation in local government.

Chapter 5
The informal organisation

Introduction

The main emphasis of the classical writers on organisations that we examined in the previous chapter was upon the formal characteristics of organisations, particularly in terms of organisational structure. Little attention was paid to the individuals within organisations in terms of their beliefs, values and their relations with each other. This chapter begins by examining these informal relations and assesses their importance in terms of our understanding of how organisations operate. This informal perspective is not meant to replace the formal approach but rather to supplement it and to develop a fuller understanding of how organisations operate. The classical approach used the methodology of the physical sciences to illustrate a view of organisations. Those that study the informal aspects of organisations tend to do so from perspectives drawn from the social sciences, particularly sociology and psychology.

The human relations approach

This approach is associated with the famous Hawthorne experiments at the Western Electric Company in America between 1924–32 (see Mayo, 1971 and Roethlisberger and Dickson, 1939). The original intention behind the research was to measure the effect on the individual worker of variations in the work conditions. The researchers used control groups from amongst the workers to assess the effect upon productivity of such variations. The first phase of experiments was concerned with the variation in the lighting. The results of this first phase were, much to the researchers' surprise, that productivity increased no matter how much the lighting was varied. The conclusion drawn was that it was the fact that the group was working as a team that was important. Also the workers felt a certain status and a privilege to be singled out for special treatment. Thus, it was argued that the increase in productivity was a direct result of improved relations among the workers. Subsequent experiments tested the effect of rest periods, the duration of work and the use of a payment by piece-work system. The results of these experiments seemed to indicate that:

- informal group dynamics were important;
- informal group norms would develop which could undermine formal working relations. The researchers found that the workforce would work more easily with one supervisor rather than another;
- informal group norms developed over what was to count as an acceptable day's work despite what management thought. Those individuals that worked above or below these group norms risked being ostracised by their fellow workers;
- such informal group norms were important to the workers even to the extent that an individual worker might refuse promotion if it meant leaving the group;
- if management took an interest in the workforce and allowed them some control over their environment then the workforce would feel less alienated from the workplace;
- where norms of co-operation and high output are established because of a feeling of importance, physical conditions may have little impact.

The methodology, the results and the interpretation of those results have all been questioned and criticised (see Parsons, 1978) but the Hawthorne experiments do suggest a number of considerations:

- Individuals will interact in much more unpredictable and complex ways than the classical writers would have us believe. Taylor assumed, for example, that workers were rational and would be motivated by an increase in wages and hence by linking wages to productivity the worker would produce more. The Hawthorne researchers argued that this does not necessarily follow.
- Productivity may be affected by the dynamics of changing social relations at work.
- Working in a group and feeling part of a team is important.

The Human Relations approach, as its name suggests, thus concentrates upon the people dimension within organisations and how they interrelate with each other. We shall return to this later in the chapter when we examine the impact of groups and of culture within organisations.

The individual

A number of writers have concentrated upon the psychological make-up of individuals and indicated that we need to be aware of the individual's nature.

Maslow's hierarchy of needs

Maslow (1943) argued that individuals have a number of basic psychological and physiological needs which an individual tries to satisfy. These needs are:

- physiological: for food, drink, shelter, etc;
- safety and security;
- social: to relate to others, have friends and so on;
- esteem: to have the respect of others;
- self-actualisation: to achieve full potential.

Maslow argued that as one need is met then the individual moves on to the next need. Thus as the need for basic sustenance is met we move up the ladder to the next step, which is the satisfaction of the need for safety. As each need is met the individual moves up the hierarchy. We shall examine these ideas in more detail when we come to look at motivation and morale within organisations. For the moment we need to take account of individual needs coming into the picture.

McGregor's Theory X and Theory Y

McGregor (1960) argued that within organisations the style of management is also important in determining how an organisation operates. He suggested that there are two different approaches based upon the basic perceptions that the manager had of the workforce. The first perspective, Theory X, assumes that (a) the average person is lazy and does not care to work; (b) most people must be coerced, directed and controlled if the organisation is to benefit by employing them; (c) the average person lacks ambition and has no interest in taking on responsibility.

In contrast to this, Theory Y assumes that (a) for most people work is natural; (b) people are interested in their work and will exercise self-direction; (c) given the right conditions then people will seek responsibility; (d) people are committed to organisational objectives since rewards are associated with the achievement of these objectives.

The importance of this approach is to suggest that it is perceptions that are important and depending on how the management views the worker then a different style of management will develop and a different set of relationships between the management and the workforce will exist.

Herzberg on motivation and hygiene

Herzberg (1966) argued that we need to take into account not just the needs and motivations of the individual worker but also the context within which they are operating. He thus developed a theory which argues that there are two sets of factors at work. The first set of factors are concerned with the content of work and the amount of job satisfaction that an individual receives – the motivation factor. This factor includes:

- the sense of achievement;
- the sense of responsibility;
- the sense of recognition;
- advancement at work;
- the content of the job itself.

The other factor is associated with the context of work and the work environment. Herzberg terms this the 'hygiene' or 'maintenance' factor. He argues that by maintaining the job environment at an acceptable level then feelings of dissatisfaction can be avoided. The hygiene factor includes:

- the level of salary;
- the quality of supervision;
- working conditions;
- interpersonal relations with supervisors;
- company policy and administration.

In Chapter 8 – on motivation – we shall examine research on the civil service which draws heavily upon the two-factor analysis developed by Herzberg.

Argyris on self-actualisation

Argyris (1957) suggests that whilst the individual may seek to actualise or achieve his or her full potential the organisation does not always allow this to happen. This is particularly the case for individuals working in the kind of formal organisations that were described in the previous two chapters. The individual is frustrated by the formal constraints imposed by formal organisations and creates informal activities. The individual becomes apathetic and disinterested, reduces the speed of work and the care taken over work. Group norms are developed that condone such behaviour. Eventually the organisation will modify its form in order to take account of the individual.

Groups in organisations

Although psychological explanations tend to concentrate upon the individual worker within the organisation, we can also examine the role of individuals as members of groups and note how the existence of different groups, both formal and informal, have an important role to play in developing our understanding of organisations. According to Mullins (1989) a group consists of a number of people who share (a) a common objective or task; (b) an awareness of group identity and boundary; (c) a minimum set of agreed values and norms.

The classical writers completely ignored the existence of such factors. Organisations consist of both formal group and informal groups. Thus, formal groups are created to achieve specific organisational objectives and are concerned with the co-ordination of work activities. Formal groups can be split into:

- team groups such as research teams or inter-departmental working parties;
- task groups centred around administrative tasks such as finance or personnel;
- technological groups centred around a piece of technology such as in assembly line production. In local government this might take the form of computer services;

- decision-making groups such as committees (particularly prevalent in local government and an integral part of local government structure);
- problem-solving groups cutting across different divisions such as working parties or task forces;
- representative groups such as the British Medical Association representing the views of doctors, or trade unions representing the views of their members.

We would expect individuals to belong to more than one of these groups. Problems may arise when loyalty to one group may be in conflict with membership of another group. We can imagine the dilemma that an individual might face if, for example, she works in the personnel department of an organisation and has to give redundancy notices to members of the same trade union. Such formal groups do, however, perform a number of useful functions:

1. Certain tasks can be performed only through the combined efforts of a number of people working together – e.g. a police or a medical operation. Sometimes such tasks require groups working together. A car accident, for example, may involve all the emergency services such as the police, fire service, ambulance service and surgeons.
2. Groups may encourage companionship and provide a source of mutual understanding and support from like-minded colleagues.
3. Membership of a group may provide an individual with a sense of belonging. Maslow, if we recall, suggested that this is one of our basic needs.
4. The group may provide guidelines for behaviour such as a professional ethic or a code of conduct.
5. It may provide protection for its members as with a trade union.

Strong and cohesive work groups can have beneficial effects for the organisation where they share common goals and values. At the same time the existence of strong groups may have a detrimental effect upon the organisation where the group puts forward its own interests at the expense of the organisation as a whole. The Hawthorne experiments that we discussed earlier indicated that peer group pressure was more important in determining an acceptable level of output irrespective of the demands of management.

Homans (1950) suggests three concepts for understanding individual behaviour in social groups: activity, interaction and sentiment. The more the people share activities, the more likely they are to interact with one another. The reciprocal is also true; interaction in one sphere of activity often leads to shared activity in unrelated spheres.

Increasingly, the importance of group working within organisations is recognised and much of the work of public sector organisations has a team element. For example, the National Health Service uses quality circles to ensure quality in its service. A quality circle usually involves relatively permanent small groups of between five to 15 people from the same work group who meet periodically to consider quality problems. The features of such groups are trust, involvement, the commitment to improvement and recognition for success. (See Chell, 1987, pp. 214–19.)

Professional groups

Within the public sector we find that professional groups usually have a tremendous impact upon the culture of an organisation and their influence is felt widely throughout the decision-making channels. It is, therefore, worth exploring in some detail their role. Dawson (1988) indicates that the characteristics of professional groupings include:

1. The commitment to a particular body of training: accountants, lawyers, doctors have to sit examinations set by the professional bodies.
2. Specific and lengthy training – usually over a period of years so the non-committed will fall by the wayside.
3. A restricted entry – usually through the attainment of other examination passes such as A-Levels and, increasingly, degrees.
4. Prescribed codes of ethics and standards of behaviour – there are both formal and informal codes which indicate how the member of the profession is expected to behave. In serious breaches of these codes, the professional can be struck off the professional register.
5. A proclaimed concern for client groups – doctors exist to serve their patients, teachers to educate their students.
6. Peer group evaluation, control and promotion – the work of the professional is usually assessed by other professionals.
7. Possession of a status and a mystique associated with the profession. Doctors are held in high regard by society, teachers used to be and social workers strive to be.

Such professional groupings have a number of implications for organisations. Firstly, we can ask, given the existence of a professional code, to what extent is the professional committed to the profession before the organisation? An architect working in local government may insist upon designing buildings that conform to a professional standard rather than to fit the needs of the authority. Winning design awards may be more important than building affordable, practical housing estates. The architect may wish to design the most aesthetically pleasing school using the best materials, the educationalist may be concerned that the school has appropriate classroom sizes for the different educational activities, and the accountant will concentrate upon costs.

Such different perspectives may lead to organisational conflict between the professional group and the organisation as a whole. Secondly, the professional may insist upon controlling the work that he or she does rather than allowing the administrator to impose control. Doctors may not, for example, be happy with interference in their work by somebody who lacks their medical expertise. Thirdly, self and peer evaluation seem to indicate that professionals are unwilling to be held to account for their actions by outside individuals or groups. Again, the medical profession will argue that an individual without medical expertise cannot pass judgement on their performance. Finally, professional groups have distinct cultures, norms and values and these cultures may come into conflict. The administrative civil servant may operate within a legal culture with a concern for following regulations and statutes. The architect or the engineer working within the civil service may believe this to be unnecessary red tape and their culture may be dominated by a concern to do the best possible job conforming to the highest professional standards.

The role of the professional within the civil service has traditionally been that of the 'specialist on tap'. In other words the generalist administrator calls upon the economists, the statisticians, etc. for information but it is the generalist who is 'on top'. The generalist dominates the decision-making procedure and it was this tradition that was heavily criticised by the Fulton Report (1968) on the civil service. The report argued that the specialist should be encouraged to develop managerial skills and be allowed to play a bigger role in the strategic decisions of the organisation. Such a view has more recently found favour in the National Health Service where the medical profession is encouraged to develop managerial skills. The local government dimension is slightly different with specialists in charge of the different departments. Thus the Chief Housing Officer will have expertise, experience and relevant professional qualifications. It is also the case that the generalist administrator is becoming more 'professionalised' with qualifications available through the Business and Technician Education Council (BTEC), the Institute of Personnel Management (IPM), the Institute of Chartered Secretaries and Administrators (ICSA) and so on.

Ultimately our interest with professional groups within organisations is a concern with power and the extent to which professionals have power as a result of their expertise. Following on from that is the question of accountability. If an important concern in the public sector is with accountability then we can question whether peer accountability is sufficient. In the public sector there has to be accountability to the public or the client. A major theme in local government is to control the power of the professional. The concern with professional power is developed in Chapter 6 and our concluding chapters show how the recent changes in public sector organisations may affect the power of the professionals.

Discretion

In Chapter 3 we examined the role that formal rules may play in bureaucratic organisations. It is also the case that informal rules exist within organisations and that discretion is exercised even within the most seemingly formal organisation. Discretion always exists even over such matters as the pace of work, the attitude to work or the willingness to perform tasks. Smith (1981) sets out the issues for us:

- *How is discretion defined?*

Discretion is concerned with the element of choice that an individual has when making a decision. The mechanical following of rules would leave little scope for discretion to be exercised. Thus:

> A public officer has discretion wherever the effective limits on his power leave him free to make a choice among possible courses of action or inaction. (Davis, 1969, pp. 4.)

● *How is it controlled?*

In practice there will not be complete freedom of choice for the individual. Group norms and values will act as constraints and even informal rules can be as rigid as formal rules. Professional codes of conduct will constrain individuals and ultimately the law will deter extreme interpretation of rules.

● *What are the consequences of widespread discretion?*

Discretion will allow officials to exercise some autonomy in their work and may allow the official to respond to the individual needs of clients rather than applying a set of standard rules. It may encourage, though, the arbitrary nature of decision making so that, for example, the receipt of benefits comes to depend on the attitude of the official and how he interacts with the claimant.

● *What models do we have to provide guidelines?*

Throughout the public sector individuals exercise discretion over a wide range of issues. For example, the social worker exercises discretion in individual case work. The police officer exercises discretion in areas such as minor traffic offences.

● *What factors will influence the use of discretion?*

1. The need for accountability – no matter how much discretion those working in the public sector exercise they will ultimately be accountable for their decisions either to superior officers or to the public through the tribunal systems.
2. Resources – the reason why discretion is used in the first place may be because of limited resources. If all minor traffic offences were prosecuted it would clog up the system.
3. The clarity of formal rules – if the rules are clear, specific and cover every eventuality there would be no question of them being open to interpretation. Often, though, legislation is general in nature allowing interpretation by officials to meet individual cases.

Any organisation will have a mixture of formal and informal rules and will allow discretion. However, we need to be aware that they all influence behaviour.

Culture

A more recent approach to the informal organisation is to consider the beliefs and values of individuals and groups as part of an organisational culture. Writers are concerned with such issues as: Does culture belong to the organisation or to the individuals within it? Is it thus greater than the sum of the individual parts? We also need to consider the extent to which organisations have one dominant culture, or the extent to which they consist of sub-cultures. In the light of the previous discussion we would be concerned with the extent to which professionals have their own sub-culture which is distinct from the organisational culture as a whole. However, Schein (1987) suggests that organisational culture is concerned with the

> ... *basic assumptions* and *beliefs* that are shared by members of an organisation, that operate unconsciously, and that define in a basic 'taken-for-granted' fashion an organization's view of itself and its environment. These assumptions and beliefs are *learned* responses to a group's problems of *survival* in its external environment and its problems of *internal integration*. (Schein, 1987, p. 6.)

Our first concern is with deciding what culture does. Here we can offer a number of different possibilities:

1. Culture will specify the goals and objectives of the organisation. In the private sector an organisation's corporate identity will perform this function and will contain such phrases as 'service with a smile', 'the customer is always right', 'the ultimate driving machine', and so on. Some universities and polytechnics compete to convince us that they are 'centres of excellence'. The NHS is 'working for patients' and the local authority is 'serving the public' or 'caring for the client'. Such phrases try to give us an image of what the organisation is about and individuals within the organisation are expected to adopt such a culture and to pursue the goals that it prescribes.
2. Culture will specify the relations that exist within the organisation and define what is to count as legitimate or illegitimate behaviour. In the Hawthorne experiments that we discussed earlier it was group pressure that determined the appropriate behaviour of individuals rather than formal guidelines, and informal sanctions were imposed if the individual did not conform to the group norms and expectations. In the civil service, the relationship between the civil servant and the politician is partly governed by the need for confidentiality. Civil servants who leak information are criticised by politicians for a breach of trust. After the Ponting case (1985) the head of the civil service, Sir Robert Armstrong, issued a code of conduct in an attempt to guide the behaviour of officials (Armstrong, 1985).
3. Culture also specifies what qualities are valued within organisations such as loyalty, confidentiality, dynamism, hard work, the ability to sell a product, and so on. Each organisation, and different groups within that organisation, may value different qualities. Difficulties arise when individuals are asked to develop qualities which they do not possess or which they have previously dismissed as

irrelevant or not worth posessing. Thus to ask the civil servant to cut costs irrespective of the effect on the quality of the service provided may be difficult not only if the civil servant does not possess the appropriate financial skills but also if the civil servant takes pride in the quality of service provided. Similarly, if the official is expected to trim advice so that it is politically acceptable she may find this unpalatable if she takes pride in offering impartial advice.

All organisations exist within some wider context and we would expect an organisation's culture to reflect this. Thus it may be unrealistic to expect a democratically run workplace when the prevailing political and social ethos is authoritarian. We would, however, expect a match between the organisational culture and the wider culture of society at large. Thus we can pose the question. To what extent is the traditional hierarchical nature of bureaucracy at odds with a less deferential and more egalitarian society? Can we expect individuals to enjoy equal rights and participation in their social lives and yet work under an authoritarian structure at the workplace that gives them little responsibility and allows them little scope for participation?

Apart from the societal context within which the organisation operates we would also expect the history of the organisation to influence its present culture. Past values and beliefs are transmitted to new members through formal induction programmes and informal working practices epitomised in such phrases as: 'We do things this way in this office'. The transmission of values ensures continuity and allows the organisation to survive changes in personnel. The former head of the civil service, Lord Bridges, describes departmental life in the civil service and suggests that:

> . . . in every Department a store of knowledge and experience in the subjects handled, something which eventually takes shape as a practical philosophy, or may merit the title of a departmental philosophy . . . in most cases the departmental philosophy is nothing more startling than the slow accretion and accumulation of experience over the years . . . Every civil servant finds himself entrusted with this kind of inheritance. He knows that it is his business to contribute something of his own to this store of experience; and that he should play his part in moulding it and improving it to meet changing conditions. Equally he knows that it is something he will ignore at his peril. (Bridges, 1950, p. 16.)

It may happen that individuals are taken over by the organisation and by groups within it, particularly where the corporate identity and image is a strong one. This transmission of culture is aided by the tendency to recruit in 'one's own image' where members of interview panels tend to look for similar qualities that they themselves possess when recruiting new members. The Oxford and Cambridge arts and classicist graduate at the top of the civil service may, consciously or subconsciously, favour individuals from similar backgrounds because such candidates will possess similar qualities to themselves. Not to do so is to admit that one's own qualities are not required by the organisation. Politicians may apply the same criteria. Margaret Thatcher is supposed to have applied the acid test of 'Is he one of us?' when making her senior appointments.

Thus we are concerned with organisations as social systems that have shared understandings, norms and values and have a common language. The new recruit into any organisation or group has to learn these norms and the codes of speech that groups employ before they can feel part of the group. Young and Sloman discovered this sense of intimacy in the Treasury. They quote an Under Secretary commenting upon informal communications networks: 'Some of these people I've known for twenty-five years and we can of course communicate with each other almost in code.' (Young and Sloman, 1984, p. 25.)

The difficulty arises, as we saw with professional groupings, of sub-groups existing within an organisation that do not all share the same goals or values. To what extent does an organisation exhibit a common, homogeneous culture? We can imagine that a small advertising agency may well share a common culture, but a large government department, such as the Home Office, with multiple functions and goals is unlikely to exhibit the same homogeneity. Similarly, the picture we have of the civil service drawn from such programmes as *Yes Minister!* only depicts a small number of Mandarins at the top of the civil service. We can legitimately ask what does a senior official based in Whitehall and acting as a policy adviser to a minister have in common with an administrative officer working in a local branch of the Department of Social Security other than the fact that they are both civil servants? Of course, it may well be that there is a dominant culture within an organisation which is formed at the top and is transmitted downwards through formal and informal mechanisms. This point is important if it is the case that the leaders at the top of the organisation are the ones who create the image and identity of the organisation.

Handy (1985) has analysed the different types of organisational culture and offers a four-fold typology:

- **The power culture**

    The organisation stresses the role of individuals rather than committees. Individuals are power-oriented and politically aware. Control is exercised at the centre and it is characterised by informal webs of influence rather than formal procedures. It is not characterised by bureaucracy.

- **The role culture**

    Here the stress is upon formal rules and roles and authority is vested in these roles. It is characterised by formal procedures and offers the individual security, stability and predictability. It is, therefore, characteristic of a bureaucracy.

- **The task culture**

    This is job-oriented and is concerned with getting the job done. It is concerned with utilising resources to meet the organisation's objectives and is characterised by the requirement of efficiency. The culture adapts itself to change and is driven by the need to provide goods and services for the customer.

● **The person culture**

The individual is at the heart of this organisation and this culture, according to Handy, is not often found. The organisation serves the individual rather than the other way round. Control mechanisms or hierarchies are virtually impossible and influence is shared. The commune would possess this type of culture.

Traditionally bureaucracy has been described as a role culture, but there is no reason to suppose that the different cultures cannot all exist within the same organisation particularly if the organisation is as large and diverse as a government department or a local authority. Indeed the contingency approach to organisations would argue that, depending upon the dominant activity, an organisation should consist of different sub-cultures reflecting different activities.

In the public sector the concept of a role culture would seem to have some relevance. However, we may wish to use a different set of criteria:

● *A political culture* – given that government takes place within a political context then we may wish to consider the political dimension as the most important. Thus, we might be interested in the relationship between the politician and the official; the relationship between the different parties particularly where there is a hung council; the role of interest groups and their relationship with departments and so on.
● *An administrative culture* – which is concerned with rules, roles, authority and fits in with the concept of a role culture.
● *A legal culture* – particularly important in local government where much of the work may be governed by statute, or may involve the regulation of activities.
● *Market culture* – where public sector organisations are exposed to the market through competitive tendering, contracting out, internal markets and so on.

Each of the different cultures may express the roles that organisations perform. Problems arise where there is a clash of cultures. Thus, it would be unrealistic to expect officials to be responsive to the market when their traditional activity has been conditioned by the need to follow statutes. The creation of the Training and Enterprise Councils by central government to run the bulk of the country's training has encountered problems of culture clash. The businessmen brought in to run the Councils have been frustrated by the tight operating and financial practices imposed by the Department of Employment. Such practices sit uneasily alongside the entrepreneurial freedom that business leaders are used to (see *Guardian*, 23 March 1990).

Within government there will be strong traditions which have to be overcome if a new culture is to develop. Depending upon the strength of the existing culture then change is not easily brought about. The strength of the civil service culture is commented upon by Hennessy who suggests that, after three decades of travelling up the hierarchy, senior civil servants become indistinguishable from each other:

> Their habits, modes of thought, patterns of speech, style of drafting will have rubbed off on one another to the point where but a few free or tough or independent spirits resist mutation into a sludgy administrative amalgam. (Hennessy, 1989(a), pp. 521–2.)

Where sub-cultures exist they could weaken the hold of a dominant culture and may respond to change more readily.

Conclusion

Taken together the formal and the informal approaches almost complete our picture of how to understand organisations. We need, however, to add one further ingredient – that of power. Although we have introduced the concept of a power culture from the work of Handy, it can be argued that *all* organisations are really concerned with power. From this perspective, all organisations are political in that they are characterised by bargaining, compromises and conflicts between individuals and groups.

Further reading

Most introductory textbooks on organisational theory will have chapters on the Human Relations approach to organisations. Litterer (1969) is generally good on the informal organisation. Schein (1987) is very detailed on the relationship between culture and leadership. Adler and Asquith (1981) edited a very good collection of essays by different authors on welfare and discretion. Ham and Hill (1984) link discretion to the policy process. Kakabadse (1982) examines culture in a social services department. Handy (1985) explores the concept of organisation culture in detail and is also good on the workings of groups.

Chapter 6
Power and conflict within organisations

Introduction

All organisations, whether in the public or the private sector, are involved in politics. This may be more explicit within the public sector because of the fact of government organisations being led by politicians and their work involving the implementation of a political party's policies. And yet private sector organisations are also political in the sense of competition between ideas and individuals within the organisation. There is conflict between departments, between hierarchies and over decisions that are made. All organisations are concerned with who makes decisions, who controls resources, who determines which issues are discussed, who sets the agenda and how is conflict between individuals and groups resolved. We are also concerned with the political environment within which all organisations operate. Decisions taken by politicians concerning the economy, for example, will affect those organisations engaged in business.

We need, therefore, to examine who has power within society and locate that within the context of the power of the state. Through such an examination we can see who has power over decisions and which groups and individuals can achieve their aims. There are a number of general theories that are concerned with such issues and we shall briefly investigate these before moving on to an examination of power within organisations. All the theories that we examine have variations and we shall be concerned to pick out the main themes that the different interpretations of these theories have in common.

Pluralism

This theory suggests that within society power is fragmented between different groups all of whom are in competition with each other. Depending upon the issue, different groups will get their own way and no one group dominates power within society. Political power can result from a variety of factors including wealth, control over information, status, popularity and legality. Pressure group politics is a manifestation of this where individuals organise into groups to achieve their aims.

Examples of such groups range from trade unions and professional associations through to environmental groups trying to save the whale or local groups that are concerned with juggernaut lorries travelling through a small village. The issues are numerous and diverse but groups form to try to influence decisions concerning these issues.

Pluralism is a development of democratic theory and recognises that often individuals can best get their views heard by combining in groups to give them a stronger voice. Pluralism presupposes that groups have access to the decision-making process and that power is widely spread. Although power is widely spread it does not necessarily mean that it is evenly spread between all groups. However, in society the groups that we might think of as having an influence upon the decision-making processes will be the trade unions, representatives of the business world such as the Confederation of British Industry (CBI), the bureaucracy and political parties.

In organisational terms, a pluralist approach would suggest that organisations are made up of different groups each with access to the decision-making processes and with the ability to influence those processes. Thus, for example, in the National Health Service groups such as the consultants, junior doctors, administrators, nursing staff, GPs and so on, will all be striving to influence the organisation and to get their views accepted by the organisation. In local government we might find groups composed of councillors, officers, local businessmen and women, client groups, voluntary agencies, all attempting to get their views accepted. Stoker and Wilson (1986) argue that a range of resources are available to the competing groups involved in local decision making such as access to contacts, position in the hierarchy, control of information and so on. They identify a number of actors involved in the decision-making processes in local government and suggest that the picture of who has power is sometimes not clear.

Similarly, the conventional picture of decision making within health authorities is that of consensus between different coalitions of interests represented by practitioners, politicians and administrators, each with different resources and power bases. Pluralism, then, seems to be concerned with competition between different groups involved in making decisions. Critics argue that this does not seem to be very realistic. Some groups seem to have more power than others. Big business or some trade unions, for example, seem to have exercised power consistently over long periods of time. Similarly, within organisations is it not the case that certain groups consistently seem to be able to get their own way? Thus, in the National Health Service it may well be the consultants that always seem to get their own way and the nurses rarely so. In the civil service it may well be the small number of Permanent Secretaries heading government departments that make decisions. In local government it may well be a small group of chief officers and committee chairpersons that control decisions. More widely, it may well be that central government usually gets its own way over local government. If this is the case then society and organisations, far from being pluralist in nature, are, in fact, elitist so that on any given issue there may be a small group that exercises a great deal of power. Indeed many of the pluralist writers were acutely aware of inequalities in the distribution of power.

Elitism

Elitist theories argue that power is always in the hands of a minority. Within society power is in the hands of a small number of individuals and groups who may be prominent in industry, in financial or in political circles. It is these elites that dominate society. Those who support the arguments of the elitist theories will point to the tendency for senior politicians from all parties to come from similar social and educational backgrounds. Similarly, it is often the case that senior officials within the civil service all seem to come from the same sort of background. The absence of women and members of ethnic minorities and the continuing dominance of Oxford and Cambridge arts and classicist graduates amongst the senior civil service and the 'high fliers' are said to support these criticisms. C. Wright Mills (1956) advances the notion of a power elite composed of men from similar social and educational backgrounds sharing similar values.

We can legitimately ask, however: What is wrong with this state of affairs? Indeed, Schumpeter (1976) argued that democracy is really about competition between competing elites for the votes of the people and that democracy did not require mass participation. From a different perspective it can also be argued that it is right and proper that, for example, the Mandarins of the civil service should have power, because, after all, they have the expertise and knowledge in government matters. The politician may have been democratically elected but the politician does not have the same experience as the career official. We can characterise this as rule by the non-elected with power in the hands of a bureaucratic elite. Those familiar with the television programme *Yes Prime Minister!* will recognise this characterisation. Similarly, it can be argued that the consultants and their professional body, the British Medical Association (BMA), should dominate decision making within the National Health Service since they have the medical knowledge and expertise which the politician, the administrator and the patient do not possess. Such arguments are powerful ones and, as we shall see later, possession of specialised knowledge is an important source of power.

There are also strong arguments, however, to suggest that a more pluralistic decision-making process is the best way for society and organisations to operate. Expert knowledge may be too narrow in its focus. A decision made in the light of wider considerations may be a better decision. To what extent can it be the case that a decision-making process that is dominated by white, male, middle-aged and middle class civil servants is likely to be appropriate for all areas of social and economic policy? Such decision makers may have little experience of the issues that affect women or ethnic minorities, for example. In the long run a more efficient and effective – not to say democratic – decision may be one that draws upon different points of view and has considered several possibilities.

Marxism

To do justice to the many writings of Marx and the vast body of work that has accumulated around his writings is impossible within the confines of this book and we shall, therefore, merely attempt to discuss one or two ideas and indicate their impact upon organisations.

Marx was very much concerned with conflict; indeed for him the driving force of history is based upon conflict between different groups or classes within society. This conflict comes about because of economic differences between different classes based around who has control over economic production. Thus, for example, one of the most important features of capitalism is the pursuit of profit and owners can increase their profit by exploiting the workforce. This inevitably leads to conflict between these groups. Within organisations such conflict may take the form of strikes or go-slows because of the attempt by owners and managers to control the workers.

Inevitably, as capitalism developed it made sense to introduce more machinery, to move to a division of labour and to a conveyor-belt system of production. We saw in our discussion of bureaucracy that such developments can lead to a more efficient and effective organisation. And yet the individual worker is forgotten in all of this. In a drive for improving productivity and hence greater profit the values, needs and concerns of the worker are ignored. The worker becomes, in Marx's terms, 'an appendage of the machine' and is alienated from the workplace, from the job and from fellow workers. The provision of welfare benefits merely preserves an exploitative and inegalitarian system and Marx argues that the bureaucracy becomes merely the tool of the ruling classes.

Braverman (1974) argues that scientific management and the work of individuals such as F. W. Taylor, that we looked at in an earlier chapter, encouraged the development of the control of the worker by management and that the transformation of work advocated by scientific management led to the de-skilling and to the degradation of the worker. Such effects also apply to the office worker who similarly experiences an increased division of labour, the mechanisation, simplification and routinisation of tasks, and strict management control.

Corporatism

Corporatist theories argue that major interest groups are incorporated into the decision-making apparatus of the state. Conflict is kept to a minimum by allowing such groups to share power. An example of corporatism at work may be that of Britain in the 1960s where the unions, represented by the Trades Union Congress, and big business, represented by the Confederation of British Industry, seemed to have easy access to government. Corporatism is a development of pluralism that allows for the domination of a small number of powerful groups. Schmitter defines corporatism as:

. . . a system of interest representation in which the constituent units organised into a limited number of singular, compulsory, non-competitive, hierarchically ordered and functionally differentiated categories, recognised or licensed (if not created) by the state and granted a deliberate representational monopoly within their respective categories in exchange for observing certain controls on their selection of leaders and articulation of demands and supports. (1979, p. 13).

In the context of Britain in the 1960s, for example, government recognises the legitimate right of the Trades Union Congress to be consulted over issues which affect its members. In return, government expects the Trades Union Congress to respect that right and to control its members. Rhodes (1981) utilises this definition of corporatism in an examination of the policy networks within which public sector organisations operate.

We have thus examined some of the general theories of power within society and within organisations. We now need to narrow our focus and concentrate upon the concept of power itself. We shall accordingly define the concept, examine its usage, and investigate the sources and limits of power.

The definition of power

Immediately we have difficulties since there seems to be no generally accepted agreement on the meaning of power. In the language of political philosophy, power is deemed to be a concept that is 'essentially contested' which means that although the concept has featured prominently in political philosophy over the centuries and is now a major concern of organisation theorists we are still left with disputes over its meaning. We can, however, offer a very general working definition, which seems to feature in most discussions. Thus we take power to be the ability of one person or group (A) to get another person or group (B) to do as A wants. From this very general definition we can see that power is relational in character. Power is not something that is possessed such as blue eyes or red hair but manifests itself in terms of relations with others. Indeed it is often the case that a powerful person is not necessarily somebody who is physically strong but will depend upon the extent to which that person can get others to do as he or she wishes. Indeed it may well be that the most powerful person is someone who does not have to resort to physical force at all. We can see this idea expressed in international relations between states: the USA could not defeat Vietnam despite the fact that in terms of military equipment the USA had the most powerful weapons. Military hardware alone is not sufficient to ensure military victory. We have to take into account the skill of the leaders, the morale of the troops, the influence of world opinion and so on. In organisational theory Pfeffer (1981) argues that power is a relational concept that can only be understood in terms of interactions between individuals and groups.

We can see that power is related to other concepts such as force, influence, authority or manipulation. Power is one of a cluster of concepts that are all concerned with the ability of one person or group to affect another person or group as expressed in our general definition of power. However, we do not need to embark upon a lengthy discussion of differences between these concepts as such differences will be explained as they bear upon our concern with power in public sector organisations (see Connolly, 1974, for treatment of these conceptual issues). What we can do is examine the concept of power from a number of different perspectives.

The basis of power

Power in any form will be based upon something. In general terms we can suggest that power is based upon a number of different factors:

● **Economic power**

This will be based upon the possession of scarce resources such as coal or oil or manpower and the extent to which those resources are in demand. Also the existence of alternative resources will limit the power of the individual or the group. Thus the power of a group like the miners will depend upon the demand for coal compared to other forms of energy. Hence their power to influence the government will depend upon the extent to which alternative forms of energy are readily available. The economic power of the individual may also depend upon the possession of a particular skill or knowledge that others want. Thus the government may offer extra financial rewards to try to recruit scarce science teachers.

● **Political power**

This will be based upon legitimacy, i.e. that which is accepted within a particular society as conferring the right to rule. Sometimes 'might is right' has been accepted as a legitimate form of political power, whereas at other times and in different societies hereditary succession has been accepted as the legitimate source of political power. In democratic societies the will of the people, as expressed in elections, is deemed to be the appropriate legitimation for political power. Thus our elected representatives are entitled to make decisions on our behalf.

● **Military power**

This may be based upon weaponry but, as we have seen, other factors are also important. An extra dimension is introduced which depends upon the perceptions of these factors by the opposition. A crucial element in determining the power of an opponent is whether you believe that the opponent has the will to use its forces.

Two general points arise out of the above discussion. (1) The basis of power will depend upon the context within which it is exercised. Thus the will of the people as a basis of power may not be accepted easily in a society with a tradition of monarchical rule. (2) The basis of power may change. What is to count as a scarce resource, for example, may change over time. In times of low unemployment labour will be in a strong position because it is in demand by employers and is not easily substituted. At other times labour will be in a weak bargaining position if, as in times of high unemployment, the employer can easily acquire alternative sources of labour off the dole queues. Individuals who possess certain skills may also find their power diminished if those skills are made redundant by developments in new technology.

- **Organisational power**

What then is organisational power dependent upon? We can identify a number of factors:

Information Organisations rely upon information in order to function and it is likely that the individual or group that has control over information will have power. Thus, part of the explanation for the power of the official over the politician may well be the extent to which the politician relies upon the official for information in order to make decisions. Critics argue that because of the control of information officials are in a position to slant their recommendations to one course of action that they prefer rather than one they do not prefer. If, on the other hand, there are alternative sources of information and advice then the monopoly position of the official will be undermined. Politicians may thus seek to use special advisers or use research units or policy units outside of government for their advice. The Conservative governments throughout the 1980s have taken advice from the Centre for Policy Studies and the Adam Smith Institute in drawing up their policy proposals. Similarly political parties also have their own policy teams which draw up policy documents.

Knowledge Linked to the power acquired through the control of information is that acquired through the possession of some specialised knowledge or skill, particularly where that knowledge cannot be easily substituted. The power of the officials stems from their understanding the processes and procedures that characterise the bureaucratic organisation. The politician may not possess this knowledge. This will be the case where, for example, a minister stays in a government department for only a limited period of time. The average stay is two years and this is considered insufficient time to master the workings of a complex government department. Other examples include the power of the medical profession within the National Health Service as a result of their medical expertise; the power of the professionals in local government, be they accountants, architects or social workers. The power of such groups will be enhanced if the organisation requires their expertise in order to function. The type of knowledge required within organisations may, however, change over time. In times of financial stringency and the adoption of Value for Money strategies in government those with financial expertise may acquire power. Similarly, in those organisations that are becoming increasingly reliant upon information technology then those with computing skills may become more powerful.

Personal power and charisma   Power may depend upon the personal skills or charisma of certain individuals who, because of their particular characteristics, induce others to follow them. Successful politicians may have it; captains of industry may have it; captains in sport may have it. We can legitimately ask to what extent such personal qualities are important as a source of power within the public sector. According to Weber, bureaucracy is characterised by rational-legal authority rather than by charismatic authority. Given the constraints placed upon officials by formal rules and regulations we may wonder to what extent there is the opportunity for officials to express personal qualities. The attributes of the official are traditionally considered to be formal, anonymous and impersonal in character; hardly the stuff of charisma. And yet even with formal organisations there will be some discretion and there will be opportunities to impose oneself on the organisation. The police constable on the beat will occasionally be in situations where leadership skills have to be shown; team leaders will need to elicit the support of other team members, and some supervisors are more readily followed than others.

Resources   Those who control resources – such as financial or legal – will have power within organisations. We have seen how the control of resources, particularly scarce ones, within society will determine who has power. The same arguments can be applied to organisations. The resources of organisations will include people and money and those who control these in terms of salaries, promotion or budgets will have power. Middle management will have power over those lower down the organisation if middle management determines pay, promotion and bonuses. This argument presupposes that others seek and value these resources. If, for example, an individual does not seek promotion then it will be difficult for those who control promotion to have power over that individual. Where such resources are controlled at the top or are determined by national agreements, as with much of public sector salaries, then the power of middle management will diminish. A further dimension is where one organisation is dependent upon another for resources. Local government depends upon central government for much of its finance and such dependency will limit the scope of local government work. At the same time local government is responsible for implementing central government policy and hence we may find mutual dependency between organisations. Rhodes argues that any organisation will be dependent upon other organisations for resources. He uses the term 'power-dependence' to describe this mutual dependency and suggests five resources that are used in the relationship between central and local government. These are: (1) Constitutional-legal resources that are allocated between local authorities and central government by statute. (2) Hierarchical resources. These may take the form of, for example, central government circulars that guide the work of local authorities. (3) Financial resources. (4) Political resources, such as the access to decision making bestowed on politicians by their election into office. (5) Informational resources, so that the group or individual who has these resources is in a powerful position. Rhodes also suggests that central government and local government will be dependent upon each other 'to different degrees in different circumstances' (Rhodes, 1981, p. 101).

Professionalism We have seen how public sector organisations are made up of professional groups and have briefly discussed their importance for organisations. We can locate that earlier discussion within the context of power by arguing that membership of such groups can confer power upon individuals, particularly if that group has status and prestige. Doctors have a high status based upon their profession and the perception of that profession by the public at large. In contrast, social workers may not have the same status and their power will be less. The concept of a profession is, as we have seen, based upon claims to specialised knowledge and skills developed over time through training. Where certain skills and knowledge are not valued then the profession will have little status. We can expand the argument concerning the power of occupational professions to cover any group. Thus a trade union will have power within an organisation if the union represents all workers and those workers have skills and knowledge that are in short supply. Organisations may also be made up of different groups and professions and when these groups seek to assert themselves then the organisation may well be characterised by competition between groups. This argument fits in with the pluralist notion of power that we discussed at the beginning of the chapter.

Authority A final source of power is that of authority. There are individuals within organisations who have power by virtue of the fact that they occupy a certain position within the organisational structure. This power is not necessarily dependent upon their personal qualities and nor will it depend upon their control of information or their expertise. We may not like or respect our superiors, for example, but they will have power over us just because they occupy a position above us in the organisational hierarchy. Of course, the higher up the organisation an individual progresses it is likely that they will possess skills and expertise, but it does not necessarily follow. In theory, Parliament is the supreme legislative authority in the United Kingdom, but it could be argued that real power, as opposed to authority, is located elsewhere in the hands of the Cabinet or Prime Minister or leaders of industry. The power of Parliament will be limited where a government has a working majority in the House of Commons. Similarly, in the case of a local authority, formal authority to make decisions will rest with the full council; but in reality it may well be that power is in the hands of a few councillors and chief officers such that the locus of decision making may be far removed from the full council meeting.

Power, then, is not the same as authority, even though the two will be closely related. Indeed it may well be that power is not linked to the position of an individual within the formal structure of an organisation at all. An example here may be the power of the receptionist within an organisation to project an image of that organisation since the receptionist is often the first point of contact that we have with organisations. Not only that but the receptionist may control access to individuals within the organisation and hence play an important role as 'gatekeeper' to the organisation. The civil service recognises this: 'Reception staff will convey the image of the office to the public, and they should therefore be carefully selected for the task.' (Cabinet Office, 1988, para. 2.23, p. 12.)

Despite this, receptionists are usually low down in the formal organisational structure.

Power and decision making

We have examined the concept of power within organisations and we now need to see how it is exercised. Power is only seen when it is put to use. This often manifests itself within decision making in terms of who gets their own way within organisations. We can approach decision making from several dimensions. We will follow the approach adopted by S. Lukes (1974) who suggests three different dimensions.

First dimensional view

This view is associated with the pluralist view that we discussed earlier. An early version of pluralism and decision making was developed by R. Dahl in *Who Governs?* (1961). This book was a study of decision making in the town of New Haven, America, in the 1950s over issues such as urban development and public education. Dahl focused upon the making of decisions over which there was an observable conflict of opinion and he studied how that conflict was resolved between the different individuals and groups involved. Dahl argued that power is fragmented between the different groups involved in the decision-making process since different groups got their way on different issues. Thus when there is an observable conflict between different groups then whosoever gets their way has power. It may well be a different group on different issues. We might, therefore, examine different groups involved in the policy process concerned with, say, education. Such groups would represent parents, teachers, political parties, the Local Education Authority, local business, school governors and the Department of Education and Science. According to Dahl, we can see which group gets its own way on a particular issue and conclude that this group has power. We would expect different groups involved in the policy process to have power on different issues.

Second dimensional view

This first view was criticised, in particular, by Bachrach and Baratz (1962) for being too narrow. They argued that some groups can consciously or unconsciously put up barriers to the public discussion of issues. Dahl concentrates upon issues over which there is an observable disagreement and yet it may well be that certain issues are kept off the agenda altogether. Some issues may be filtered out because they are too controversial and hence public discussion may be confined to relatively safe or non-controversial issues. We need, therefore, to be aware of the power of the group or individual who decides what is discussed in the first place. Stringer and Richardson (1980) show how information can be managed and how the presentation of statistics by government departments can keep problems off the agenda. One example they give is that of Home Office statistics on drug addicts that show only those addicts that are registered. Low numbers might indicate that there is no drug problem. Yet what about all those addicts that acquire drugs illegally and hence are not registered?

Another example of the differences between the two views is the location of power within central government in Britain and the role of the Cabinet. The first view would suggest that in Cabinet issues are 'up for grabs' and whichever minister gets his or her own way on an issue has power. The second view would point to the fact that in reality it is the Prime Minister who, in setting the agenda for Cabinet discussion, decides what is to be discussed in the first place and consequently has power.

The relationship between central government and local government further illustrates this point where local government will have the power to make policy and spend public money but within limits set by Parliament and central government.

Third dimensional view

This is the most radical view and is the view endorsed by Lukes himself. Lukes argued that both the previous views are unsatisfactory in that power is only seen to operate where there is conflict. Yet a person or group may have power by shaping beliefs, values and desires. Thus the power of advertising is such that we believe that our lives will be unbearable unless we possess the latest dishwasher, video recorder or television set. This, Lukes argued, is the most insidious form of power in that we can be manipulated into a course of action or believing in a set of values without realising it. From this perspective, political power in Britain is in the hands of the Prime Minister not just because she controls the agenda but also because we would never question her right to do so. Ultimately the attempt to undermine the power of the Prime Minister can be portrayed as an attempt to undermine the whole system of parliamentary democracy as we know it and this will not even be considered. We are 'indoctrinated' into believing in the value of parliamentary democracy just as we are indoctrinated into believing in the merits of this or that soap powder. The extent to which the majority believe in parliamentary democracy or advertising will be an indication of how much power those who propagate such views have.

Similarly, those within organisations who can persuade others to put the good of the organisation before that of the individual or group will have power. Thus, nurses are persuaded that they must put organisational goals such as the welfare of the patients before individual and group goals. Any attempt to win better pay or conditions through industrial action is criticised by the government as selfish and, insofar as many nurses agree with this, then such prevailing beliefs are a very powerful tool in the hands of government.

The major problem with Lukes' view is that if there is no observable conflict then how do we know that power is being exercised at all? It is all very well to use the language of manipulation or indoctrination but how do we know that this in fact is what happens? Individuals may freely endorse an organisational culture or set of values and who is to say that they have been indoctrinated?

A more fruitful line of enquiry is to examine the concept of conflict within organisations and to show how power is exercised in practice.

Power and conflict

If organisations are pluralist in nature such that different groups and individuals can influence the decision-making process then we would expect competition between these groups who will represent different interests. Competition may be no bad thing if it encourages the development of new perspectives, sets standards and encourages groups to improve their performance. Conflict, on the other hand, may lead to tension, to inter-personal friction, and to the pursuit of individual or group goals rather than the pursuit of organisational goals. Competition characterises a healthy organisation and conflict an unhealthy organisation. Competition will be channelled into avenues that benefit the organisation, and one of the major tasks of management is to manage and resolve conflict. From the perspective of power we can suggest, similarly, that power can be used to aid or hinder the organisation.

What then are the possible causes of conflict within organisations? Hall argues that there will be four components in a situation of conflict: (1) The parties involved. (2) The field of conflict. (3) The dynamics of the situation, or how the parties react to each other. (4) The management, control or resolution of that conflict. (Hall, 1972, p. 153.)

In the first instance we can suggest that individuals will enter into organisations from a diverse range of social, economic and educational backgrounds which will give them different perspectives and different values. At the same time individuals will enter into organisations for different reasons and will have different expectations of that organisation. Some will see the organisation as offering a career; others as a stop-gap before moving on; still others as a means to earn as much money as possible in order to pursue life outside the organisation. These differences will inevitably lead to disagreements within the organisation. There will also be conflicts and disagreements arising from the organisation itself which will result from a number of factors.

Incompatible goals

Individual goals may well be in conflict with organisational goals even where there is a strong commitment to one goal by the organisation. It is worth repeating that there may also be competing goals within the organisation itself. Thus, for example, the prison service may wish to pursue the twin goals of the punishment of offenders and at the same time their rehabilitation. These two goals may prove to be incompatible and yet each will have its supporters. Within the National Health Service there may well be a commitment to provide the best possible medical care that the state of medical knowledge will allow and yet this may be tempered by the requirement to act within tight financial constraints. The two goals may be in conflict. Many organisations will face the problem of which goals to prioritise in the light of competing goals.

In the public sector there is also the added dimension of the politician–official relationship. The goals of the politician may well be in conflict with those of the official. When the politician pursues the goal, for example, of reducing the size of the public sector, is it likely that there will be a whole-hearted commitment to this goal when this may directly threaten the job security and promotion prospects of the official?

Centre versus periphery

There may well be conflict between the different parts of an organisation as a result of its geographical and physical dispersal. There will be conflict between central and local government and also within the same authority or department. The region or local office may feel that it is being dictated to by a central office that has no understanding of local needs and conditions. A decision made in Whitehall may look very different in the North East of England. At the same time, the central office may argue that local offices are too parochial and that central control and the imposition of a uniform provision of service has to be of paramount importance.

Interdepartmental conflict

Different departments may wish to pursue their own interests at the expense of other departments or of the organisation as a whole. Within central government there will be conflict between the spending departments and the non-spending departments. Between the spending departments there will be competition for resources. Indeed, as we have seen elsewhere, Public Choice Theory is based upon the premise that bureaucrats are in competition with each other to expand their budgets. Each year there will be competition between the departments of Education, Health, Social Security, Defence and so on, to ensure a slice of the public expenditure cake. Within local authorities there will be similar competition between personnel and finance, between education and social services.

The professional versus the official

If different groups within the organisation resent or do not understand the work and contributions of other groups then there will be conflict. The National Health Service administrator may be critical of the doctor who is profligate in the use of equipment and resources and at the same time the doctor may resent having to account for expenditure to the administrator who may lack the medical expertise to understand why such equipment and resources were used. Similarly, within the civil service the engineer or architect may resent being bound by the rules and regulations of administrative practices and accountability rather than those of the profession.

Structural differences

Disagreement may occur between different levels within the organisation where one level controls the resources that the other wants in terms of information, salary increases, promotion and so on. These differences may be exacerbated in a more formal hierarchical structure where clear divisions exist between the different levels.

Personal differences

It is likely in any organisation that individuals will have different opinions, there will be personality clashes and there may well be conflicts of interest where an individual is required to pursue a particular course of action that they cannot, in all conscience, perform. The public sector is likely to throw up issues that may require the individual to go against the organisation's instructions. The former civil servant, Clive Ponting, was taken to court for disclosing information about the sinking of the Argentine ship, the *Belgrano*, during the Falklands conflict. Ponting's defence was that he was acting in the public interest since he felt that the government was trying to mislead Parliament. As an individual who had access to this information he felt that he could not, in all conscience, keep quiet about it.

Finally, we can suggest that there will be:

- competition for resources in terms of budgets, status, prestige and staff;
- competition for goals, particularly where those goals remain unclear or there is no agreement on objectives or priorities. The goal of a local authority may be expressed as 'Serving the public' but this is rather vague and can be interpreted in any number of different ways;
- competition for territory. Handy (1985) makes the point that organisations can be seen in territorial terms, characterised by empire building. There will be violation and jealousy of the resources or territory that another group or department has at its disposal. For example, the Civil Service Department was created in 1968 to oversee manpower and training issues within the civil service. These functions had previously come under the Treasury. The Civil Service Department eventually lost a running battle with the Treasury and was disbanded in 1981, with some of its functions returning to the Treasury. There may also be overcrowding in some areas. Certain issues quickly become topical and every group wishes to be involved. At the end of the 1980s environmental issues rose to the top of the agenda and suddenly we were all 'greens' as attention was directed towards environmental issues.

Conclusion

To what extent, though, is the exercise of power, the endless competition, healthy or unhealthy? As was suggested earlier, competition may generate new ideas, stimulate and channel energies, set standards for others to follow. It may also waste time and energy; it may be unproductive; it may lead to hostility and to low morale. Whatever the form power takes or the extent to which conflict exists, it is important for us to recognise their existence within organisations. It is in this sense that we can say that every organisation is political and every organisation is concerned with the use, and abuse, of power. Bacharach and Lawler (1980) argue that organisations comprise bargaining systems and we need to understand how they work to understand organisations fully. The research by Thompson (1986) on decision making within district health authorities found much evidence of bargaining, not just between the different coalitions of politicians, administrators and the medical profession but also within these coalitions. Perhaps this is not suprising if we agree with the English philosopher, Thomas Hobbes, who argued that the pursuit of power is part of human nature.

Further reading

For general theories of power and the state the book by Cox, Furlong and Page (1985) is very useful. Pfeffer (1981) and Bacharach and Lawler (1980) both examine power within organisations. Rhodes (1981) examines power in the context of relations between central and local government and is well worth reading. For those interested in a case study approach then Thompson (1986) is most illuminating. Finally, for those interested in the radical approach to power, Lukes (1974) is required reading.

Chapter 7
Leadership

Introduction

Increasingly the qualities of leadership are deemed to be desirable for those working in the public sector. In the private sector the quality of leadership has long been recognised as a key factor affecting organisational performance. The Local Government Training Board publication *The Leadership Audit* (1987b) recognises the importance of leadership for local government officials. Management development within British Rail has been built around a leadership programme for their top managers. A recent scrutiny of public sector job advertisements reveals such phrases as: 'You will be expected to take a lead on all aspects of work in the Division.' 'The General Manager will be required to play a leading role.' 'You must be able to demonstrate leadership.'

We shall examine the different theoretical approaches to leadership and apply these approaches to public sector organisations as well as asking a number of questions.

- How do we define leadership?
- Who are the leaders?
- What does leadership consist of?
- What do leaders do?

Each of these questions will be addressed in turn.

How do we define leadership?

Writers often distinguish between management and leadership. Ackerman (1985) argues that there are a number of important differences. He suggests that management is synonymous with organisations but that leadership can exist outside of the organisation. According to this author, management may be related to formal authority within an organisation and managers get others to do their bidding because of their organisational position. Individuals follow leaders because of the additional attribute of charisma and the personal attraction of the leader. As Stewart puts it:

Managers have subordinates. Leaders have followers: people who recognise and find attractive the leaders' sense of purpose. Leaders are those who can get the people with whom they work, whether subordinates or not, to be convinced co-operators. Leaders make others feel that what they are doing matters and hence makes them feel good about their work. (1989, p. 4.)

There are many different definitions of leadership, but they do seem to have certain features in common and a useful general definition is that given by Kossen: 'Leadership is the ability to influence the behaviour of others to go in a certain direction.' (1983, p. 201.)

This definition of leadership is similar to that of power that was used in the previous chapter. This should come as no surprise since leaders possess a certain amount of power. However, Kossen's definition of leadership can encompass:

- the military leader who is concerned to win support of the troops to pursue the goal of military victory;
- the political leader who is concerned to persuade the citizens that her way is the right way;
- the team leader at work who is concerned to ensure that members of the group are all pulling in the same direction towards greater productivity or an improved service.

Another feature of this definition is that it does not specify at what level within the organisation the leader is. Thus, if an official lower down the organisation can influence those at the top to move in a certain direction then we could designate that person a leader. This may occur where a lower level official may have specialised knowledge or is considered an expert in some area.

Leadership, traditionally, has been seen as a form of activity that is expressed in terms of a relationship – that between the leader and the led. More recent theories, which we shall examine later, suggest that the idea of individuals being led is too passive and that the capacity for leadership may be in all of us. We shall need to study, not just the individual characteristics of leadership, but also the reaction to leadership by others. Leadership is also apparent in many different spheres of activity – the military, the political, the organisational and so on – and it may exist at different levels.

If we return to the definition of leadership as the ability to influence others to go in a certain direction then this ability may be required at many different levels within the organisation. At one level it may be expressed by a Commander-in-Chief who is determining the strategic objectives of the military and has to convince the generals. At a different level it may be the squad leader who has to define these overall goals in operational terms and who has to lead the squad in battle. In the same way the Chief Superintendent of Police may be concerned to define strategic goals for the police force as a whole while the individual police constable may need to exercise leadership in an operational situation and direct others in that situation. Here we might use the term 'street-level' leadership. Similarly, the manager in charge of a local authority department may need to give a lead to others in defining the role and objectives of that department.

The ability to give direction to people is necessary not just at the top of an organisation. Its necessity will depend upon the context and the situation. Stewart (1989) argues that, despite the traditional subordinacy of the nurse to the doctor, nurse managers, for example, will need to demonstrate leadership not least in terms of acting as a role model for younger nurses and for maintaining morale. There are situations, like the operational one that the police find themselves in, where an individual has to take the lead. We can expand, therefore, Kossen's original definition so that our definition of leadership is the ability to influence the behaviour of others to go in a certain direction within a given context.

Who are the leaders?

Traditionally, we have perceived leadership as belonging to those at the top of organisations and have described others within the organisation as followers, subordinates or the led. This is likely to be the case in formal hierarchical establishments where it is felt that the proper locus of decision making is at the top. Where there is an increasing use of decentralised structures and accountability we would expect individuals lower down the organisation to take on more responsibility. The traditional view of the leader may, then, be questioned and our model of leadership may have to be widened to encompass the different locations of leadership. Indeed, Bradford and Cohen (1984) argue that the image of the leader as hero is inappropriate for today's organisations. There is a mythology of the 'good leader' where such a person:

- knows what is going on at all times within the department;
- has more technical expertise than those lower down;
- should be able to solve any problem that crops up;
- should be the primary person responsible for how the department is working.

This image, according to Bradford and Cohen, is outdated. It is the image of the tough, resourceful 'lone ranger' figure who rides in to rescue the town from the wicked cattle baron. What happens when our hero is not there? Surely it is better for the townsfolk themselves to develop the necessary skills to fight their own battles? Our 'post-heroic leader' will allow others to take responsibility, develop their own skills, solve their own problems and develop their own goals. Our leader, according to this approach, will allow others to develop, to act as an enabler rather than as a director of subordinates.

This view, though, has implications for the public sector where convention has it that it is the role of the politicians and not the officials to determine goals and take responsibility. Indeed the idea of civil service leadership is a contradiction in terms within a democracy. The problem with decentralising responsibility and accountability within public sector organisations is that traditionally it is the politician who is held to account rather than the official. Thus if leadership is to be practised throughout the organisation then it has to be consistent with political objectives and compatible with the role of the politician.

At the same time Painter (1989) argues that senior officials within the civil service need to be aware of their responsibilities in offering professional leadership and articulating the values of the civil service as an organisation. Senior officials have a duty to protect junior officials and to set standards for those lower down.

What does leadership consist of?

We are all familiar with the cliché 'Leaders are born and not made', and whether this is true or not it does suggest to us that leadership is dependent upon an individual possessing certain characteristics. This idea has received much support and it is known as the 'trait theory' of leadership. The theory states that individuals possess certain characteristics so that they are predisposed to act in a certain way within a given situation.

Trait theory

Kossen (1983) has suggested that possession of certain characteristics is required for leadership:

- the ability to solve problems creatively;
- the ability to communicate and listen;
- a strong desire to achieve;
- many interests and sociability;
- a positive and sincere attitude towards subordinates;
- self-confidence;
- enthusiasm;
- self-discipline;
- manners;
- emotional stability.

Kossen also says that these characteristics can be learned and developed, thereby suggesting that leaders may be made as well as born. One of the problems, though, is that there is no general agreement on what these characteristics should be. A workshop on leadership skills in local government produced a list of ten key skills:

1. *Vision* – creating a sense of what the organisation is about and where it is going.
2. *Prioritising* – the ability to distinguish between, for example, the urgent and the merely important.
3. *Motivation* – through recognising achievements and rewarding staff.
4. *Inter-personal skills* – such as listening, suggesting, being positive.
5. *Political sensitivity* – to the needs of councillors and to organisational power.
6. *Resilience* – to remain steadfast in the face of adversity.
7. *Charisma* – difficult to define but it attracts others.

8. *Risk-taking* – in areas such as delegating work to other staff.
9. *Flexibility* – to respond to new ideas and practices.
10. *Decisiveness* – when the situation demands it. (Local Government Training Board, 1987)

In her work on the National Health Service, Stewart (1989b) produces a similar list:

- pointing the way or creating a vision;
- symbolising what matters in terms of the values of the organisation;
- getting others to share these values;
- creating pride in the organisation;
- making people feel important;
- realising people's potential;
- self-sufficiency and relying on oneself.

The problem with such lists is that they do not specify any order. Is flexibility any more important than decisiveness? May the two, in fact, be in conflict with each other? We can imagine a situation where a decision needs to be made quickly and the official does not have the scope to take into account individual or local circumstances. Likewise, we may not wish a budget-holder to take risks with taxpayer's money and to ensure equity the official may need to follow formal rules rather than respond flexibly to each new case.

It may also be that we look for different attributes in different parts of the public service. In the civil service, for example, recruitment is dependent upon the selector's perceptions of:

1. Penetration of thought.
2. Fertility of ideas.
3. Judgement.
4. Written ability.
5. Oral expression.
6. Personal contacts.
7. Influence.
8. Drive.
9. Determination.
10. Emotional stability.
11. Maturity. (See Chapman, 1984.)

Once again, though, such a list may be too general and does not indicate any order of preference. It may be that for any individual to succeed in any organisation then he or she will need some or all of the qualities listed above. Likewise the ability to listen or to communicate or show enthusiasm and self-confidence know no organisational boundaries.

There is one feature that is included in the local government list of characteristics that may be unique to the public sector and that is the requirement that our public sector officials have political sensitivity. Thus our official, in dealing with the politician, needs to be aware of the political impact of his or her advice and be sensitive to the needs of the politician. In drafting reports, for example, the official will need to be aware of the ruling party's political values. This issue has been of particular importance within central government in recent years as the traditional task of the civil service – that of offering objective, impartial advice – has come under scrutiny. Recent Conservative governments have stressed a greater concern with commitment to putting policies into practice and getting the job done. However, any organisation has to be aware of the environment within which it operates. The businessman has to be sensitive to the needs of the customer or to the demands of the shareholders.

The approach to leadership purely in terms of individual characteristics is also deficient in that it does not take into account the relationship between the leader and the followers. If we recall our definition of leadership we stressed that leadership involves a relationship. This relationship may take a number of different forms. There are a number of theories that discuss this relationship and they are generally known as 'style theories of leadership' where the focus is upon the style that a leader adopts in dealing with others.

Style theories

A common approach is to suggest that there are different styles of leadership such as:

- *Autocratic* – identified with a strong domineering leader where power and control are centralised.
- *Participative* – the leader gives up some power and authority to subordinates.
- *Laissez-faire* – the absence of direct leadership. The leader may believe that the most important role for them to play is that of a co-ordinator.

An example of the first might be Mrs Thatcher, insofar as it is said that she dominated her Cabinets. However, she cannot control every aspect of government and she will give up some of her authority to, for example, the Chancellor of the Exchequer where financial matters are concerned. Thus it may be that style theories are too simplistic. Different situations may require different styles of leadership and a good leader may be one who uses a combination of different styles. Where there is a task to be completed and deadlines to be met an autocratic approach may be appropriate. Where the issue is one that requires a consensus decision it may be that a more participative style is required.

Not only is the particular situation important but also the attitudes towards the leader by the followers are. A leader may believe that individuals need coercing into following a particular direction, or alternatively may believe that encouragement is the key. The model of the post-heroic leader that we discussed earlier is certainly based upon the premise that individuals will respond to encouragement.

One of the better known theories concerned with leadership styles is that put forward by McGregor (1960). As we saw in Chapter 5, he suggested that the style adopted depends upon the perception that leaders have of their subordinates. A leader who believes that their subordinates are lazy, lacking in ambition, self-centred and resistant to change will adopt an autocratic style of leadership. The emphasis here is on securing the compliance of the subordinate through direction and control. McGregor calls this Theory X. In contrast to this is Theory Y, where he argues that if the leaders see subordinates as willing and able then the leader will be less inclined to pursue an autocratic style but instead prefer a participative style of leadership and encourage subordinates to accept responsibility and authority. Blake and Mouton (1964) argue that leadership behaviour is based upon a conflict between two opposing forces within the individual – a concern for the task to be done and a concern for people. Blake and Mouton construct a matrix with concern for task on one axis and concern for people on the other axis. They identify five main leadership styles to be plotted on the matrix, depending upon the various commitments to either people or the task.

So far, then, leadership can be seen as a number of different factors, comprising;

1. An individual's characteristics.
2. The organisational context – some organisations will value different characteristics.
3. Different styles that leaders prefer.
4. Different styles appropriate to different situations, depending upon whether the situation is task-oriented or people-oriented.
5. The perceptions by leaders of the qualities and values of those they are seeking to influence.

Contingency theory

This group of theories suggests that leadership will be a combination of different factors, depending upon the situation. Different leaders will choose different approaches, depending upon the context. It depends upon what 'best fits' the situation. This is an expression used by Handy (1985) who suggests that there are a number of leadership variables and the best combination is one appropriate to a particular situation. The variables that Handy uses are:

- the leader's style, which may change;
- expectations of the leader's behaviour;
- the objectives of the group;
- the environment of the organisation.

Fiedler (1967) suggested that the elements of a leadership situation are three-fold:

- leader member relations and the extent to which there is support for the leader;
- the task itself; is it simple or complex?
- position power; to what extent does the leader have the power to reward or punish other members of the organisation?

A leader must assess whether favourable factors exist, i.e. good relations, high task structure and strong position power, before selecting an appropriate style. Fiedler found that extremely favourable or unfavourable conditions required a task-oriented or autocratic style of leadership. Those situations deemed to be moderately favourable required a people-oriented style. The leader could be matched to the situation which suited his/her style or the situation could be changed to suit the particular style.

A more recent approach emphasises not just the relationship between the leader and others but also stresses the changing nature of this relationship.

Developmental approach

This approach stresses the fact that as individuals 'mature' in an organisation then the leader should take account of this and allow the relationship to develop as a consequence. Thus we might expect to move gradually to a more participative or laissez-faire approach. Banner and Blasingame (1988) suggest that there are nine stages in this development:

1. *Attention* – leaders initially pay attention and give time to subordinates.
2. *Support* – help the employees in their work.
3. *Feedback/information sharing* – show how the employee's work fits into the wider scheme of things.
4. *Nurturing* – move towards the sharing of ideas.
5. *Emerging autonomy* – the employees begin to define their own role but still need guidance.
6. *Setting limits* – autonomy plus limits determined by the leader.
7. *Personal competence* – employees are highly 'mature', i.e. they are high achievers who take responsibility for results.
8. *Independent personal and professional growth* – employees begin to lead themselves.
9. *Loyalty and commitment* – the leader and the organisation are now seen as 'family' by the individual.

This approach takes into account the changing nature of the relationship between the leaders and others and indicates how it may develop. It is a more sophisticated account than the simple trait and style theories that we began our account with.

What do leaders do?

Leadership is concerned with performing a number of different tasks and below we explore some of these tasks in detail.

Providing a vision

We have discussed the notion that leaders will influence others to go in a certain direction. In order to do that our leaders must, themselves, have a clear idea of where that direction lies. Increasingly, management theory stresses the most important role is that of the visionary where the leader:

- creates a vision;
- communicates it to others within the organisation;
- shows its relevance to their work;
- ensures commitment to that vision.

Peters and Austin (1986) use the image of the leader as 'chief salesperson' where leadership is involved in creating an image of the organisation and symbolising what it stands for. Within the public sector we tend to think of politicians as providing the vision for the organisation, expressed in terms, depending upon the ideology of the party in power, which include:

- reducing poverty;
- promoting equality and freedom;
- pursuing justice;
- caring for the welfare of the population;
- promoting enterprise;
- educating the population.

Perhaps we should also expect the officials to provide a vision for the organisation even though less grandiose in scope? We can imagine a departmental head in a local authority urging his/her staff to be the most efficient and effective, the most caring or the friendliest department. Such visions can be utilised at all levels within an organisation and are not the sole prerogative of those at the top. Indeed, they may be considered to be much more practical than the visions given to us by politicians and hence may be more likely to have support. It is difficult to operationalise the politician's objective of promoting freedom and equality.

Overall perspective

Linked to the notion of creating a vision is connecting that vision to the overall perspective of the organisation. Both require standing back from the day-to-day running of the organisation and examining the wider picture. One of the major criticisms that is made of senior management is its unwillingness to let go of the reins of an organisation, to delegate routine tasks and to concentrate upon the longer term. Leadership has to see the work of the organisation within a wider context and to be aware of the environment within which the organisation is working. Garratt (1987) suggests that leaders need to be aware of the wider economic, social and political contexts, the uncertain world within which organisations operate, and to take account of this external environment. Stewart (1989) argues that the call for leaders in the National Health Service is precisely because the National Health Service increasingly operates within an uncertain and changing environment. We would expect leaders at all levels to be aware of the wider context of their work. Departmental heads will need to be aware of other departments within the organisation, will have outside relationships involving clients or customers, and will need to work with other agencies. People in departments dominated by the professions will need to be aware of developments within the professional field and keep up-to-date with the latest techniques or equipment. At whatever level it manifests itself, leadership is concerned with standing back from the day-to-day routine of affairs.

The Fulton Report (1968) on the civil service was critical of the generalist class within the civil service and suggested that a greater role in management should be found for the specialist classes. However, recent writings on leadership would seem to support the retention of the skills of the generalist administrator. We have suggested that a feature of leadership is the ability to stand back and take the wider perspective. This means not being bound by the commitment to a narrow specialist view. The generalist administrator is concerned to take this wider view and not be bound by a narrow perspective. This role would fit easily into the modern view of leadership.

Similarly, in local government the tradition that senior officers are specialists with professional expertise has been questioned. The suggestion is that there needs to be a move away from the narrow professionalism of the past towards a more generalised and politically aware professionalism. The concern is with taking a wider perspective, looking outwards rather than inwards.

Transmitting the vision

We suggested earlier that leadership is concerned with influencing the behaviour of others. This may take a number of different forms:

- coercion;
- manipulation;
- threats;
- promises;
- explanation;
- persuasion;
- setting an example.

The more extreme forms of influence, such as coercion or threat, are unlikely to be sustained over any length of time. If a leader constantly has to threaten individuals, it is unlikely that those individuals will come to share the vision of the leader. Of course, it may be that under certain circumstances a more autocratic relationship is appropriate. For example, where a decision has to be made quickly then it may be more appropriate to tell an individual what to do rather than persuade him. This may be appropriate in an organisation like the Army where discipline and the carrying out of orders is essential to the success of that organisation. Here there also may be more compliant subordinates who prefer this more authoritarian style – there may be individuals in any organisation who do not want responsibility and who prefer to be told what to do. We suggested earlier that leadership will need to take account of different situations and the different relations that leaders will have with others. The perceptions that individuals have of the leaders is also important here.

The Developmental model that we discussed earlier suggested that the relationship between the leader and others will develop through various stages and it is up to the leader to know what is appropriate at any given time and with any given individual.

Relations with others

We have stressed the notion that leadership is concerned with a relationship and we have indicated what forms this relationship might take. Many difficulties faced in the public sector will stem from the formal, hierarchical structure within which such relationships take place. As we have seen, such organisations tend to be dominated by formal rules and by committees which may lend themselves to the more autocratic style of leadership. Hence it will be necessary to take account of the structure in determining what leadership role is most appropriate. It will be pointless advocating a more participative style of leadership if the structure does not allow participation and informal rules to develop.

A further problem is that the promotion, pay and career development of officials may be outside the control of immediate superiors and hence it may be difficult for the departmental head to have much impact upon the work, the responsibilities, the morale and the development of individuals within the organisation. As we saw earlier with Fiedler's model of leadership, position power is an important factor. In the civil service it may not exist lower down the organisation. The Developmental model of leadership advocated by Banner and Blasingame will require greater responsibility and the identification of leadership lower down the organisational structure than has traditionally been the case within either central or local government.

Conclusion

We have examined the various models and explanations of leadership, from the traditional concern with leaders and their subordinates to a more recent approach which suggests that leadership needs to be more enlightened and to allow individuals to develop their own leadership skills. We illustrate these points diagrammatically in Figures 7.1 and 7.2.

Thus if we were to compile a checklist of leadership it would comprise the following:

1. Take an integrated view.
2. Learn to delegate tasks and responsibility.
3. Know the staff.
4. Help and allow individuals to develop.
5. Provide direction.
6. Be constructive and positive rather than destructive and negative.
7. Trust and have faith in the staff.
8. Treat staff with respect and value their abilities.

Figure 7.1 The traditional model of leadership.

Stewart's prescriptions for the leader in the National Health Service urge:

- do not be afraid to think of yourself as a leader;
- have a strong belief in what needs doing;
- be willing to convey the vision to others;
- show enthusiasm and commitment in pursuing the vision;
- show a passion for excellence;
- show a positive attitude to setbacks;
- encourage others and do not let disappointments show. (1989, p. 17.)

Finally, then, we also need to locate our concept of leadership within: (a) the political environment within which the organisation operates and hence be aware of political objectives; (b) the organisational structure that exists; (c) the 'fit' between the structure of public sector organisations, and the preferred leadership style. It is no good advocating a more participative style of leadership if the organisation is dominated by a bureaucratic structure.

Figure 7.2 The 'enlightened' model where individuals are seen as equals within the organisation.

Further reading

There are many general textbooks on the subject of leadership. The ones that we have found useful are Kossen (1983), Selznick (1957) and Chell (1987). There are also a number of texts that are prescriptive in giving guidelines to improving leadership performance. Bradford and Cohen (1984) and Wright and Taylor (1984) both fall into this category. A similar approach based upon research in the National Health Service is offered by Stewart (1989). We found Local Government Training Board (1987b) instructive for the local government context. The short article by Painter (1989) is also useful for the dimensions of leadership in the civil service.

Chapter 8
Motivation and morale

Introduction

Lack of motivation and the existence of low morale is of concern to all organisations. From an organisational perspective, motivation is linked to performance. A highly motivated individual, it is argued, will perform better than one with a low level of motivation. Organisations, therefore, have an interest in ensuring that motivation is high in individuals and morale is good throughout the organisation. Within the public sector one of the implications of attempts by government to reduce the size and change the structure of public sector organisations has been declining morale – or so commentators would have us believe.

> There is ample evidence that pay levels in the NHS are too low and that there are insufficient rewards. These pay levels have resulted in low morale within the Service and have made it increasingly difficult to recruit and retain staff. (Institute of Health Service Management, 1988, para 2.8.)

We find similar accounts in the press. The lack of public confidence in the police and the declining status of the police profession was commented upon by a police constable: 'I want to leave the station wearing my uniform and feel proud, that it means something, honour and dignity. But now, that uniform feels like a rag.' (*Guardian*, 21 February, 1990.)

Problems arise when we attempt to *measure* motivation and morale. The approach to understanding organisations that concentrates its focus on people within organisations needs to be aware of what it is that motivates people within those organisations. We have already examined the Human Relations approach to organisations, and this is a precursor to examining what it is that motivates people to perform within organisations. We shall be concerned with a number of general questions about motivation and morale:

1. What is motivation?
2. Why is it important within organisations?
3. Is it linked to performance?

4. Can we measure it?
5. Does motivation vary between individuals and between different types of occupations?
6. Is there anything distinctive about motivation and morale within the public sector?

In order to answer these questions we need, in the first instance, to examine theories of motivation and then discuss their practical relevance.

Theories of motivation

A number of theories are built upon some conception of human nature. The theories make certain assumptions about individual needs and desires and how individuals are motivated to satisfy these needs and achieve our desires. Depending upon what view of human nature we take then we will arrive at different explanations of what motivates us.

Maslow's hierarchy of needs

We discussed Maslow's theory in Chapter 5 and so we do not need to reproduce his basic arguments. But it will help our present purposes if we show his theory of basic needs in the form of a diagram (see Figure 8.1).

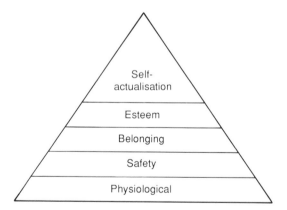

Figure 8.1 Theory of basic needs.

Although Maslow was not concerned specifically with individuals within organisations, we can suggest a number of implications where concern would apply.

1. Our needs change so that our motivation will change. It may well be that throughout our careers we are motivated by the desire to satisfy different needs.
2. The higher up we go in an organisation then what motivates us will also change.

3. Motivation is a reflection of position within the hierarchy. If we are at the bottom of the organisation we may be motivated by the desire to satisfy physiological needs. In the first instance we go to work in order to eat and drink and provide ourselves with shelter. At the top of the organisation we may be motivated by the desire to satisfy self-actualisation needs. At the top the individual may be earning enough money to satisfy the basic physiological needs.
4. Managers need to be aware of these different needs and recognise the stage at which individuals have reached in the satisfaction of their needs. Giving an employee more money may not motivate him/her if that individual needs to satisfy the desire for respect and the esteem of colleagues. That may be satisfied by giving the individual more responsibility or more challenging work.
5. Satisfaction in terms of needs says nothing whatsoever about improving performance. Individuals may be more content and morale may be high, but does this necessarily lead on to an improved performance?

Although Maslow offers us useful insights into individual psychology, his theory is open to a number of criticisms:

1. The basic components of Maslow's theory are often presented as a pyramid, but this seems to imply that those needs situated at the top of the pyramid are more important than those at the bottom. This is open to debate. It also seems to imply that relatively few of us ever reach the stage of self-actualisation.
2. What exactly is self-actualisation? Although it can be linked to the idea of attaining personal meaning through work, much of our potential may be attained outside of work in terms of sport or hobbies.
3. Are there only five basic needs? Do we know what they are? Can we prove it? There is no evidence to suggest that Maslow's assumptions are correct or incorrect.
4. Are there clear dividing lines between the different levels? It may be that people wish to satisfy a number of needs at the same time.
5. It may be that individuals can satisfy their needs outside the organisation altogether. Thus, an individual's need to belong may be satisfied by close family and friendship ties.

McGregor's Theory X and Theory Y

As we saw in Chapter 5, McGregor argued that the style of management adopted is a function of the manager's attitudes and assumptions about human nature. We can wonder to what extent McGregor's Theory X is appropriate for the modern organisation since it implies direction and control through a centralised system of organisational structure. In other words, this theory will apply to the traditional, formal organisation. Under Theory X motivation occurs only at the physiological and security levels of Maslow's hierarchy. In contrast, Theory Y focuses upon the top three tiers of Maslow's hierarchy and implies the integration of individual goals with those of the organisation.

An important feature of McGregor's approach is that it shows how management assumptions are important in determining motivation and morale. It is in this sense that the scientific management approach and that of the Human Relations school that we discussed in earlier chapters are both managerialist in that increased efficiency of the organisation is the context for both approaches. McGregor's approach suggests that motivation also depends upon relations with others as well as the individual's own nature. However, we need to be aware that:

- individuals respond differently to different types of management style. Thus, some individuals may welcome the opportunity to exercise responsibility whereas others may not be interested and prefer the security of being directed by others;
- situations may also respond to different styles of management. Thus, for example, in a police operational matter it may well be that one individual must make a decision and make that decision quickly. Clear direction has to be given and control over colleagues exercised.

Downs and bureaucratic motivation

Although rarely included in standard textbook discussions of motivation, the work of Downs (1967), as representative of Public Choice theorists, is important. Public Choice theorists explicitly examine the motivation of bureaucrats and suggest that, in crude terms, the most important motivator is the desire to increase one's share of the budget which leads to increased status. The assumption is that it is much more difficult to assess the work of a public manager than it is of a private sector counterpart. There are no sales or profit figures to judge the bureaucrats' work. Public Choice theory argues that bureaucrats are judged by the size of the budget that they control and by how much they can increase it. It is a fairly cynical thesis but one that is not without its merits, as those who work in the public sector might testify.

Downs argues that bureaucrats do exhibit personality traits but these may differ. Not only that but they do have different ways of achieving their maximum personal utility. He goes on to argue that:

1. Bureaucrats are made up of different types of officials.
2. These officials can be characterised in two ways: (a) purely self-interested; and (b) mixed-motive.
3. The purely self-interested officials are of two types: (a) climbers – motivated by power and prestige and the pursuit of both. These types of individuals are the ones who are said to stab you in the back in order to achieve their ends; and (b) the conservers – motivated by the desire to retain the status quo. They resist change because they feel threatened by it and are the ones who constantly refer to the rules and regulations before they will do anything. They tend to be characterized by the phrase 'its more than my job's worth . . .' and may be termed petty officials.

4. Mixed-motive officials are of three types: (a) zealots – they are especially obsessive about particular pet policies even though no one else may share their enthusiasm and although it may be detrimental to the organisation as a whole; (b) advocates – concerned with getting things done and loyal to a broader set of policies; (c) statesmen – concerned with the good of the state or society as a whole. They comprise the classical concept of the public official who is anxious to promote the 'public interest'.

The assumption is that organisations are made up of different types of individuals who have different motives. Not only that but motivation can be expressed in terms of self-interest, however that may be perceived, and in terms of serving organisational interests. And yet we can offer a number of criticisms of this approach:

1. Only the most senior officials may be in a position to have some impact upon determining their own interests. The theory will not apply to the vast majority of officials.
2. If Public Choice theory as a whole is based upon the concept of maximising budgets it may be the case that most officials have no control over budget allocation. As Dunleavy (1985) argues, different kinds of government bodies will vary in their control over their budgets.
3. As officials move up the hierarchy they may be more involved in policy advice rather than managing budgets or people.

Herzberg's two-factor theory

From Herzberg's theory we can suggest that motivation is thus concerned with both the content and the context of work. According to Herzberg (1966), job enrichment through increasing responsibility and providing more challenging work can lead to job satisfaction. If we received job satisfaction, we would be motivated to work harder. At the same time if the hygiene factors were a poor working environment, poor salary and poor supervision then we might ask: 'Why work here'? We might be able to do the same job elsewhere under better working conditions.

However, like many of the theories we have been looking at, it leads to oversimplification. What satisfies one individual may not satisfy the next. Some workers do not seem to be particularly interested in the job content of their work. As long as the context of work allows good working relations and a pleasant environment then morale may be high but individuals may not be particularly motivated to seek responsibility.

Expectancy/valence theories

These theories attempt to link the value of rewards, the probability of receiving these rewards and the effort put in. This simple proposition is linked most closely with the work of Vroom (1964) and Porter and Lawler (1968). Expectancy theories are concerned with the relationships among the inputs that make up motivation.

The motivation to perform is seen as a function of the beliefs that individuals have concerning future rewards multiplied by the value they place on those rewards. Thus individuals desire certain goals and they put a value on these goals. To determine motivation we need to break the model down into two components:

- expectancy
- valence (or the value which an individual places on an outcome)

Thus:

1. Individuals believe that acting in a certain way will lead to certain outcomes (the performance – outcome expectancy).
2. Individuals believe that these outcomes have positive value for them (valence).
3. Individuals believe that they are able to perform at the desired level (effort – performance outcome). Here 'Can I do it?' is the question.
4. Expectancy is the perceived probability that effort will lead to perceived outcomes.

The individual will want to know the answer to two questions:

1. What am I most likely to get out of this if I do it? (*Expectancy*).
2. How much do I value what I am likely to get out of it? (*Valence*).

The theories are based upon individuals' perception of what they expect out of work and recognise that individuals place different values on rewards and the effort that they have to expend in order to achieve those rewards. There is thus believed to be a direct correlation between expected rewards and performance.

However, such theories have limited predictive capability in that we cannot measure the individual's perception of values. Unless we assume that all individuals are the same then presumably we may all have different values and different perceptions of how to satisfy these values. We can also legitimately ask to what extent people are rational in the sense of making some kind of calculation concerning the best way to satisfy their needs.

Although we have offered a fairly simplistic version of these theories we can still see that even a simplified version is very complex.

Adams and equity theory

This theory brings in the element of comparison such that an individual will compare his/her ratio of input (effort) to output (pay) with a similar ratio for some other relevant person. Other theories are based upon the individual. This group of theories is based upon how we perceive others in comparison to ourselves. We desire to be treated equitably (Adams, 1965). Thus:

- It is perceived equity that motivates behaviour and provides satisfaction.
- Perceived inequity will lead to dissatisfaction and conflict between individuals.
- The individual is motivated to change the situation back to an equitable one.

The theory is based upon exchanges and the equity of those exchanges. If we work extra hard for our employers we expect some kind of reward in return. Not only that but we expect that reward to be a fair and just one. The organisation must ensure that employees *believe* that they are being treated fairly in comparison with others. This comparison may be based upon pay since this can be easily measured. It may also involve comparison with other professions and other occupations and not just with rewards within the organisation.

The administrative officer working within the civil service may compare pay and conditions with similar jobs in the private sector such as a building society. Indeed this may more likely be the case if there is a uniform salary within the civil service which is not based upon performance.

However, most of the research in this area is based upon employee reactions to pay inequalities. This may be too narrow a base if it is the case that pay is only one factor in determining levels of motivation. It may be used by the employer to induce individuals to be over-competitive with each other.

A major problem is that there is no reason why we choose the referents that we do other than the fact that they may be someone we know or whose occupation we have information about. Thus, there is no particular reason why we should choose one referent rather than another. We may choose a professional sports person as our referent and bemoan the fact that our salaries do not compare despite the fact that we may have as much talent in our chosen fields. It is difficult trying to build a theory on such subjective criteria.

Summary

Each set of theories offers us insights but none is conclusive. However, we are left with a number of general points:

- views on human nature are important;
- the role of management is crucial;
- the content of work is important;
- the context of work is important;
- individual perceptions of reward and the relation between performance and reward are important;
- the notion of a fair or equitable reward compared to others is also important.

Implications for managers

Increasingly it is recognised that the role of management is of crucial importance in securing motivation and morale. The Griffiths Report (1983) on management in the National Health Service suggested that the presence of a general management process is important in: 'securing proper motivation of staff. Those charged with the general management responsibility would regard it as vital to review incentives, rewards and sanctions' (para 9c, p. 13).

Given the theories that we have explored above we can suggest that the manager needs to:

1. Be aware of the individual needs of employees (Maslow).
2. Be aware of the assumptions that they are making concerning human nature (McGregor).
3. Be aware of the organisational context of work and not just concentrate on the job itself (Herzberg).
4. Calculate that outcome which each employee values (*Expectancy*).
5. Make sure that the desired levels of performance are attainable (*Expectancy*).
6. Link desired outcomes to required performances (*Expectancy*).
7. Make sure that employees are treated equitably (*Equity*).

Such a role for management assumes that:

- it is possible to measure motivation;
- rewards are linked to performance;
- management has the time and the expertise to assess individual performance;
- organisations can be individualised and take account of the many different needs of employees.

The public sector

As we indicated at the beginning of the chapter, there is a growing interest in issues of motivation and morale within the public sector. The extent to which it is being seriously addressed throughout the sector is less clear. However, efforts in this direction are increasingly being reported on:

- Lawrence and Santry (1989) report on the work being done in a division of the Department of Trade and Industry and indicate the techniques used. These included the introduction of specific work targets, a more open and informal management style, the establishment of a quality circle.
- The Local Government Training Board (1988b) report that morale and motivation can be improved by defining the core values of the organisation and communicating these to employees.

One piece of research looked specifically at the civil service and was carried out by Livingstone and Wilkie (1981). The exercise was concerned with the motivation of junior and middle managers within the civil service and in broad terms used Herzberg's two-factor analysis described briefly above. Livingstone and Wilkie presented a number of factors leading to dissatisfaction:

- Failure to achieve.
- Lack of a challenge.
- The feeling of being an unimportant cog in a large machine.
- Ungrateful or demanding clients particularly in the – what was then – Department of Health and Social Security.

- The lack of autonomy and responsibility.
- The lack of promotion prospects.
- Salary – a low proportion identified this as a source of dissatisfaction. Dissatisfaction was mostly aimed at individual anomalies or inappropriate differentials within the organisation rather than those outside.
- The manager's inability to delegate responsibilities or to communicate to those lower down.
- The lack of training to carry out the job.
- Departmental practices were often unworkable.

Livingstone and Wilkie also identified a number of factors leading to satisfaction, the most important of which were:

- A sense of achievement – successfully completing a task or overcoming a challenge.
- Recognition.
- Decent colleagues.
- The physical environment.
- A degree of autonomy in one's work.

Livingstone and Wilkie make a number of comments concerning their findings. They suggest that relatively junior and often youthful staff do not shirk opportunities for taking responsibility when the opportunity is there and they, in fact, associate responsibility and autonomy with a high degree of job satisfaction. Thus an improvement in performance is often related to the content of the job rather than to pay. Thus an interesting, worthwhile and challenging job was deemed to be a motivator. Unfortunately the tradition in the civil service is to bring about changes in structure rather than changing job content or levels of responsibility. Just to redesign the structure misses the point.

Many respondents felt that the most effective barriers to change were the attitudes, beliefs and behaviour of senior management itself. In the civil service the prevailing ethos is one of control of subordinates rather than allowing discretion. Paradoxically, attending courses at the Civil Service College often led to more dissatisfaction when contrasted with the reality of civil service life. Livingstone and Wilkie conclude by arguing for the decentralisation of control and the democratisation of work processes.

Comments

The sample may be biased insofar as Livingstone and Wilkie used middle management as their study and it may well be that at this level individuals are reasonably well paid and hence money is not as important as other factors. If they had interviewed the – what were then termed – clerical officers and assistants, they may well have come up with different results. In the Department of Trade and Industry case, reported above, junior staff were short of money and welcomed the opportunity to earn more through overtime.

However, their work does cast doubt on two recent developments within the civil service. Firstly, merit pay; if it is the case that money is not the most important motivator then linking pay to performance, as with merit pay, is not likely to improve performance. We look at this in more detail below. Secondly, recent changes in the structure of the civil service with the development of the agency model through the Next Steps programme will not improve matters unless it is linked to changing roles and relationships. Changing the structure alone is insufficient to improve performance. Indeed the Next Steps Report found that: 'People who had recently resigned from the Civil Service told us that frustration at the lack of genuine responsibility for achieving results was a significant factor in encouraging them to move to jobs outside.' (Efficiency Unit, 1988, para 2.3, p. 3.)

A surprising feature of the Livingstone and Wilkie research is the lack of a commitment to the public service ethos. Certainly in certain professions such as teaching, nursing or social work it is generally considered that a desire to serve the public is of paramount importance.

A more recent report from the Department of Social Security indicated low morale and a lack of confidence in the organisation. It suggested that lack of job satisfaction is related to:

- *pressure*, with too much work and too little time;
- *recognition and regard*, with efforts going unnoticed by both employer and the public at large;
- *career development and training*, where it exists it leads to a happier employee;
- *communications*, where people prefer formal communication from the department rather than relying on the 'grapevine';
- *pay*, which was perceived to be poor both in terms of the duties involved and pay for similar jobs elsewhere;
- *the quality of service*, where the feeling of providing a quality service improves morale. (1988, pp. 16–7.)

Performance-related pay

Throughout much of the public sector performance-related pay is being introduced. In the National Health Service it was introduced in 1986 for General Managers and has since been extended to other levels of management. It is linked to the achievement of individual and organisational objectives. In the civil service merit pay has been extended to cover all grades from April 1990. It is linked to an appraisal system usually based upon a banded assessment of performance. For example:

Band 1 – Outstanding.
Band 2 – Performance significantly above requirements.
Band 3 – Performance fully meets requirements of grade.
Band 4 – Performance not fully up to requirements of grade, some improvement
      necessary.
Band 5 – Unacceptable.

We have already suggested that theories of motivation seem to indicate that money is only one of many factors that have a bearing upon motivation and morale. Another problem is that of trying to assess performance when there may be no tangible product to measure. If we recall, the main advocate of scientific management, F.W. Taylor, argued that pay should be related to an individual worker's output. This may be fine when we can identify the output in terms of manufactured goods but it may be more difficult to measure the output of a government official. Thus judgements are made on subjective grounds concerning the performance of the individual and this will be open to interpretation. Not only that but where the nature of the work requires working in a team then how is the performance of the individual team member assessed? However, we examine performance indicators in more detail in later chapters.

Conclusion

There are a number of problems in discussing motivation and morale.

1. How do we measure motivation and morale? We can measure productivity but with motivation we can only make certain assumptions that improved motivation may lead to improved performance. It is probably easier to measure lack of motivation. Thus, for example, a high level of absenteeism may be a sign of low morale; high staff turnover and the inability to retain staff may be a sign of low morale (witness the number of teachers that leave the profession every year); industrial action or strikes may be an indication that morale and motivation are low. Thus if we want signs of low morale in the civil service, for example, we could point to the 1981 civil service strike.
2. A second general problem is associated with the esteem with which a profession is held by society as a whole and, as far as the public sector is concerned, the attitude towards it of the government of the day. Thus, commentators have suggested that the Conservative Party came into power in 1979 and was committed to reducing the size of the public sector. Not only that but a change in methods of working, in its ethos and what were seen as its privileges, such as index-linked pensions, was to follow. There is evidence to suggest that this did in fact happen.

    Within the civil service the Priestley pay bargaining system was abolished which linked civil service pay to rates in the private sector. Equity theory that we examined earlier suggested that a feature of motivation was the individual's perception of equity compared to others. At one stroke the Conservative Government undermined that principle.

    The banning of trade unions at the Government Communications Headquarters (GCHQ), the naming and blaming of civil servants in the Westland Affair, and the Rayner Scrutinies were all seen as undermining the morale of civil servants. The former Labour Party leader, Michael Foot, suggests that there may be another reason:

Does not the Prime Minister appreciate that one of the reasons for the very low morale in the Civil Service is that she has appointed so many confirmed Thatcherites to some of the best jobs? (*Hansard*, 18.2.1988, p. 1152.)

In local government developments such as compulsory competitive tendering, or the introduction of GCSE in schools, have been said to undermine morale.

3. There are a number of factors that are to be considered when looking at motivation and morale within public sector organisations and these operate at many different levels. These factors are both external and internal to the organisation and are a reflection of individual needs and the organisational context. We can represent this in Figure 8.2:

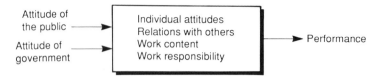

Figure 8.2 Motivation and morale factors.

Further reading

Steers and Porter (1979) offer a good general introduction to the concept of motivation. The collection of essays in Vroom and Deci (1970) also provide a useful introduction. The article by Fowler (1988b) describes the history of performance-related pay and offers a guide to the future use of such systems. The Livingstone and Wilkie article (1981) on motivation in the civil service and on the application of one of the main theories of motivation is well worth reading.

Chapter 9
Planning and decision making

Introduction

The concept of planning can be applied in its various ways to a whole range of activities. The common theme is that planning is used to solve problems. Because of the wide range of problems that the public sector faces there will be different approaches to planning in different situations.

One view of the administrative task is to see it as planning and decision making (Simon, 1976). If we accept this view, we need to consider what decision making is about and then examine the various prescriptions on how best to make decisions.

This chapter discusses the notion of planning, examines different approaches to planning and looks at the changes in attitudes to planning that have taken place. In so doing, we will look at two approaches to decision making – the rational and the incremental models – and assess their suitability to modern public sector organisations.

Planning

According to Wedgewood-Oppenheim, planning 'can be seen as a process whereby aims, factual evidence and assumptions are translated by a process of logical argument into appropriate policies which are intended to achieve aims' (Wedgewood-Oppenheim, 1982, p. 107). This definition assumes that organisations have aims which are clearly stated and they have the capability to gather information and use it in a positive way to develop policies. At this point we must note that policies need to be put into practice – a theme that will be developed later in the chapter.

As we have already stated, decision makers in organisations will formulate aims or objectives which they wish to achieve or, in other situations, a commanding authority will impose objectives on organisations. In order to achieve those objectives, an organisation will need to plan its activities: it will need to take account of factors internal to the organisation such as its assets, the qualities of the staff, the task to be achieved, etc. as well as environmental factors such as demand for services, government policies and so on.

In Chapter 4 we considered the idea of systems theory which enabled decision makers to take a holistic view of organisations and how those organisations relate to their environments. The activity of planning illustrates the usefulness of this approach for organisational analysis. It is often difficult for people in organisations to see the wood for the trees, and it is very easy to concentrate on large amounts of internal detail while ignoring important trends in the outside world. For example, organisations may tend to concentrate on improving minor internal processes while failing to plan for the single European market.

Organisations need to be adaptive to respond to the changing environment and therefore the process of management and organisational structuring 'should have an environmental orientation' (Haynes, 1980). To be fully effective, managers must concentrate on the total organisation and environmental changes instead of on artificial internal segments.

What do public sector organisations plan?

The concept of planning can be applied to a wide range of activities. We identify a number of areas where planning has, or is having, influence. The list of these areas is by no means exhaustive.

National planning

Nations in what was formerly the Soviet Bloc were characterised by national planning. Instead of leaving economic decisions to the free hand of the marketplace, economic decisions were made by highly centralised states which were responsible for resource allocation and the planning of economic activities. This method of planning was widely criticised for its inefficiency and its inability to adapt to changing demands.

Western economies are based on a mix of the free market and state planning and have tended to move towards greater use of market forces. However, the state still intervenes in many areas of social and economic activity including the provision of welfare services – hence the existence of the public sector.

Town and country planning

As Elcock (1986, Chapter 9) points out, town and country planning can be traced back to the Victorian era when enlightened industrialists sought to improve areas such as Bournville in Birmingham and Saltaire in West Yorkshire. The Town and Country Planning Act 1946 formed the basis of the modern planning system, requiring local authorities to make plans for their local areas, and to control land use in those areas.

Though the system has now been modified for some years, local authorities still play a crucial role in the shaping of the local environment by, for example, forecasting the need for roads for travel to work or leisure, and thus plan on the basis of that need. Planners seek to influence behaviour, for example, by deciding that particular zones will be devoted to industrial estates, others to shopping centres and residential use in order to harmonise traffic movement and so on. The Skeffington Report of 1969 emphasised the importance of public participation in the planning process, and local authorities were urged to publicise plans and encourage the public to contribute to the process. Critics of the planning system argued that the resulting system was bureaucratic and slow moving because of the problems of dealing with competing interests and the long cycles of committee meetings that local authorities use. Recent initiatives, such as the creation of Urban Development Corporations, have sought to speed up decision making and involve people with business experience. These initiatives, however, have not been without criticism.

Corporate planning

Traditionally, local government exhibited one of the dysfunctions of bureaucracy mentioned in Chapter 3 – that it was run on departmental lines with departments such as housing, education and public works providing services in isolation from each other. As Haynes points out, the planning process reflected this in that it 'usually took the form of a series of isolated, departmental exercises which lacked any common framework of reference apart from the central control of financial input' (Haynes, 1980, p. 82). As the scale of local government grew and the environment began to change more rapidly, it became apparent that services needed to be more closely integrated in order that they would meet the needs of the environment. The late 1960s and early 1970s saw a plethora of government-sponsored reports which sought to influence the way in which local authorities were organised and the services that they provided. For example, the Seebohm Report on Personal and Allied Social Services (1967) pointed to the need to anticipate events and to conduct research on future needs.

The Bains Committee on The New Local Authorities: Management and Structure (1972) recommended that local authorities should adopt a corporate approach which would enable the authority to provide a range of integrated services to meet the changing needs of the local community. Like many other ideas that we consider in this book, it is not an idea which originated in the British public sector. Corporate approaches had their origins in business thinking in the United States of America, were implemented in large multinational corporations in the 1950s, and eventually found their way into public sector thinking in Britain in the late 1960s.

Corporate management and planning required that the local authority adapt its internal organisation in order to provide a set of integrated services to the local community. Particular emphasis was placed on the links with other service providers in the area. For example, the then new local authority social service departments needed, according to the Seebohm Report, to develop close working links with health authorities and local authority housing departments. The internal organisation of the local authority was to be integrated by appointing a chief executive officer as the senior official of the organisation. A chief officers' management team, as well as parallel political structures including a policy and resources committee (consisting of senior elected members), was recommended to co-ordinate the decision-making process. These proposals were adopted with (often unquestioning) enthusiasm by many local authorities. This, together with the development of central research capabilities, underpinned the transition that local authorities had made from town and country planning to corporate planning.

Strategic planning

Strategic planning involves those at the top of the organisation formulating the organisation's objectives and developing strategies to achieve those objectives. In Chapter 3 we examined the concept of bureaucracy and the features of the bureaucrat. In order for strategic planning and decision making to be effective, a different set of values needs to be held by senior officials. Vision, leadership, the ability to be proactive, flexible and forward-thinking are the essential qualities that need to be present. Senior managers should be able to look to the external environment in order to obtain messages about likely future trends, for example in the demand for services, resources that may be available, changes in the legislative framework, etc. They need to develop strategies to enable the organisation to make the appropriate policy choices and implement them in order to enable the organisation to meet the needs of the environment.

Strategic planners use techniques such as SWOT analysis. This involves an analysis of the internal Strengths and Weaknesses of the organisation and the Opportunities and Threats to the organisation (hence SWOT). The idea is to improve the overall organisational performance by eliminating weaknesses and developing strengths. Opportunities are to be maximised and threats either avoided or turned into opportunities (see Sharplin, 1985, pp. 54–6, 190–4 where it is referred to as WOTS-UP analysis).

As with corporate planning, strategic planning has its origins in the private sector. But in the light of recent developments in the public sector such techniques may be particularly useful in enabling managers to plan the future direction of the organisation. As National Health Service hospitals are forced to compete with each other for business they may begin to see other hospitals as competitors. With the advent of compulsory competitive tendering in local authorities, direct service organisations are forced to compete with private sector organisations for contracts to provide certain services and as a result they are beginning to use strategic planning techniques (see the section below on business planning).

Writing about local government, Clarke and Stewart argue that a strategic perspective 'places a premium on the role of the chief executive and its support; it also demands that senior management of service and support departments set their separate sectional interests within a wider strategic perspective. The latter must give their departmental organisations purpose and direction but this must be rooted in what the authority as a whole is trying to do' (1988, pp. 14–15).

Policy planning

Governments and other public sector organisations plan and manage policy areas such as housing, education and law and order. The complex nature of policy provision for many policy arenas involves a large number of actors in local authorities, central government, voluntary bodies, pressure groups, inter-governmental bodies, local authority associations, professional bodies and so on (see Hambleton, 1986). For example, Malpass and Murie document the complex machinery which administers housing policy (1987, pp. 136–77).

Business planning

The introduction of compulsory competitive tendering through the Local Government Planning and Land Act 1980 and the Local Government Act 1988 means that direct service organisations may see themselves as agencies with a degree of independence from the actual client, for example, the social service department requiring the cleaning of office buildings. As such they are in a position to see themselves as running a business and may adopt the whole gambit of business techniques when addressing their organisational problems.

It is impossible to make a technical distinction between strategic planning and business planning: both use techniques such as SWOT analysis. Private sector consultants such as Peat Marwick McLintock have offered their services to local government to enable them to apply business planning ideas to strategic and operational levels of the organisation.

Expenditure planning

As we have observed in earlier chapters, one of the major concerns of government – one which can be traced back to the last century – is the control of the level of expenditure by the state. Various strategies have been adopted to reduce the level of expenditure. These will be examined in detail in the next chapter.

The planning process

The examples above illustrate the fact that different things can be planned. However, planning is only a part of an administrator's work. Ideas need to be put into action. Therefore we need to consider a model of decision making which can be applied to the planning process. The model – known as the rational model – involves a cycle of decisions which need to be made so that an organisation can achieve its objectives.

The rational model

The cyclical process shown in Figure 9.1 is an adaptation of decision-making models that economists have used to maximise the utility obtained from the use of scarce resources (see for example, Haynes, 1980, Chapter 4). The model has been used widely by political scientists and, interestingly, underpins the Business and Technician Education Council's guidelines on problem solving on public administration and business studies courses.

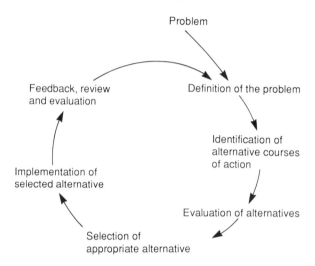

Figure 9.1 The rational model (1).

It begins with the identification of a problem or issue which requires consideration. At this stage there will be a decision to do nothing or pursue the issue. If the issue is pursued then it needs to be defined and a fuller understanding of the nature of the issue needs to be gained. Analysis based on a partial understanding of the issue is likely to be flawed. In matters relating to the social sciences, the number of variables is large and hence it is often difficult to establish valid theories of cause and effect. This, together with the political dimension, means that it is hardly surprising that problems such as the inner cities tend to be defined and redefined over the years.

If the rational model is followed, the decision maker is then required to identify possible courses of action to solve the problem. For example the Review of Railway Finances chaired by Sir David Serpell was given the following terms of reference 'to examine the finances of the railway and associated operations, in the light of all relevant considerations, and to report on options for alternative policies, and their related objectives, designed to secure improved financial results in an efficiently run railway in Great Britain over the next 20 years'. (Department of Transport, 1983, p. 1).

The terms of reference are reproduced here in full because they provide an interesting example where the overall objective behind the policy development is clear – improved financial results or, in other words, reducing the size of the state subsidy or Public Service Obligation as it is correctly known.

The Committee considered the long-term options for the railway network. They did this by 'producing a set of mathematical models which linked variables (demand, service levels, unit costs and infrastructure) in such a way that, as changes were made in one or more of these variables, the estimated consequences for the others, and for financial results could be evaluated' (Department of Transport, 1983, p. 63). This resulted in the production of a set of options. These varied from what was essentially the retention of the existing system with a few modifications, to an option referred to as a Commerce Railway consisting of about 16 per cent of the existing network (meaning that to travel from Manchester to Leeds one would need to go via London).

Given that decision makers often deal with complex problems, there is a requirement to think beyond the obvious and usual solutions to such problems and to consider innovative solutions. Techniques such as 'brain storming' and 'lateral thinking' can be used to generate such alternatives (see Mullins, 1989, Ch. 14).

Once the alternative courses of action have been identified they need to be evaluated, and particular attention is devoted to the implications of each option. In the case of transport planning – for example the location of a third London airport – planners used a technique known as cost-benefit analysis in order to establish the costs and benefits of each option. This involved costing up the advantages and disadvantages of each of the proposed courses of action and selecting the preferred option on the basis of the balance of each calculation. Problems arise firstly in trying to forecast events and make realistic costings of programmes, and secondly in making costings of intangibles such as the cost of noise pollution in the case of a new airport (for a thorough critique of this technique see Self, 1975 on the Roskill Commission on the third London airport).

The selection of the preferred option is often a political process and so subject to the values that politicians bring to the process as discussed in Chapter 2. However, once the preferred solution has been selected, we have a policy in the form of a statement, perhaps an Act of Parliament or a government circular. The next stage is to implement it or put it into action. Academic research tells us that this rarely happens perfectly and so we need to examine the effects of the policy in practice. This takes the form of obtaining feedback and evaluation. As we shall see in later chapters the public sector is making increasing use of performance indicators in order to assess the effect of policies. Suffice it to say at this point that because of the complex and changing world in which the public sector operates, implementation of policies may solve certain problems but is likely to throw up further problems which in turn need to be solved: hence the cyclical nature of the policy-making process.

Criticism of the rational model

One of the implicit assumptions of the model is that those who are making decisions are rational actors. We have noted in Chapter 2 that politicians bring values, policies and priorities to the process and these will, of course, influence the process. Peter Self cites a former head of the civil service, Lord Bridges:

> However complicated the facts may be, however much your junior may try to persuade you that there are seventeen arguments in favour of one course and fifteen in favour of the exact opposite, believe me, in four cases out of five there is one point and one only which is cardinal to the whole situation. (Quoted in Self, 1977, p. 3).

Similarly, administrators may not have the open-mindedness, breadth of imagination, intellectual or organisational resources, or the time to generate the full range of alternative courses of action and assess their implications. A career official may be reluctant to present an option to a political master in the knowledge that it would be politically unacceptable.

Personal experience shows that the best ideas never work perfectly in practice. Lewis Gunn provided civil servants with a number of conditions which would have to be satisfied if perfect implementation of policies were to be achieved (Hogwood and Gunn, 1984, pp. 198–206; see also Hood, 1976). It is helpful to look at these to realise the complexity of planning for the world of public sector organisations.

The circumstances external to the implementing agency do not impose crippling constraints

As we have seen, public sector organisations work in a world where they are heavily dependent on the co-operation of other organisations to get things done. For example, local government depends on Parliament and government to determine the financial framework.

That adequate time and sufficient resources are made available to the programme

For example, the local authorities implementing the Griffiths Report on Care in the Community (1988) are dependent on central government making the resources available to complete the changes from long-stay institutions for the elderly to community care.

That the required combination of resources is actually available

The predicted demographic downturn will mean that in the future there will be labour and skills shortages for many organisations. At the time of writing, the comparatively low levels of public sector pay mean that schools and benefit offices in the south-east of England have difficulty in recruiting and keeping staff.

The policy to be implemented is based on a valid theory of cause and effect

In other words, if we do X now then Y will happen. The theory behind the Community Charge or Poll Tax was that individual flat rate charges for most members of the community would focus attention on the level of spending by the authority and increase local accountability. Critics say that this is not the case and cite 'poll tax capping' as evidence. If accountability had been enhanced, profligate councillors would have been dismissed from office and replaced by more prudent ones.

That the relationship between cause and effect is direct and there are few, if any, intervening links

Often the theory of cause and effect is extended to cover a whole series of events. For example, we may assume the if we do P then Q will happen; if Q happens then R will then occur. The longer the 'chain of causality', as Gunn calls it, the more likely it that there is going to be a weak link in the chain. For example, if a verbal message is to reach its audience then the reduction in the number of people passing the message will reduce the possibility of the message being distorted.

That dependency relationships are minimal

One of the problems that the Conservative government faced in the 1980s was that it depended on over 400 local authorities in England alone to implement large parts of its policies, for example housing, education and social services. These are political organisations, many of whom were opposed to the policies, some of whom were obstructive to their implementation. One solution that government has used is to replace or override them with more compliant organisations such as the urban development corporations referred to above.

That tasks are fully specified in correct sequence

If an office development is being built, the foundations are built first, the cosmetics such as paint and carpets last.

That there is perfect communication and co-ordination

We have already referred to the problems of co-ordination in organisations – individuals and groups within the organisation need to identify with the objectives of the project. The success of the organisation will depend, in part, on the effectiveness of the communications systems in the organisation.

That those in authority can demand and obtain perfect compliance

As Gunn states, this situation is difficult to achieve and is probably undesirable. Leaders of large organisations will inevitably find problems in getting those at lower levels in the hierarchy to comply with their objectives – a problem illustrated by the frequent leaks of confidential memoranda and reports in Whitehall.

As we indicated above, the rational model may generate untried solutions. Organisations may take giant leaps and consequently deal with the unfamiliar. One of the strengths of organisations is the expertise that officials have accumulated over time. This expertise, based on past practice, may not be appropriate to new solutions. Organisations may be less ready to deal with radical solutions because of the dangers of dealing with the unfamiliar.

Alternatives to the rational model

In this section we discuss two points. Firstly, we will introduce an alternative model of decision making – incrementalism – and secondly, we will consider whether it is an approach that can be commended to policy makers.

An increment is a small step from the existing position. Most public sector officials will be paid on a salary scale which has a number of incremental points on it and each year the official will advance a small step towards the top of the scale. Policy making can be conducted in a similar fashion; indeed, research testifies to its popularity.

Herbert Simon (1976) argues that decision makers seek to be rational and behave like economic men in maximising the utility of any decision. However, the circumstances in which they operate mean that, in practice, they settle for being satisficers. In other words they aim to satisfy and to perform to satisfactory standards. The barriers to rationality outlined above, in terms of the lack of organisational, intellectual resources and time mean that the well-intentioned official will settle for satisficing or getting by.

In particular, Hogwood and Gunn (1984) cite five types of limitation to explain why the opportunities for rational decision making are limited:

● **Psychological limitations**

Decision makers lack the complete knowledge of the issues, do not have the skills or understanding of the values that underpin decision making which are necessary to behave rationally.

● **Limitations arising from multiple values**

In situations where there is a collective rationality there is likely to be a conflict of interest and because different people weigh values in different ways, there is no rational way of resolving the conflict.

● **Organisational limitations**

In earlier chapters we have discussed the limitation of organisations as tools for solving problems. The high degree of specialisation in terms of function, the implications of departmentalism and the inadequacy of management information all mitigate against rational decision making.

● **Cost limitations**

Rational behaviour is expensive. As Hogwood and Gunn point out, it is likely that the costs of rational behaviour will outweigh the benefits.

● **Situational limitations**

All decisions are taken in the light of past events, the demands of pressure groups, the expectations of the future – all of which mitigate against rationality. We can add to this the uncertain environment in which decision makers operate. For example, local authority treasurers are faced with a high level of uncertainty in planning budgets because of the lack of information on resources available from central government and the uncertainty about the number of community charge defaulters.

So far we have presented a pessimistic view about decision making – that incrementalism is adopted as a decision-making technique because of the impossibility of the rational model. However, writers such as Lindblom (1959), have argued that an incremental strategy of 'muddling through' may be a positive one. Again it is Hogwood and Gunn who summarise the case in favour of incrementalism:

1. Making objectives explicit is a hostage to fortune and the failure to do so may reflect a shrewd awareness.
2. Giant leaps into the unknown are dangerous and therefore wiser counsel may preach limited change from the existing position.
3. In practice, it is unlikely that problems are solved in one go. A better approach is to adopt a serial approach and solve them over a number of stages.
4. Because of the number of agencies and interests in any policy issue, the conflict of competing interests means that rational approaches are unlikely to succeed.
5. The nature of policy making means that those involved in the process are open to negotiation and compromise as a method of solving problems.
6. Although a rational approach may produce the best policy, there may not be widespread agreement on it. Compromise may be a better alternative.

The two models summarised

Figures 9.2 and 9.3 demonstrate how the two approaches to decision making can be used to move from the current state of affairs to a desired situation. Supporters of the rational model may seek to move to the desired situation in one strategic move. However, the problems that we have considered mean that it is likely that we may

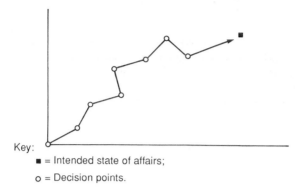

Key:
■ = Intended state of affairs;
o = Decision points.

Figure 9.2 The incremental model.

miss the target and actually arrive at an unintended situation. The incremental model demonstrates how a successive number of small steps may enable decision makers to move slowly towards the intended state of affairs with the facility to re-address the situation at each stage in the process.

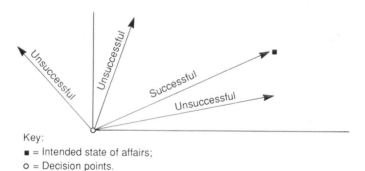

Key:
■ = Intended state of affairs;
o = Decision points.

Figure 9.3 The rational model (2).

The rise and fall and rise of planning

As we have already discussed, planning and the use of rational techniques were highly popular in the late 1960s and early 1970s. This was a period of growth in the size of government in terms of budgets and the areas of service provision. Added to this there was a belief in the economies of scale of large organisations – hence the 1970 White Paper on the Reorganisation of Central Government and the 1972 Local Government Act which reduced substantially the number of local authorities creating much larger organisations. Rational techniques were introduced to try to solve what were perceived to be problems at the time.

Planning and the rational model fell into disrepute in the mid to late 1970s for a number of reasons. Firstly, changing external factors meant that many plans became rapidly out of date and so they could never be implemented properly. These included:

- the economic environment changed with the Labour Government obtaining a loan from the International Monetary Fund in 1975 which had conditions attached to it requiring cuts in public expenditure;
- the imposition of cash limits on areas of public spending;
- the election of the Thatcher Government in 1979;
- the growing uncertainty of the environment in terms of reductions in the amount of capital and revenue money available;
- the effects of high levels of inflation particularly on the costs of long-term capital projects;
- the changing requirements of central government in terms of what was required through legislation and circulars;
- the changing demands of the clients of public services (or 'customers' as we are now urged to call them).

Secondly, there was growing disillusionment with planning as a technique to solve problems. As we saw above, there are limitations with the rational model as a method of solving problems.

Despite these criticisms, recent approaches to decision making have sought to pursue the rational approach. The new agenda for the public sector emphasises organisational planning – the setting of objectives, measuring performance against those objectives, etc. Business plans are used to achieve economy, efficiency and effectiveness.

Conclusion

In this chapter we have examined approaches to planning and decision making. Many factors contribute to the effectiveness or otherwise of the various techniques. These include the formal organisation, the informal organisation and the nature of the environment. We need to examine these issues further. Perhaps the key issue of the 1980s was resources. In the next chapter we examine how resourcing issues have affected organisational performance.

Further reading

The literature on the policy process is examined in Barrett and Fudge (1981), Hogwood and Gunn (1984) and Burch and Wood (1990). A more applied approach is offered by Hogwood (1987). On local government and its relationship with central government, see Hambleton (1986), Chandler (1986) and Rhodes (1988). For a critique of corporate management see Dearlove (1979). Much of the older work remains salient - see Lindblom (1959) on 'muddling through' and Simon (1976) on the administrative man.

Chapter 10
Resourcing the public sector

Introduction

At the heart of the debate about the role of the public sector is invariably the issue of finance. Some critics of the public sector maintain that it is inherently inefficient and unable to control its expenditure. Though this point of view is not a new one, it took on increased importance in 1975 when the Labour government obtained a loan from the International Monetary Fund which was conditional upon a reduction of the level of public expenditure. The Conservative governments elected in 1979, 1983 and 1987 instigated a range of policies which sought to reduce further the overall level of expenditure. Although this strategy has met with limited success in terms of reducing the overall level (Dunleavy, 1990), it has had severe implications for the management of public sector organisations.

This chapter examines the processes of revenue raising, allocation, spending and control. These activities are considered in the context of the two models of policy making – the rational model and the incremental model – which were examined in the previous chapter. Examination of the budgetary process in the public sector provides interesting evidence on how organisations actually behave and the applicability of these models as descriptions and prescriptions for their behaviour. To this end, three case studies of budgetary behaviour are discussed: resourcing in central government, local government and the National Health Service. As we shall see, the role of finance is inextricably linked to the programmes they are financing.

Getting: The revenue-raising process

Revenue can be raised from a number of sources. These vary from service to service and will reflect political choice. Some services are financed out of general taxation and are made available for all of us to consume. Alternatively there may be a direct cash relationship between the service provider and the customer. In some cases, such as defence or law and order, we all stand to benefit from the service and it would be difficult to envisage how it could be financed other than out of direct taxation. In other cases, the decision about how to finance a service will reflect the political and ethical values that underpin the policy. For example, the National Health Service was founded on the principle that there would not be a financial exchange between the doctor and the patient. It was thought that if people had to pay at the point of delivery then this might deter some people from using the service. Critics of the Conservatives' policy on health point to the decline in the number of people having eye tests since the introduction of a fixed charge for the service. The so-called ring fencing of local authority housing revenue accounts in 1990 has meant that current spending on housing has to be financed out of the revenue raised from rents alone. This means that the council housing customer will normally pay the full cost of the service while the owner-occupier will enjoy a subsidised mortgage. This reflects the Conservative government's concern that people should not be drawn into what is called the 'dependency culture'. Instead they prefer to promote the values of a 'property-owning democracy'.

The unsuccessful policies aimed at reducing the level of direct taxation (Gamble, 1988) intended to create an 'enterprise culture'. On the assumption that people are motivated by monetary reward, it was argued that this would provide incentives for them to work harder and for entrepreneurs to create wealth and jobs. It was also assumed that if people had more of their gross income to spend as they chose then they would purchase goods and services that they wanted rather than the state spending money on goods and services for which there may be little or no demand.

Other criteria will influence decisions about the sources of finance. The Layfield Committee on Local Government Finance (1976) argued that in order to achieve a vital local democracy, a larger share of the revenue of local authorities must be raised locally, thus enhancing local accountability. Other criteria for a suitable tax are that it is easy to collect, the yield is predictable, it is cheap to collect, and that it is fair. An interesting exercise is to analyse current and possible forms of local taxation against this checklist.

Spending

Spending by public sector organisations has to comply with complex and changing legal regulations, and is exposed to scrutiny at a number of levels. It is quite possible for one organisation to be audited at five levels, as well as being accountable to internal decision-making bodies, political masters, and the law.

All organisations will make the distinction between capital and revenue or current expenditure. While there are exceptions, capital expenditure is defined as:

'Expenditure on new construction, land, and extensions of and alterations to existing buildings and the purchase of any other fixed asset (e.g. machinery and plant) – including vehicles – having an expected working life of more than one year' (Likierman, 1988, p. 219); while current expenditure on goods and services 'includes direct expenditure by central and local government on providing services (e.g. health or education) . . .' (Ibid., p. 220).

In general terms, capital expenditure will commit future current expenditure. For example, it is capital expenditure that will finance the development of a new leisure centre while current expenditure will be used to pay for the running costs, for example staff, heating and lighting, etc. Decision makers therefore need to plan budgets and commit resources for the future if capital programmes are to be undertaken. Equally, when cuts in expenditure are considered, capital programmes are usually the first victims.

In our discussion on accountability in public sector organisations in Chapter 2 we pointed out that a principal focus of processes of accountability was finance. Repeated attempts to cut back the global total of public spending have placed an increased emphasis on control of public spending. We will see that various strategies can be adopted, many of which will be discussed in more detail in the next two chapters.

The creation of the Audit Commission in 1982 has increased accountability. It appoints auditors for local authorities to ensure probity and promotes improvements in economy, efficiency and effectiveness. As well as investigating the activities of individual authorities, it publishes papers which compare practice and offer suggestions for improvement. The National Audit Office scrutinises the accounts of government departments on behalf of Parliament and periodic audits of the National Health Service (Perrin, 1988). Since October 1990 the Audit Commission's area of work has extended to cover the National Health Service.

The role of the budget

When we speak of budgeting in the public sector we are not referring to the Chancellor of the Exchequer's spring Budget statement. This is only a part of the public spending process which focuses on demand management and changes in levels of taxation. The budgetary process will vary from organisation to organisation but all will share the common theme of allocating resources through a political process. It is political, not necessarily because politicians are involved, but because it involves the representation of organisational interests and has scope for bargaining and conflict.

One of the traditionally cited differences between public and private organisations is the role of the budget. In the private sector, a budget will be a set of projections about likely future activity. A motor manufacturer will only be in a position to estimate revenue because they do not know how many cars they will sell. In the public sector, sources of money will often be precise and known for the forthcoming year. It is debatable how well this distinction holds up today. Large commercial organisations need to allocate budgets to programmes such as research and development and design. These will be needed to finance long-term programmes. In the public sector there is a great deal of uncertainty about the assumptions implicit in budgets. Local authorities will be unaware of the yield of the Community Charge, the level of pay settlements and the level of inflation. Hence budgets are made amidst uncertainty.

Organisational culture and public spending

As we considered in earlier chapters, public sector organisations are divided into large departments and they will develop cultures of their own. At the heart of these organisations is a central finance department, whether it is the Treasury in central government or the treasurer's department in a local authority. Heclo and Wildavsky's study of the Treasury, *The Private Government of Public Money*, portrays the organisation as a nuclear family with a distinct culture and a set of norms and values all of its own. They act as guardians of the public purse when dealing with members of spending departments who seek additional resources. The authors summarise Treasury norms as:

1. Decide by reacting.
2. Let others do the technical work.
3. You know as much as anybody and more than most.
4. Above all, be sceptical – especially of enthusiasts.
5. Probe, delay and question again.
6. As a rule, cut by bargaining rather than absolute no's.
7. A reputation for toughness inhibits would-be spenders.
8. Be on guard against hidden and built-in expenditure escalators. (Heclo and Wildavsky, 1981, 49–50.)

John Stewart demonstrated how the budgetary environment can impact on the culture of public sector organisations. He analysed local government spending and labour-force figures in the post-war period leading up to the late 1970s. He identified two periods – firstly a period of budgetary growth (until 1976), and secondly a period of reduction in growth leading to a standstill and in some cases cutbacks (1976 onwards). He argued that a period of continued budgetary growth is likely to build expectations that the pattern of growth will continue. If growth is perceived as being the norm by those in the organisation then it 'would begin to influence their behaviour and through their behaviour the procedure and structure of the organisation' (Stewart, 1980, p. 11). This is characterised by:

1. The environment will generate demands which could be met by the increment in the budget without challenging the existing budget thus leaving existing programmes of expenditure untouched. The allocation of the increment becomes the key decision.
2. Procedures established to control the level of spending evolve over time to become bidding procedures for the increment. Hence the emphasis on growth at the margins.
3. Organisations tend to emphasise the benefits of policies rather than their costs, looking at the objectives to be achieved rather than the resources available.

4. Uniform provision of services as opposed to discrimination or targeting services towards groups with high needs become the norm.
5. Capital development was a dominant feature in budgets because of the assumption that, for example, in the case of a swimming pool, the revenue expenditure would be available in future years to heat and staff the pool.
6. Choices tend to be about when to implement a given policy rather than whether to implement it. (Stewart, 1980.)

The overall characteristic of a period of growth is that of a consensus among decision makers. The possibility of conflict is reduced because of the expectation of the continued availability of the increment to avoid the questioning of the existing budget (or baseline as it is often referred to). However, if the assumption of growth is removed, then there is a change in the experience of those involved in the process which leads to a change in expectations. The main characteristics of a period of standstill are:

1. The environment continues to present new and changing demands but these cannot be satisfied by the allocation of the increment.
2. Consensus becomes difficult to achieve and decision makers become reluctant to create future commitments. Capital programmes are cut.
3. The budgetary process focuses more clearly on the resource allocation process with more thorough scrutiny of existing commitments. Control procedures are strengthened.
4. Greater control over the staffing levels results in the freezing of posts.
5. Cash limiting of expenditure is used to control the expansion of budgets through inflation.
6. Attention becomes focused on costs of programmes rather than benefits, and resources available instead of objectives to be achieved.
7. Political consensus disappears and relationships become increasingly adversarial.
8. Uniform provision is replaced by targeting of services at the most needy. (Stewart, 1980.)

Thus we can see a very different style of behaviour resulting from a change in the budgetary environment. If we were to move from standstill to cutbacks, we would expect to see further changes in behaviour. For example:

1. Voluntary redundancies or compulsory redundancies.
2. Increasingly departmental behaviour in order to protect oneself.
3. The use of voluntary and private organisations to save costs.
4. Increasingly close scrutiny of discretionary expenditure and consideration given to alternative methods of achieving existing goals.
5. The use of creative accounting techniques such as lease-back arrangements if legal.
6. Increasingly power exercised by central budgetary control staff and auditors.
7. Further adversarial relationships.

8. 'Sore thumbs' and 'shroud waving' to demonstrate the effect of cuts or potential cuts. (See Elcock *et al*, 1989, p. 178.)

Thus the environment in which budgetary choices take place will be an important determinant on budgetary behaviour.

In order to understand fully the effect of resource issues on the public sector we need to examine what happens in practice. To this end we present three case studies. It is not our intention to supply the reader with the full details of the various initiatives; instead we seek to examine the effect of these initiatives on organisations.

Case Study 1: Central government

Control of public expenditure until the 1960s was highly fragmented and largely revolved around the consideration of annual estimates: there was little or no attempt to plan expenditure programmes for the medium or long term. Concern about this led to the appointment of the Plowden Committee on the Planning and Control of Public Expenditure which reported in 1961. The committee recommended a system of annual surveys of planned public expenditure for years ahead. This led to the introduction of the so-called PES system. The PES (Public Expenditure Survey) involved 'the cost projection of existing policies' (Heclo and Wildavsky, 1981, pp. 216–7). The committee (known as the Public Expenditure Survey Committee, PESC) consisted of an inter-departmental group of departmental finance officers and Treasury officials who prepared information for decision makers. They then compared total spending implications of policies against available resources and different expenditures against each other. This was done by costing programmes up to five years ahead. According to one senior civil servant, Otto Clarke, PES was designed to achieve the effective collective responsibility of ministers for public expenditure, regular ministerial appraisal of public expenditure for five years ahead, and increased stability of public expenditure (see Hennessy, 1989a, p. 179).

The idea was then to introduce greater rationality to the public expenditure process. However, the eventual effect was, as Heclo and Wildavsky observe, to enshrine incrementalism. They state: 'If PES makes it less likely that new monetary programmes with large spending implications will be introduced inadvertently, it also helps to assure departments that their on-going programmes will not suddenly be disrupted' (Heclo and Wildavsky, 1981, p. 238). In other words, it did not lead to the questioning of the validity of existing programmes, but instead re-costed them, thus providing updated costings (see Pliatzky, 1982, p. 98).

In an attempt to remedy this weakness, a further system was introduced – Programme Analysis and Review (PAR) in 1970. Spending departments were to carry out reviews of programmes by questioning existing commitments and to ask whether they should exist at all and not only how they should be carried out (see Pliatzky, 1982, p. 99). It was a system that was widely criticised for making heavy demands on officials, raising sensitive issues and increasing the level of conflict. It required staff with specialist skills – economists and statisticians – who were not available. Both officials and politicians saw the system as an unwanted intrusion and not for them (see Heclo and Wildavsky, 1981; Gray and Jenkins, 1985). Hennessy wrote the following obituary: 'To be brutal and brief, PAR became slow, top heavy, and a victim of the relentless, interdepartmental grind' (Hennessy, 1989a, p. 236).

The election of the Thatcher government in 1979 was to see a new approach to the management of the civil service. The intention was to seek lasting cultural changes in the service to transform it from a reactive bureaucracy to a more proactive business-like organisation. Four initiatives merit examination: the Rayner scrutinies, the Management Information System for Ministers (MINIS), the Financial Management Initiative (FMI) and agency status.

Following her election to power, Mrs Thatcher abolished PAR and introduced a new system of scrutiny of departmental expenditure – the Rayner scrutinies. Sir Derek Rayner (now Lord Rayner) from Marks & Spencer stated that the reviews aimed to:

(i)   examine a specific policy or activity, questioning all aspects of work normally taken for granted;

(ii)   propose solutions to problems and to make recommendations to achieve savings and increase efficiency and effectiveness; and

(iii)   implement agreed solutions, or to begin their implementation within 12 months of the start of the scrutiny. (Cited in Gray and Jenkins, 1985, p. 118).

The subjects of the scrutinies varied from payment of social security benefits to the organisation of the coastguard (Gray and Jenkins, 1985). The emphasis was on action and results rather than the collection of pages of analysis – the report produced by the scrutiny team was to include recommendations for the minister to act on.

Several other initiatives have been undertaken, often influenced by the work of the Efficiency Unit. Michael Heseltine was unusual among ministers in having an interest in the detail of the management and internal working of his department. This interest led to the creation of (MINIS). This was introduced by Heseltine in the Department of Environment in 1980 and later in the Ministry of Defence. The basis of the system was to establish what was happening, who was responsible, what the targets were and whether they were being monitored (see Greenwood and Wilson, 1989, p. 125). Interestingly, Heseltine recalled that nobody could remember the questions being asked before. The system involved a cyclical process of establishing what is done, how many people do it, what is achieved, linked to a number of performance indicators. These statements were then considered by ministers and senior civil servants who then made decisions which were implemented. The system was received with scepticism both by fellow ministers (despite enthusiasm from the Prime Minister) and civil servants (see Hennessy, 1989a, p. 608–9).

However, this led to a more widely implemented Financial Management Initiative (FMI). FMI aims to produce:

a system in which managers at all levels have (a) a clear view of their objectives; and means to assess and wherever possible measure outputs and performance in relation to those objectives; (b) well-defined responsibility for making the best use of their resources, including a critical scrutiny of the output and value for money; and (c) the information (particularly about costs), the training and the access to expert advice which they need to exercise their responsibilities effectively. (Cited in Metcalfe and Richards, 1987, p. 183).

Greenwood and Wilson identify four features:

1. Top management systems: the creation of an information system for senior managers particularly concerning resources, activities, and the review of policy programmes.
2. Statement of objectives: clear statements of what departments were setting out to do were required. This has proved difficult because of the intangible nature of the activities of many departments.
3. Decentralisation and delegation: particularly the delegation of decision making and budgets to cost centres so that decisions are made by those responsible for carrying them out.
4. Performance measurement: measuring the relationship between inputs and outputs, and the effectiveness of policy programmes. (See Greenwood and Wilson, 1989, p. 129–34.)

Our principal concern here is the delegation of decision making down the hierarchy. A key element of the FMI has been the use of delegated budgeting and the creation of cost centres to hold managers to account for their expenditure. This involves a move away from the traditional form of centralised bureaucratic administration and will inevitably meet with resistance from those at the centre who seek to control.

However, the thinking behind the FMI was that if the budgetary process works and if officials have the information and the skills to use the process then good management will result. This has implications for the organisation as a whole: 'in the rhetoric of the FMI, departments are expected to move from structures based on centralised but separate responsibilities for finance, personnel, policy, executive operations and performance improvement towards structures that decentralise and cluster these responsibilities in "businesses".' (Metcalfe and Richards, 1987. p. 194).

The National Audit Office Report on the FMI (1986) found, in practice, that departments differed in the extent to which they had adopted the FMI. It was also found that middle and lower management had reservations about the new arrangements. In the Ministry of Defence, for example, there was very little participation by those at the lower levels of management. Similarly, in the Department of the Environment, managers felt a lack of decision-making capability to accompany the new processes.

The theme of decentralisation is one that is pursued further in the Next Steps Initiative. Described by the Treasury and Civil Service Committee as 'the most ambitious attempt at Civil Service reform this century' (1990, para 1), it involves the creation of executive agencies to perform the administrative work of large parts of the civil service (see Chapter 12). The project, which aims to cover three-quarters of the service work by the end of the century, is intended to give chief executives of agencies a higher degree of autonomy from central control. Implicit in the idea is a distinction between the policy-making work of advisers to ministers and the day-to-day administration of the departments. The new relationship, which will be set out in framework documents agreed between the minister and the chief executive of the agency, will cover areas such as recruitment and staff management, planning and financial arrangements. It is intended that managers will have greater freedom to make the service meet the needs of the environment. For example, the role of the Employment Service will be very different in an area with high levels of unemployment compared with one with low levels of unemployment. It is envisaged that staff will be consulted on the work that they do. Already 'wish lists' have been made where staff indicate what they want to see from agency status and these suggestions have been acted on.

The project is at its very early stages and it is difficult to predict what the eventual impact will be. Hood and Jones offer four possible fates for the project:

- major changes resulting in total success;
- superficial adoption with mix of success and failure;
- a step to a further radical initiative;
- termination after enthusiasm wears off. (Hood and Jones, 1990, p. 82–3.)

The key to the success of the project is the relationship between the agencies and the host department, and the degree of freedom that the agencies will be allowed. Given the history of Treasury control over financial matters, it will require a substantial cultural shift if agencies are to have the financial freedom which is crucial to the success of the project.

Case Study 2: Local government

In the previous chapter we discussed the ways in which local government has changed its approach to planning. Changing approaches to resourcing issues arise out of the same organisational thinking, particularly the experimentation with rational techniques. The traditional local authority budget was characterised by:

- a narrow focus by senior officers and politicians with limited control over the process. Departmental estimates were prepared in isolation from the other departments;
- the core budget of established expenditure went unchallenged – the focus of the debate was the increment;
- because of the isolation of the various departments whilst preparing the budgets, there was little co-ordination, and little prioritisation of bids for new expenditure, and no attempt to assess the overall impact of the individual estimates of the departments. (See Elcock et al, 1989, 69–71.)

Although we do not need to reconsider *all* the issues relating to the corporatisation of local government during the 1970s, it is important to remind ourselves of the widespread adoption of policy and resources committees, consisting of the senior elected members (with sub-committees specialising in land, finance, personnel and performance review). There were parallel structures on the officers' side with chief officers' management teams consisting of the senior departmental heads. The intention behind these structures was to focus thinking on the overall co-ordination and control of the activities and resources of the authority.

This period saw experimentation with rational techniques such as Planning, Programming and Budgeting Systems (PPBS). This is an attempt to bring together the annual budgetary process with the policy planning process by linking the analysis of objectives and activities with the outputs of the authority. As Table 10.1 indicates, this is an example of an attempt to implement the rational model of decision making discussed in the previous chapter.

Table 10.1 The PPBS cycle

Stage
1   Identification of needs and strategic problems in the environment.
2   Formulation of objectives related to those needs.
3   Assessment of alternative ways of achieving those objectives.
4   Assessment of the resource and environmental impact of the alternatives.
5   Decision taken and implemented.
6   Results are monitored and, if necessary, adjustments and revisions are undertaken in relation to the strategy and overall objectives.
7   The cycle returns to stage 1.

Variants on PPBS such as Zero-Based Budgeting (ZBB) have been experimented with. This technique according to Henley *et al.* (1983, p. 69), is more suited to situations where restraint or cutbacks are called for. It involves the selection of a zero-base which, confusingly, is rarely zero but may equate to a minimum level of service consistent with the law. Hence there is a gap between the zero-base and the existing budget. This is the area which is subjected to scrutiny and would enable the consideration of, say, a reduction in the level of environmental services together with an increase in spending on education. Inevitably this process will address difficult questions and may generate difficult solutions which may in turn have severe effects on existing interests both inside and outside the organisation. For example, it may require the termination of a service, thus affecting the clients of the service.

A number of problems are associated with these techniques. Experience has shown that they call for more work from officials, and that they meet with resistance from officials (see Jenkins, 1978). Haynes states that PPBS makes an 'inherent demand for self-criticism and the need for a creative dissatisfaction with the status quo' (1980, p. 79). Elcock *et al.* (1989, pp. 85–6) point to the sheer volume of paper that ZBB exercises consume, the possibility of losing sight of overall objectives, and thus the possibility of incrementalism by default.

Paul Griffiths' study of the 1986–87 budgetary process in Mid-Glamorgan County Council illustrates the influence of a number of factors in the budgetary process: culture, the environment and the relationship between members and officers. Firstly, the council had a large Labour majority with political decision making often restricted to the Labour group and with little debate in committees. There was a political culture of stability 'thriving on the creation of symbolic dragons – the English, the Tories, the Church of England, Twickenham' (Griffiths, 1987, p. 215), a lack of a corporate revolution and an inherent conservatism reflected by one councillor who believed that borrowing money to finance capital expenditure was tantamount to creative accounting. The changing policies of the Welsh Office meant that a standstill budget would result in a 14 per cent increase in the rate and a 2 per cent cut in the budget would mean a 5 per cent increase.

Following criticisms that budgetary behaviour had been too incremental in the past, one group of officers conducted a Zero-Based Budgeting exercise which assumed a core budget of 85 per cent. The exercise involved the generation of a number of options including a growth in the budget, standstill and a re-ordering of priorities. The results of the officer-led exercise were presented to the Labour group. They committed themselves to simple pro-rata savings rather than a re-ordering of priorities, reflecting the changing demand for the education and social services. This was, according to Griffiths, due to some members not understanding the budgetary data and the closed nature of the decision-making process and also the lack of debate in committees. He concludes: 'In the end the rationalist aspiration of the officers was overridden by the conservative political values of the members' (Griffiths, 1987, p. 223).

During the 1980s central government sought to increase its control over spending by local authorities. This strategy has been pursued through a number of means – there were over 40 Acts of Parliament which changed the finance system culminating in the introduction of the Community Charge. It is not our purpose to review these initiatives, merely to point out that this has been the single most important factor responsible for the change in budgetary climate in local government in recent years.

In addition, the Audit Commission has, as mentioned above, promoted better financial management. One of the major themes of the 1980s was the decentralisation of services to make them closer to the public. This involves the creation of small teams who need to be able to turn their hands to a wide variety of tasks. This move away from the traditional specialisation which was a feature of local government, has meant that generic workers need to develop financial skills and take responsibility for budgets. For example, a housing neighbourhood office manager may be responsible for budgets covering empty properties, rent arrears, maintenance, staff such as wardens, office expenses and income from garages (Audit Commission, 1989a).

Case Study 3: The National Health Service

The National Health Service provides an excellent example of an organisation facing the problem of making a best fit with its environment. Among the problems it faces are:

- the continuing popularity of the service amongst the general public. This has meant that it has become a politically sensitive issue;
- demographic trends show that the proportion of elderly people is set to rise dramatically over the next ten years. This section of the population makes a high demand on health care resources;
- developing medical technology means that more and more types of illnesses can be treated, thus increasing demands for treatment;
- the consensus on which the National Health Service was founded in 1948 was based on a service financed out of taxation. Though charges for certain services have been introduced and increased, the majority of funding comes from central government sources;
- the academic literature on professionalism cites the medical profession as a prime example of a highly professionalised body. Doctors exercise considerable power and often come into conflict with politicians;
- the rate of inflation for the health service tends to be higher than the overall rate of inflation. This means that to stand still in terms of health service provision, funding has to increase over and above that for other services.

The National Health Service is accountable to central government and decision making has to be seen in the context of the central government initiatives on financial control discussed above. Indeed proposals for the service to be administered by local government have fallen by the wayside because of the determination of central government to control the cost of the service. The service has been the victim of organisational reforms in 1974 and 1982, which reflected the conventional wisdom in the administrative thinking of those times. These reforms created a service which was controlled at the top but left some regional autonomy in relation to the allocation of funding and service organisation (see Klein, 1989).

New directions in National Health Service budgeting have emerged during the 1980s. According to Perrin (1988) it is possible to budget by subjective costs (such as staff, supplies and equipment), functions (such as nursing, catering and estates), specialties (such as neurology, geriatrics and general surgery), or by the units that comprise the district. The problem is to devise a system that enhances financial accountability.

The Griffiths Report (1983) saw the introduction of general managers at regional, district and unit levels. This reform was intended to give the service a clearer management direction. In order to enhance management accountability, budgets were allocated to units. As Perrin (1988) points out, improved accountability was dependent on managers having financial skills, and the creation of effective decentralised structures with staff (especially clinicians) able to understand budgetary information.

Following Griffiths, the Körner Report (1984) recommended that district budgets should be linked to specialties such as X-rays or operating theatres. If a patient was sent for an X-ray, the cost would be attached to the department, giving clinicians information on the cost of their work. Again the aim was improved financial accountability. Problems that arise include the unwillingness of clinicians to see themselves as resource managers. They may believe that this conflicts with the clinical autonomy that they traditionally enjoy. Also, the quality of the information may not be sufficiently high to enable effective decision making.

Budgeting techniques are only one solution to the problems of the health service. According to the King's Fund Institute (1988), decision makers are faced with a number of options. Amongst these are:

- *more public expenditure*: the King's Fund researchers provided a tentative estimate that spending would have had to be just under £400 million higher in 1987/88 if it was to match 1981/82 levels, taking into account changing demand and technology;
- *supplementary and alternative sources of funding*: a number of alternatives exist. These range from private insurance schemes, to shops in hospitals and changing for services;
- *the creation of internal markets*: this would allow general practitioners to make decisions about which hospital or clinician to use. It is argued that the doctor would have the information to decide from where the best value for money could be obtained.
- *expansion of private health care*: the private sector in health care has grown considerably. Like all decisions about the future provision of health care, it is dependent on the value systems of the decision makers. If private provision is considered acceptable, it is highly attractive in deflecting demand away from the public sector. However, the King's Fund researchers argue that limited private sector expansion may lead to 'distortion in NHS planning priorities, cost inflation and possible adverse effects on NHS labour supply' (King's Fund Institute, 1988, p. 24).

Internal markets form the basis of government thinking about the reform of the National Health Service. This reflects the view that if the logic of the private sector is introduced into public sector organisations then greater efficiency will be achieved. This theme is pursued in more detail in the next chapter.

Conclusion

The above three case studies bring out a number of points about resourcing the public sector which demonstrate that resourcing issues are not the sole province of the technical experts in the area: accountants and economists. Instead resourcing issues impinge on all of us. We can make a few more concluding points:

- The environment affects budgetary behaviour. In a period of growth, the increment is the focus of debate; with cutbacks the baseline is questioned – leading to increasingly adversarial relations.
- As we saw with the Treasury, organisational culture will impact on budgetary behaviour. In the National Health Service clinicians may see their role as providing health care, not managing budgets. Managers and staff need to be motivated towards financial management.
- The structure affects budgetary behaviour. Decentralised structures may mean that budget holders are closer to the point of service delivery, but usually they will not be financial specialists. The introduction of local cost centres may result in people identifying with departmental objectives rather than the objectives of the organisation as a whole. Central finance department may be reluctant to concede power to the periphery by, for example, allowing cost centres to vire money from one budget heading to another. This may reduce the flexibility which decentralisation aims to promote.

Further reading

The importance of organisational culture is examined in Heclo and Wildavsky's study of the Treasury (1981). More recent material on the Financial Management Initiative is contained in Gray and Jenkins (1985) and Metcalfe and Richards (1987). There is little substantial work yet published on the Next Steps, though the Treasury and Civil Service Committee (1990) contains a number of useful appendices. The public spending process is covered by Likierman (1988), and Heald (1983) provides an economist's perspective on public expenditure.

In local government finance, work by Tony Travers (1988) is useful as are the case studies on local authority budgeting edited by Elcock and Jordan (1987) and the ensuing more theoretical book by Elcock *et al.* (1989). The Audit Commission publishes management papers (see, for example, 1989b) which highlight the latest developments. On the National Health Service, see Perrin (1988), and Harrison (1988) on general management. The journal *Public Money and Management* contains topical articles covering the whole of the public sector.

Chapter 11
The new agenda

Introduction

We have seen how in recent years the environment within which public sector organisations operate has changed:

- a changing society and economy has meant that government, and in particular local authorities, have had to respond in shaping their services to meet the changing needs of local communities;
- a continuing concern with financial restraints has meant that the public sector cannot respond to changes by growth or by throwing money at a problem;
- a willingness on the part of central government to pass legislation affecting the size, role and scope of other organisations in the public sector;
- attempts to change the culture of the public sector so that it becomes more 'businesslike';
- declining public acceptance of government's ability, and the professionals who work within it, to make decisions on behalf of the public.

To make more sense of these changes we need to examine the concept of organisational change itself and apply this to changes within and around public sector organisations. We shall, therefore, raise some of the theoretical issues surrounding change in the public sector and in the next chapter show how the public sector has responded.

Dimensions of organisational change

Organisations exist in a changing environment, be it economic, political, social, legal and so on; the economy continues to suffer from periodic booms and slumps despite the best efforts of politicians and economists; the political environment changes with new parties coming into power and new ideas permeating the political scene; and the legal context changes as a result of legislation passed down from the European Community to central government and from central government to local government. Demographic changes in society in terms of birth rates, death rates, or the mobility of the workforce will have an effect upon government in terms of the services it provides.

Change then is a *constant* in that it will always occur. What is not constant,however, is the *pace* of change, and this is what makes change so difficult to predict and to deal with. Witness the tremendous changes that occurred throughout Eastern Europe during 1989 and 1990 and the problems that the rapid pace of change has brought with it. It is the *rate* of change that causes organisations problems. If the rate and extent of change could be calculated in advance then organisations could prepare and take account of any changes and hence control it. Where the pace and extent of change is not predictable, organisations are forced into crisis management and react to changeratherthan controlling it. Irrespective of these outside influences upon change, some organisations are better equipped to deal with it than others.

We have already distinguished between open organisations and systems and closed organisations and systems. The latter tend to comprise of formal rules, stress routine and predictability and to be inward looking. Such organisations are designed for stability. In contrast to this, the open organisation stresses flexibility and is characterised by discretion and responsiveness to the environment. A closed system is often characteristic of a bureaucracy. If this is the case then a bureaucracy may have difficulty in coping with unplanned organisational change. Indeed, a number of writers have strongly contended that the end of bureaucracy is in sight (Bennis, 1966) and have heralded the coming adhocracy (Toffler, 1970) characterised by the responsive organisation rather than inertia and red tape. Such writers argue that the bureaucratic form of organisation is no longer viable since it cannot cope with:

- rapid and unpredictable change because it relies on routine, and the tall, thin organisational structure does not allow it to respond to the outside environment since all decisions have to be passed up the hierarchical chain of command for comment;
- the complexity of modern organisations needs new and different structures to allow for the many different tasks, locations and people that the modern, large government machine requires;
- the modern organisation requires people with diverse and transferable skills so that the division of labour and traditional professionalism is broken down;
- changing management thinking requires a more participative management style where senior managers give up some of their control to those lower down the organisation.

Thus, it is argued that bureaucracy is changing. What then are the catalysts that are likely to bring about such changes?

External change catalysts

The impetus for change may well come from outside the organisation itself and may take a number of forms.

1. **Ideas** The importance of ideas is often underestimated because their impact is difficult to measure; and yet changes in political, social and economic ideas will change organisations. The early 1980s saw the commitment to reduce the size of the public sector and this, in part, was the political impact of the economic theories of monetarism and the stress upon the individual associated with the political thinking of the New Right. Different ideas concerning the role of the state have an impact upon the functions that the institutions of the state are asked to perform. Thus the introduction of competitive tendering and contracting out in local government is an attempt to introduce market forces and expose parts of government to competition from private businesses.

2. **Legislation** A change in legislation will come to reflect a change in ideas. As certain ideas such as, for example, equality and equal opportunity, become widely accepted the law will legislate for this and organisations will have to respond to the requirements of such legislation. The Education Reform Act 1988 has now changed the role of the Local Education Authorities in the provision of education. Various local government Acts have made contracting out of some local authority services compulsory and this has changed the perceptions and the culture of local authorities. During the 1980s the size and structure of both the National Health Service and local government have been changed by central government legislation.

3. **Technology** The improved communication and co-ordination possibilities brought about particularly by developments in information technology continue to have an impact upon the public sector in areas as diverse as police work to the keeping of medical audit.

4. **The market** One of the most important changes throughout the 1980s has been the attempts by Conservative governments to introduce the disciplines of the market to the public sector. Competition is seen to lead to efficiency and effectiveness and to improve the service to the customer. The National Health Service White Paper 'Working for Patients' envisages the creation of internal markets within the National Health Service extending patient choice. Outside contractors have been allowed to compete for work that was previously seen as the prerogative of the local authority such as refuse collection, public transport and building work. We shall return to these issues later in the chapter.

5. **People** As we saw in the previous chapter, Mrs Thatcher has brought in outside businessmen to improve the efficiency and effectiveness of government, believing that the public sector suffers in comparison with the business world. The most notable of these have been Lord Rayner from Marks and Spencer, who instigated a series of scrutinies into the work of government departments to improve their value-for-money; and, in an attempt to improve the management of the National Health Service, Sir Roy Griffiths from Sainsburys, who has produced a number of reports. In creating General Managers to run the National Health Service Mrs Thatcher tended to look to businessmen. The advantages of such appointments are that a new perspective is brought to bear upon the organisation. Individuals coming in from outside can offer new ideas and insights and see problems in a new light. These are the reasons why

organisations frequently turn to outside consultants when attempting to bring about organisational change.

Internal change catalysts

1. **People**   Just as bringing in new blood from outside the organisation is a way of bringing about change, then promoting people or moving them around within an organisation will have an effect. Indeed some individuals, when promoted, will immediately attempt to bring about change to justify their promotion and show what dynamic individuals they are!
2. **Attitudes and behaviour**   Part of the job of management is to change people's attitudes and behaviour. This can be done formally through training courses and through changing work practices so that organisations become more people-centred. Thus, individuals may respond to change positively if they are given greater responsibility and discretion. If the individuals within an organisation are its greatest resource then effort has to be spent in taking account of their attitudes. However, changing such attitudes is extremely difficult to achieve and accounts for, as we see later, the increasing emphasis placed upon management development within the public sector.
3. **Structures**   Changing from a service dominated by the centre to a decentralised service may have profound effects upon the responsiveness of the organisation to the client and also on the morale of the workforce if it is accompanied by decentralising power. The move to such an organisational structure will also have profound effects upon existing power relations within the organisation and, as we argued in our chapter on power, there may be many vested interests to overcome and much bargaining to take place.

Obstacles to change

As a result of the political dimension to organisations conflicts and frustrations will arise as a result of change. Change is often not smooth and obstacles are put in its way as a result of:

- the self-interest of individuals who may fear that change is an encroachment upon their territory;
- the fear, insecurity, and resentment of individuals who may feel threatened by change and wonder if, for example, the new computer system means that their existing skills will become redundant or will wonder how they will cope with the new boss;
- the lack of trust that may follow if change is imposed from above and without consultation; individuals will wonder at the motives behind change.

People see change in different ways. The new manager may not understand why others resent her dynamic re-organisation and how work may be more rewarding as a result. At the same time the clerical officer may be quite happy with existing work patterns and relations even though they may appear to be inefficient. More widely, different groups interpret what the change catalyst is in different ways. Professional groups in the National Health Service may believe that an injection of funds will improve health care treatment. The government may argue that improved resource management will solve any problems. A crucial element is the way in which change is brought about. Does it involve full consultation and communication with all those that change will affect and is full account taken of the views of the workforce and their representatives? Are there proper mechanisms for bringing about consultation? Is consultation effective and meaningful or is it just going through the motions? Unless these questions are addressed by management then those that change affects may well feel that it is just imposed from above and thereby resent it.

We can ask ourselves, then, a number of general questions concerning change.

1. **Who brings about change?**   Is it internally or externally driven and is it best brought about by outside consultants?
2. **What changes?**   Is it the structure, the people, the processes, the tasks or the culture? We suggest that all these are interdependent upon each other within the organisation. Thus encouraging individuals to be more dynamic, flexible and responsive will not work if the same old hierarchical, top-down structure still exists.
3. **Who does it affect?**   And hence who is likely to obstruct it? Change may affect all the staff or just certain groups of it. The person bringing about change will have to identify and overcome entrenched interests.
4. **Are there appropriate mechanisms for change?**   Future action will depend on the answer to this question.
5. **How much will it cost?**   Change is expensive, not just in terms of financial cost – new technology does not come cheap – but also in terms of goodwill with staff and clients. However, a more important question may well be: Can the organisation afford *not* to change? In the private sector if a company does not respond quickly to new markets and products it will go out of business. Similarly, if central government is prepared to by-pass local government and encourage non-elected bodies such as Development Corporations or agencies, then local government has to respond to the challenge and show that it can do the job just as well.
6. **Is it crisis management or is change under control?**   It is difficult for government bodies to plan ahead given the short time span within which politicians operate, but if it is a flexible responsive organisation it may find it easier to deal with unexpected change.

We can now look at some of the issues that have come on the agenda in recent years.

Assessing performance

As part of the adoption of the managerialist ethos is the notion of assessing the performance of the organisation and of the individuals within it. We have already seen how advocates of scientific management linked the performance of individual workers to pay and how performance-related pay is being used throughout the public sector. We can ask, however, a number of general questions concerning the difficulties of assessing the performance of public sector organisations.

Who defines the performance?

There are a number of different perspectives that can be adopted to assess the performance of the official and these will reflect the views of the person who is doing the assessing:

(a) a political evaluation where the politician will be happy with the work of officials if they offer advice that saves the politician from embarrassment and ensures that the politician is re-elected;

(b) an organisational assessment may well be the extent to which an official staves off staff redundancies, increases the department's share of the budget, acts according to rules, is loyal to colleagues and so on;

(c) the client or customer assessment where the customer will judge the performance of the individual and the organisation by purchasing a company's goods and services. If the customer is unhappy with the performance then presumably he will go elsewhere

It is difficult to adopt these competing perspectives upon assessment. Ultimately, it may well be that officials will perform in order to satisfy the criteria laid down by those who have the power to reward or punish them, i.e. their immediate superiors.

Who owns the performance?

Presumably it is easy to determine the skill and ability of a hairdresser. Assuming they have the necessary equipment then the quality of the cut depends upon their individual skill. It is much more difficult to assign such individual responsibility to those working in the public sector. The exam pass rate of one teacher compared to another may have nothing to do with the individual teacher but everything to do with other factors including the availability of resources such as books or computers, the attitude of the parents, the ability of the students and so on. Similarly, where individuals operate as part of a team it does not make sense to assess the performance of the individual separate from the team as a whole.

Can we measure performance?

Presumably if our hairdresser cuts the hair of fifteen customers one day and twenty the next then, assuming the quality of the cut remains the same, we might consider that the performance of the hairdresser has improved. Can we measure in such a quantitative way the performance of officials who may not be producing a good or offering a clearly identifiable service? Attempts are made to assess the work of officials in terms of, say, how many claims an administrative officer deals with in a day. Yet how much of the work of government is involved in work that is easily quantifiable? How do we assess the quantity and quality of work of the social worker or the police officer?

Inputs are always easier to measure than outputs and the government has concentrated on reducing the inputs rather than improving the quality of the outputs. Thus the emphasis is on attempting to achieve the same volume of work with fewer staff irrespective of the quality of the work done. It is generally considered that evaluation must be linked to objectives but if the objectives are determined by the politicians in the first place is it fair to assess the performance of officials who may have had no input into setting those objectives? Many a government objective has been side-tracked or been overridden because in practice it has proved impossible to implement. For example, the government retreated on its proposals to implement the national curriculum for schools after it became clear that certain of the proposals would prove impossible to implement (see the *Guardian*, 1 August 1990).

Technology

The introduction of new technology will have an impact upon the organisation in a number of different ways and will affect the structure, the decision making, the organisational politics and the people and their skills within the organisation.

Structure

The increasing use of information technology could lead to either a more centralised or a more decentralised structure. It may mean that more information is stored at the centre, thereby reducing the scope for individual discretion. At the same time terminals at local offices will allow information to flow down the organisation much more quickly to the operational level. It may also mean a reduction in the tiers of middle management since many of the tasks of communication and co-ordination can be performed through the use of networked systems.

An example of information technology influencing the structure of the organisation is in the Department of Social Security where drastic changes are occurring in its London offices. Much of the work that was previously done in the local offices has been transferred to three new centres at Glasgow, Belfast and Wigan, linked to London by computer. The advantage of this is cheaper rents outside London and the easier recruitment and retention of staff. The technology will allow a reduction in the size of local offices and it is anticipated that local branches in London will become more accessible and more responsive to the local community.

Decision-making

More information will be available and the quality of that information may be improved upon. The information will allow quicker decisions to be made and permit decisions to be taken lower down the organisation. It may also reduce risk and uncertainty since modelling and simulation exercises can be carried out. The Local Authorities Management Services Advisory Committee (LAMSAC) have a number of packages that act as aids to management decision-making in local authorities. It has also developed data bases which hold information about contractors and contracts awarded by local authorities (see *Municipal Review and AMA News*, June 1988). Increasingly, moves are being made towards a common computer intelligence network linking police forces throughout Europe. Information will be pooled and available to all. At present photographs, fingerprints and documents are available to European anti-terrorist squads (*Guardian*, 26 July 1990).

Organisational politics

If we assume that knowledge is power then information technology and access to it is a powerful tool for those who control it. It may also lead to a new breed of specialists or professionals within the organisation.

People and skills

The big fear is that IT may lead to job losses and to the loss of traditional skills. Although this may be true in a particular organisation it is argued that by improving output and efficiency the economy as a whole will benefit. IT may also rejuvenate the workforce and liberate the individual from the routine work that is a part of administration. There is also a certain status associated with new skills and it may lead to job enrichment. Evidence from the Audit Commission (1988) on the police revealed large savings in administrative time through the use of computers. (See Table 11.1.)

Table 11.1 Percentage time on administration.

	Pre computers	Post computers
Inspectors	58	22
Sergeants	50	20
Constables	21	4

(Adapted from Audit Commission, 1988.)

An extra dimension to the increased use of information technology is the concern with confidentiality, particularly given the sensitive nature of much of the work of the public sector. The Data Protection Act 1984 was introduced to protect the rights of citizens concerning information about them held by organisations on computer files. This applies to all organisations but is particularly relevant to the public sector where the holding of police records, social services records, medical records and so on gives cause for concern. It has implications for the concept of open government that we examined earlier and the ethical dimension that the public sector operates within.

Human resource development

Since the early Hawthorne studies that we investigated in Chapter 5, the recognition that people are an important part of any organisation has never really been off the agenda. The most recent version of the concern with people as an important organisational resource is human resource development. Unfortunately there appears to be no clear definition of what this is. In one, limited, sense it is seen as old style personnel management with a new name. In a more radical sense it is seen as incorporating individuals into the strategic management of the organisation and recognising that long-term labour planning makes sense. According to Storey there are four dimensions to this approach:

1. It is linked and integrated into a corporate strategy.
2. It is intended to ensure the commitment of employees and not, merely, their compliance.
3. In order to ensure this commitment greater attention should be paid to the recruitment, training, appraisal and rewards of individual employees. (It is, as such, linked to the concern with performance appraisal that we examined in Chapter 8.)
4. The management of 'human resources' should be carried out by line managers and not by personnel specialists. (See Storey 1989, p. 20.)

As accountability and responsibility are located further down the organisation the role of the traditional line manager increases in importance with a greater emphasis placed upon people management. The concern with people echoes earlier theories of organisational development with its desire to release the human potential within an organisation. We suggested that one of the obstacles to change is the attitude of people within the organisation. If employees can be encouraged to be flexible and responsive then change is more easily brought about. The objectives of organisational development are:

- the personal growth of individuals through the enhancement of skills and personal attributes;
- the creation of an organisation where problems can be discussed freely and openly;
- locate decision making lower down the organisational ladder;
- build an atmosphere of trust throughout the organisation;
- increase the sense of the individual ownership of the organisation's goals;
- increase self-control and self-direction;

- change authority relations so that those with expertise, as well as those who occupy a certain hierarchical position, have authority. (Golembiewski, 1977.)

Such an approach relies upon the commitment of senior managers to developing the potential of those lower down and it requires the appropriate organisational setting.

The managerialist ethos

In our first chapter we introduced the work of Peters and Waterman (1982) and suggested that the 'excellence' culture that they described has had an important impact upon management thinking within the public sector. Supporters of such a culture argue that there is no reason why it cannot be applied to the public sector. Indeed a feature of the 1980s has been the tendency for those working within the public sector to be described as managers rather than administrators. Sir Roy Griffiths is one who subscribes to the view that the ethos of the private sector can be applied to the public sector:

> We have been told that the NHS is different from business in management terms, not least because the NHS is not concerned with the profit motive and must be judged by wider social standards which cannot be measured. These differences can be overstated. The clear similarities between NHS management and business management are much more important. In many organisations in the private sector, profit does not impinge on large numbers of people below Board level. They are concerned with levels of service, quality of product, meeting budgets, cost improvement, productivity, motivating and rewarding staff, research and development, and the long-term viability of the undertaking. All these things Parliament is urging on the NHS. (1983, p. 10.)

We can legitimately ask, though, 'What is management?'. According to Stephenson, management is a political activity and the role of the manager is to act as:

- crisis handler;
- resource allocator;
- authoriser;
- negotiator;
- monitor;
- evaluator. (Stephenson, 1985.)

According to Mintzberg, the manager has an array of ten roles to choose from which cover inter-personal roles, informational roles and decisional roles (see Handy, 1985, p. 363). Handy characterises the role of the manager as that of the General Practitioner. Which of these roles should our public sector manager be performing? The concern with the training of managers in the public sector is also expressed in the private sector. The introduction of the Management Charter

Initiative has suggested that it is possible to identify a set of generic management functions based upon a broad set of management competencies such as:

- meeting customer needs;
- managing people;
- managing financial resources;
- managing information.

This is developed alongside competencies in personal effectiveness in areas such as:

- planning and organising;
- managing others;
- knowing oneself;
- using intellect.

To what extent, though, is this a return to scientific management and the belief in a universal set of management principles that can be applied to every organisation? To what extent are the competencies so general in nature as to be incapable of practical use? To what extent does the development of general competencies take into account the different roles played by different tiers of management?

In the civil service, for example, senior officials will need to maintain good relations with politicians and to look upward to the minister rather than downward or outward. Middle ranking officials may need to look outward as they maintain good relations with the public, with clients or with contractors. Commenting upon the civil service, Manning suggests that different skills are required such as:

- communication skills;
- social, inter-personal and inter-active skills;
- decision-making and problem-solving skills;
- skills in group work;
- consultation and negotiation skills;
- technical or specialist skills.

Manning argues that: 'Consultation, negotiation and running meetings were more important for senior management; group work and team building were more valued for middle management; and job-specific, technical or specialist skills were more important for junor management.' (Manning, 1984, p. 66.)

The adoption of techniques that might be appropriate to the private sector is open to criticism and the adoption of a generic approach to management is under question. Tyson (1990) points out that the managerialist ethos is being applied to government departments wholesale irrespective of their different cultures. Dopson and Stewart (1990) have found a number of specific factors which influence the officials' reaction to the introduction of private sector practices:

1. The length of time since the first more commercial changes were introduced.
2. The degree of exposure of the organisation to political debate.
3. The degree of exposure of the organisation to public and media debate.

4. The power of the consumer to influence the manager's priorities.
5. The proportion of professionals employed in the organisation and how powerful they are in influencing policy.
6. The difficulties of attracting and retaining staff.
7. The extent to which work can be contracted out to the private sector.
8. The manager's age profile; older civil servants may be less willing to change.
9. The constraints and amount of Treasury control over tight manpower targets which may dampen the entrepreneurial spirit advocated in private sector managers.

A middle ground between traditional administrative practice and the adoption of the private sector managerialist ethos is advocated by Perry and Kraemer: 'Public management is a merger of the normative orientation of traditional public administration and the instrumental orientation of generic management.' (1983, p. x).

By normative they mean a concern with some of the values that we discussed in Chapter 2 such as equity, equality and an awareness of democracy and accountability.

Reforming the public sector: The Thatcher techniques

The period since 1979 has been one of turbulent change. As we shall see in the next chapter the public sector has been reformed although to what extent is open to debate. Much of that reform has been imposed and a battery of strategies has been used to bring about change.

Privatisation

Perhaps the most widely known of the Thatcher strategies for public sector organisations is 'privatisation' or 'denationalisation'. We define privatisation as the transfer of public sector assets out of the public sector. This can involve the sale of nationalised industries, council houses and management buy-outs of public sector enterprises. Surprisingly, privatisation did not feature in the 1979 manifesto: the programme took off in the early 1980s with the sale of British Aerospace (partly in 1981) and Britoil (partly in 1982). The programme developed increased pace after the Conservatives' re-election in 1983 with further sales of shares in British Aerospace and Britoil together with British Telecom (1984), British Gas (1985) and British Airways (1987).

The explicit rationale behind privatisation follows the free market ideas that such activities are better run in the marketplace where the forces of competition will increase organisational efficiency resulting in a better service or product for the consumer and the elimination of a liability on the taxpayer. Critics of privatisation argue that in many cases all that has happened is that a state monopoly has become a private monopoly, that the consumer has not realised the intended benefits, and that the attraction for government has been the money raised from the sale of these companies which has been used to subsidise income tax cuts.

Competitive tendering and contracting out

Traditionally, private sector organisations have supplied goods and services for the public sector, such as building work, military equipment and drugs for the National Health Service. Equally much work has been provided by the service delivering organisation: for example cleaning, refuse collection, drawing of plans and so on. This state of affairs has been under challenge during the 1980s. Virtually all large public organisations have at least considered the possibility of contracting work out to private sector organisations. Local government has faced legislative requirements to put work out to compulsory competitive tendering (the Local Government Planning and Land Act 1980 and the Local Government Act 1988). Compulsory competition does not necessarily involve the privatisation of a service. In the National Health Service competitive tendering for ancillary services (with cleaning, catering and laundry top of the list) began in 1983. Other services that may go out to tender include portering, security, medical records and non-emergency ambulance services. Evidence from the National Health Service trade union privatisation unit (1990) shows that the share of contracts for National Health Service work won by the private sector has shrunk since 1983. (See Table 11.2.)

Table 11.2   Percentage of contracts won by outside firms.

	Domestic services	Catering	Laundry
NHS	72.4	95.5	73.5
Private firms	27.6	4.5	26.5

(Adapted from Joint NHS Privatisation Research Unit, 1990.)

The trade unions also argue that 81 per cent of all contracts won by the private sector are shared between three firms, which does not indicate the healthy competition that was envisaged. According to Kristensen (1987) contracting out is aimed at achieving economies. A National Audit Office report concluded that:

> Savings from privatisation have arisen mainly from the need to draw up specifications including the rationalisation of existing operations (in domestic services), less favourable conditions of employment, greater use of part-time staff, changes in working practices and increased productivity. (Quoted in Joint NHS Privatisation Research Unit Report, 1990, p. 10).

Competitive tendering has important implications for organisational structures and patterns of behaviour. If an in-house 'direct service organisation' manages to win the contract, we have two sets of actors. Firstly, there is the client department, for example social services, who put the contract out to tender and, secondly, there is the contractor who provides the service. The basis of the relationship is the contract. In many cases, authorities are specifying the task to be completed and standards of work for the first time and are now aware of the true cost of activity. This sharpens the process of accountability – the contract becomes the focus – as the contractor is responsible for delivering the service as specified in the contract and will be judged by the client on that basis.

Use of internal market mechanisms

Internal markets, such as those proposed for the National Health Service, aim to make the allocation of resources more efficient by enabling doctors, for example, to make decisions about how to spend their budgets. It is proposed that hospitals will become profit centres competing against each other and the new self-governing hospitals will trade on their own account. Large GP practices will be able to apply for their own budgets and encouraged to shop around between hospitals for services for their patients (NHS White Paper, 1989).

Deregulation

One of the New Right criticisms of the public sector of the 1970s was the overuse of regulation and planning as a method of organising services. This, it was argued, results in inefficiency and a supply of goods and services which the consumer did not want. The solution offered was greater freedom for potential suppliers to meet the needs of the public. A prime example was the deregulation of buses (through the Transport Act 1985) which allowed private operators to seek licences to run services.

Transfer payments and vouchers

Transfer payments or vouchers represent a more radical step than compulsory competition. As Kristensen (1987) argues, while the state remains responsible for financing the service, the choice is exercised by the public. The possible gains are increased efficiency, the consumers getting the service they want, and the worse off benefiting more than the affluent. Child benefit involves making a payment to, usually, the mother of the child, who can then make a decision on how best to use the money. A criticism of this benefit is that it may be paid to people who may not need it. This could be solved by targeting the benefit at those who need it, but this would inevitably mean that many deserving cases would not get the benefit.

Another example is the case of education vouchers. Instead of the local education authority telling the parent which school their child should attend, the parents would be issued with a voucher which they could 'spend' at a school of their choice. The parents could also choose an independent school with an additional payment by them. While this proposal is controversial with critics saying that it is unworkable, we should bear in mind that a similar system already operates with mandatory grants and fees paid to students who choose which polytechnic, college or university they go to.

Charging for services

A further alternative is charging for services. The cost of National Health Service prescriptions has risen dramatically since 1979, charges have been introduced for eye tests and dental charges have been increased. This method can be used to encourage more efficient use of a service but it may mean that people who need a service do not take advantage of it. The ring fencing of local authority housing revenue accounts has meant that tenants are now paying more or less the full cost of the service instead of benefiting from a subsidy.

Withdrawal and let the market decide

One alternative is for the public sector to refuse to provide a good or service and allow the marketplace to provide it instead. Given the Conservatives' belief in market mechanisms as the most efficient allocator of resources and decision making, this would appear to be an attractive proposition. For example, the Channel Tunnel is being constructed using private sector resources only based on assumptions by Eurotunnel that it is a financially viable proposition.

Attacks on restrictive practices

Since 1979 the Conservatives have passed a number of Acts of Parliament which have challenged the power of the trade unions. Closed-shop agreements, restrictive practices and picketing arrangements have all been subject to reform. Trade unions have been banned at Government Communications Headquarters (GCHQ) and school teachers lost their pay negotiating rights. There have also been a number of industrial disputes which have led to reforms in the public sector, for example, the miners' strike, disputes in the civil service, and the strike at British Steel.

Conclusion

The overwhelming impression is one of change and the creation of a new agenda for the public sector. Conventional wisdoms have been undermined and a fundamental re-assessment has taken place concerning the functions, scope, size, processes and people within the public sector. In the next chapter we examine the practical consequences of some of the ideas that we have explored in this chapter.

Further reading

Potter (1989) links organisational change to culture, while Hoggett and Vince (1988) locate organisational change within the context of the public sector. Pitt and

Smith (1984) examine the use of technology in public sector organisations and Isaac-Henry (1987) provides a useful case study. Jones (1982) and Dopson and Stewart (1990) examine management issues in the civil service, and Gunn (1987) assesses the arguments concerning generic management. Mullins (1989) provides a detailed analysis of organisational development and the techniques used to bring it about; Davies (1988) offers a public sector focus. Stoker (1988) provides a chapter on the techniques used to change the activities of local authorities. The further reading given at the end of the following chapter will also be of use.

Chapter 12
Responding to the new agenda

Introduction

Given the rapidly changing world in which public sector organisations are living, we can now turn to look in detail at the way in which they have responded to the new agenda that has been thrust upon them.

Performance measurement

As we saw in Chapter 10, the idea of assessing performance in the public sector is not a new one: the Public Expenditure Survey (PES) dates back to the early 1960s, and Programme Analysis and Review (PAR) was a tool of the 1970s. Local government and the National Health Service have experimented with techniques to control the level of expenditure. As we saw, many of these techniques were – at best – only partially successful. In this section we are concerned not solely with financial matters but with the operation of the whole organisation.

The three case studies in Chapter 10 illustrated the problem of controlling resources in public sector organisations and how best they could meet the changing demands of the environment. The concern with performance cannot be seen in isolation from the economic strategy of the Thatcher governments. In Chapter 3 we saw how New Right theorists consider the public sector to be inefficient because the bureaucratic form of organisation provides little incentive for improving organisational performance in the way that business organisations do. Those who build large offices are rewarded with higher salaries and further opportunities on the career ladder. A former civil servant, Leslie Chapman, published an account of his experiences of waste, overmanning and inefficiency in the Ministry of Works (1979) which apparently was widely read in influential circles. The result was a strategy to reform the public sector.

Improving economy, efficiency and effectiveness

The desire to improve organisational performance has focused attention on the pursuit of greater efficiency and effectiveness. This pursuit, which dominated government thinking in the 1980s, merits detailed scrutiny. First we will define the terms, secondly we will look at how these concepts have been applied in the public sector, and thirdly, we will look at how they are measured.

Economy, efficiency and effectiveness defined

Although we recognise there is debate about the various definitions of the terms we use, we follow the most commonly used ones in order that the reader can refer to further material with ease. If we take a variant of systems approach, we can see an organisation as having inputs, processes, outputs. Take, for instance, a production process such as the manufacture of a motor car. Physical inputs such as metals, plastics and glass will be combined with designs, labour and energy and put through the production process in order to produce the output – the motor car.

The concept of *economy* relates to the inputs to the process. Jackson and Palmer define economy as 'concerned with minimising the cost of resources acquired or used, having regard to the quality of the inputs' (1989, p. 50). For the manufacture of our motor car, this will involve minimising the cost of physical inputs, labour and so on, but at the same time maintaining their quality.

Efficiency is concerned with the relationship between the inputs and the outputs. Efficiency can be defined as 'given the objectives and the means to pursue the objectives the minimising of inputs to the programme in relation to the outputs from it', and an efficient programme as 'one where the target is being achieved with the least possible use of resources. Similarly, on the way to achieving the target, the actual output should be secured with the least use of resources'. (Treasury and Civil Service Committee, 1982, para 52.)

It is about getting more for less. It can be achieved by minimising inputs in relation to outputs or, alternatively maximising outputs in relation to inputs or both. The determinant of this relationship will be the process that transforms the inputs into the outputs. In the case of the car company, it will be about making the best use of manufacturing processes, technology, and staff in order to add value to the raw materials when making the car.

Effectiveness is about achieving what we want to achieve. It is about the relationship between intended outputs and actual outputs. The Treasury and Civil Service Committee defines effectiveness as 'the definition of objectives, the measurement of progress towards achieving those objectives and the consideration of alternative ways of achieving those objectives' and an efficient programme as 'one where the intention of the programme is being achieved'. (Treasury and Civil Service Committee, 1982, para 52.)

The car company will have set a target. It might be to produce quality saloon cars and achieve a 10 per cent share of the market for saloon cars. It will then be able to compare how it actually performed against that target.

Economy, efficiency and effectiveness in the public sector

So far, we have illustrated the concepts using the example of the motor company. It is a commercial operation aiming to maximise its profits. It has to compete in the marketplace against a number of competitors who are equally keen to maximise profits. The spur to improve performance is that if the customer considers the price too high or quality too low, there are alternative cars to choose from. It has been argued that it is much more difficult to apply these concepts to the public sector. Some of the reasons offered are:

- many public sector organisations are monopoly suppliers of goods or services. For example, there is only one Department of Social Security. If the claimant is not satisfied with the service, she cannot go elsewhere for her payment. In a competitive environment there is an incentive to be efficient – inefficiency will lead to reduced profits, lower dividends for shareholders and ultimately closure. A monopolist does not have that incentive;
- the car company has a clearly identifiable product – the car. This is not always the case in the public sector. For example, what does a university produce? Is it lectures and seminars, or research, or ideas, or educated citizens or personnel for business?
- the car company has a clearly identifiable customer who will enter into a financial exchange with the company. In the public sector it is not always easy to identify the customer. For example, the civil servant in one of the new executive agencies established under the Next Steps Initiative could see several people as customers. Firstly, the customer could be the member of the public with whom she is dealing; secondly it could be the minister in charge of the service; or thirdly, it could be Parliament which is elected by, and represents the electorate; or fourthly it could be the tax or Community Charge payer (see Public Accounts Committee, 1989). Ministers may be anxious to reduce the overall expenditure on services while the public may want more services.
- the motor company has an explicitly stated objective – the maximisation of profits. Savings achieved through greater efficiency will contribute to greater profitability. Public sector organisations may not be able to produce such explicit statements. The values that underpin the public sector include a demand for equity. Would it be acceptable for a police force to concentrate its resources on preventing crime in an affluent middle class area with articulate and vociferous residents at the expense of a run-down inner city estate?

These problems make the pursuit of economy, efficiency and effectiveness in the public sector more difficult. Various initiatives have been undertaken to improve performance. Study of strategies to improve public sector performance must be seen in the context of the Conservative Government's approach to the public sector. The early 1980s were dominated by the government's efficiency strategy. The Rayner scrutinies were aimed at making lasting savings in the civil service. Critics of the strategy argued that it was not so much about efficiency as about economy. They believed the strategy was aimed at reducing the inputs to the process rather than improving the ratio between inputs and ouputs. This reflected the policy of reducing the level of public spending (see Metcalfe and Richards, 1987). They point out that such strategies cannot be seen as neutral: political decisions have to be made about what options to pursue and these will reflect the values of the decision makers.

The Audit Commission promotes economy, efficiency and effectiveness. It aims to do this by encouraging local authorities to improve their management practices. Hence their approach concentrates on improving the process which transforms inputs into outputs. This process is not as easy as it may seem. It requires authorities to consider what demands are made on the organisation – establishing what is wanted, by whom, how, and when. They need to reconsider traditional practices. The Local Government Training Board has pointed, in its various publications, to the need to change structures in order to provide a service that is closer to the public. Traditional working patterns based on the 'Purple Book' conditions of service may restrict the opening hours of amenities such as swimming baths. Demarcation disputes may mean that it takes six specialists to do a job that could be done by one generalist. Hence improved efficiency may require structural, cultural and attitudinal change. Evidence that practices have changed is provided by both the Audit Commission (1989b) and the Local Government Training Board (1985).

Measuring economy, efficiency and effectiveness

If an organisation follows the steps in the rational model of policy making, it will have decided on objectives and selected policies to achieve. The next question will be: 'How will I know if I have achieved what I set out to do?' In order to answer the question, the manager needs to measure performance. Managers in both public and private organisations therefore use measures to ascertain what they are doing and how it compares with, for example, what they intended to do or what others are doing. Profits in the private sector are known only after conducting the historical exercise of doing the accounts. Managers need information in the interim period, hence measurement.

As Jackson and Palmer argue, performance measures cannot be considered in isolation from the organisation's culture, structure and environment. The context of such measures is crucial:

> It is top management's job to ensure that there is a vision and strategy for the organisation, the achievement of which should be reflected in long and short term objectives. Unless these objectives are clearly stated and understood by those who have responsibility for them there can be no effective measurement. By the same token, objectives on their own are pointless without the ability to measure their achievement. (Jackson and Palmer, 1989, p. 25.)

The Local Government Training Board (1985, p. 60) lists some of the most common forms of performance measurement:

- **cost indicators** How much does a service or a unit of service cost? For example, how much does it cost to process a housing benefit claim?
- **productivity indicators** How much work can be done by a member of staff? For example, the number of benefit claims per person per hour.
- **utilisation rates** How efficiently are resources used? For example, the occupancy rates of classrooms in schools.

- **time targets** How long does it take to accomplish a given task. For example, to complete a housing repair.
- **volume of service** The amount of work done. For example, the number of passengers using a bus service.
- **demand/service provision indicators** The level of actual service provision compared with an indicator of potential demand. For example, number of nursery school places per 1000 children in the nursery school age range.

Large amounts of data of this kind can be collected but it is meaningless until it is put to some purpose. Data needs to be transformed in to meaningful information. This is often done by comparing data with other data. Several types of comparison can be used:

- **comparison over time** For example, comparing this year's costs with last year's costs, or comparing a school's examination success rate with previous rates.
- **standards** For example, comparing the rate of return on capital invested against government targets. Targets are set for ambulances to arrive at their destinations and authorities will compare performance against them.
- **intra-service** Comparing one unit of an organisation with another unit of an organisation providing a similar service. For example, time taken to process a claim for unemployment benefit in one office compared with another office.
- **private sector** Comparing an organisation's performance with that in the private sector. For example, comparing cleaning standards of a direct-service organisation with private sector firms.
- **other authorities** Whether all authorities or near neighbours or authorities are selected because they are similar. The Chartered Institute of Public Finance and Accountancy (CIPFA) and government departments regularly produce league tables comparing, for example, spending by local education authorities. (See Local Government Training Board, 1985, p. 60; Flynn, 1990.)

One of the most common criticisms of performance measures is that too many people insist that 'if it can't be measured it's not important'. While this is obviously not true, it merits further investigation. Research suggests that performance measurement tends to concentrate on that which is easily quantifiable. Allen *et al.* argue that 'the most fundamental criticism of PIs has been that they focus on inputs and processes, but say little about output. In other words PIs are seen to concentrate on efficiency rather than effectiveness'. (Cited in Jackson and Palmer, 1989, p. 37.)

In the case of the health service, they suggest that this means focusing on the resources used and activity rates such as admission rates, lengths of stay, etc. but little about the effect of all this on health. In a university it is easy to measure the number of lectures given, room occupancy rates, and fee income. It is more difficult to measure how effective the university is in developing the intellect of its students.

According to Mintzberg, the focus on what is easily measured produces undesirable consequences. Metcalfe and Richards summarise his argument:

First, because costs are more easily measured than benefits, efficiency often reduces to economy. Savings in money and manpower become the sole measure of improvement; the quest for efficiency becomes a search for cuts. Second, because social costs are more difficult to measure then economic costs, externalities are often ignored. Individual units concentrate on improving their own efficiency even though the overall effect is sub-optimal. Third, economic benefits are more easily identified than social benefits and efforts to increase efficiency lead to a re-definition of performance criteria in ways that lend themselves to easier measurement. The pursuit of efficiency degenerates into a numbers game. (Metcalfe and Richards, 1987, pp. 30–1.)

It seems that these criticisms have not gone unnoticed. The Next Steps reforms of the civil service are intended to bring about a change in the organisational culture and there is, as we have already seen, interest in these reforms at the very top. In its 1990 review of Progress in the Next Steps Initiative, the Treasury and Civil Service Committee paid particular attention to measuring performance. The report states:

> In setting targets for agency performance, we recommend that the emphasis should be on outputs: that is, that the performance of any operation will be measured not by how much money it spends or how many staff it employs, but how well it delivers the goods and the extent to which it meets the needs of the customers for whom its services are provided. (Treasury and Civil Service Committee, 1990, p. ix.)

Thus the focus is on the effectiveness of the agency. It is intended that staff at all levels should be consulted on how best performance can be assessed and how customer satisfaction is evaluated. In addition, performance-related pay should be linked to the achievement of targets.

Public sector organisations often have multiple and conflicting objectives. For example, British Rail objectives in their 1989 corporate plan emphasise the need to increase profitability, while the subsidy coming from government is scheduled to be reduced. This, according to the Central Transport Consultative Committee (1990), means that British Rail's quality objectives (see Table 12.1) are not being met because of the need to increase revenue and reduce the level of investment. Hence the pursuit of efficiency may lead to a failure to be effective in delivering quality.

Finally, we need to consider who is going to use the information generated by performance measurement exercises. Information generated by performance measurement can be politically sensitive. Officials may be reluctant to make information available to politicians if it shows that performance is poor as it could jeopardise the career prospects of the officials. Politicians, in turn, are sensitive to public criticism and may exercise caution in making information available to the public. Indeed, we could add another 'E' to economy, efficiency and effectiveness – electability. The politician may believe that an organisation has performed well if it contributes to electoral success.

Table 12.1   British Rail's quality of service objectives relating to the Inter-City service

---

Punctuality   90 per cent right on time and up to ten minutes late
Reliability (percentage of service to run)   At least 95.5 per cent
Train Enquiry Bureaux   95 per cent of calls to be answered within thirty seconds
Ticket Offices   Maximum queueing time of three minutes off peak and five minutes peak
Carriage Cleaning
   Interior daily cleaning   100 per cent
   Exterior wash   95 per cent (daily)
   Heavy interior cleaning   95 per cent

(Source: Central Transport Consultative Committee, 1990, p. 33.)

Jackson and Palmer (1989) argue that if performance measurement is to lead to improvement then managers need to be involved in the process from the point where it is decided what to measure. This, along with managers having responsibility for the task as well as being accountable for it, is central to successful management.

Quality

A further private sector initiative, this time originating in Japan, has begun to impinge on management thinking in the public sector – the *quality approach*. The literature on quality emphasises that in an increasingly competitive environment organisations need to improve their performance in order to gain an edge over rivals. Peter Drucker argues that the success of the Japanese economy is based not on its advantage in product design but in the leadership qualities of their managers. Faced with competition from Japan, British companies have sought to emulate their management philosophy. As with corporate management, systems analysis and other approaches, quality has hit the public sector management agenda.

A variety of approaches can be adopted. These vary from obtaining certification from the British Standards Institution that the process conforms to British Standard 5750 Quality Systems, to the attitudinal approach of Total Quality Management. Writers on quality see it as a managerial philosophy which should permeate thinking on all issues and at all levels in the organisation (see Deming, 1986). The quality approach is based on the assumptions of the Human Relations School, particularly McGregor (1960) whose Theory Y argued that people actively seek responsibility and given the right environment, have a positive contribution to make to the effectiveness of the organisation. According to Crosby, an organisation has the capacity to develop from uncertainty (where problems are dealt with as and when they occur) through a number of stages to certainty (where the organisation has a prevention system to ensure that few significant problems occur), (see English, 1990).

The Local Government Training Board has defined quality as 'that which gives the customer satisfaction. Quality assurance is about setting up systems that ensure that a service or product consistently achieves customer satisfaction' (1989, p. 42). We have argued in previous chapters that the management of organisation is contingent on the nature and task of the organisation. Hence there cannot be one simple formula for quality; each organisation has to develop its own approach. However, we can see some issues of general concern and then look at how these may be applicable to the public sector.

Bone and Griggs (1989) lists their three C's of quality:

- *Commitment:* to customers, organisational goal, personal quality, etc.
- *Competence:* in organising, solving problems, communicating, designing, etc.
- *Communication:* by both word and mouth with particular emphasis on feedback.

Most approaches to quality emphasise:

- change in the culture of the organisation and attitudes of staff;
- commitment of management to quality;
- the education and training of staff at all levels in the organisation;
- quality written into the objectives of the organisation;
- error-free work – 'get it right first time, on time, every time' – thus moving from 100 per cent inspection to the use of control mechanisms.

The Local Government Training Board summarise the steps necessary to ensure quality:

1. Know the customer's needs;
2. Design a product or service to meet the needs;
3. Guarantee performance;
4. Provide clear instructions;
5. Deliver punctually;
6. Provide a back-up service;
7. Use feedback. (Local Government Training Board, 1989, p. 42.)

Thus, the Local Government Training Board approach sees quality as an extension of the customer orientation. This makes the important assumption that the member of the public who consumes the service or the taxpayer is the customer. As we have already discussed, this assumption is a problematic one. In large organisations people are encouraged to see the first user of their service as the customer. For example, if an officer's task is to supply budgetary information to the central treasurer's department then that department is the customer.

An initial reading of BS 5750 shows how it can easily be applied to a repetitive manufacturing process or routine activities such as the payment of benefits where there is an easily identifiable output. Many of the features of the public sector require us to consider how applicable quality approaches are to the public sector. Some of the possible benefits that a quality orientation may produce include:

- agencies who compete with others for contracts (for example, direct service organisations in local authorities or the Property Service Agency or Her

Majesty's Stationery Office) can develop a competitive edge over commercial rivals and could use BS 5750 as a marketing tool;

- advocates of quality argue that after the initial investment, quality saves money. For example, getting it right first time eliminates the need to do jobs again or the need for 100 per cent inspection. Much quality can be achieved by better organisation and management. Building properties to a high standard may mean spending more at the construction stage but will incur lower maintenance costs in the long run (English, 1990). According to the project manager for the Next Steps executive agencies, Peter Kemp, under the new arrangements, departments must move towards light-handed monitoring after the event, thus relying on the agency to ensure quality (Public Accounts Committee, 1989);
- better relationships with clients because they are more satisfied with the service.

However, such a strategy generates a number of problems. These include:

- a quality policy requires long-term planning. Taking the example of building properties, local authorities may be reluctant to commit large amounts of scarce resources to the construction of high-quality accommodation when there are other priorities which are high on the agenda;
- as we have noted in previous chapters, the only certainty that public sector organisations face is uncertainty. This inevitably means that they will continue to face strategic problems;
- the absence of the profit motive means that the incentive to achieve quality may not be as high as if there was a balance sheet demonstrating what has been achieved;
- where an organisation is a monopoly provider of a service there is less incentive to improve quality;
- politicians who determine policy are not elected by virtue of their management expertise and may not be sympathetic to quality policies. However, there is evidence to show that politicians can and do demonstrate a concern for these issues (see examples demonstrated by the Local Government Training Board (1985) and the Treasury and Civil Service Select Committee (1990));
- as the Local Government Training Board points out (1989, p. 43), other values need to be assured: equity, effectiveness and efficiency. Whereas a private sector organisation can target its services towards a particular market, an environmental health department must ensure equity in service provision. Often services that are appreciated by customers may not be meeting with the objectives set by political masters. For example, what customers (or claimants) want from the benefits service may be very different from what the Secretary of State wants;
- many public sector workers (for example architects drawing plans or printers in printing units) may not come into direct contact with members of the public. Quality approaches tell us that their customers are those in the organisation to whom they provide a service and they should adopt a similar approach of getting it right first time, on time and to budget;
- if customers are highly satisfied with a quality service they may demand more. As we have noted in previous chapters, a problem in the public sector is the need

to limit demand to avoid budgetary expansion. This would cease to be a problem if customers are paying the full cost;

- the possibility that the required cultural change may not extend to those at the street level in the organisation – those who deal with the public on a day-to-day basis and are therefore crucial to the projection of a quality image;
- sceptics say that quality management is not applicable to service organisations. Advocates of quality such as Crosby (1984) argue that at the heart of most services is a production process using machinery – whether it is ovens in a kitchen or office machinery in a government department. Hence it is not appropriate to make the distinction between the two types of organisation.

Though relatively few public sector organisations have been awarded the British Standards Institute kite, many organisations have made moves towards quality. These moves include assessment of consumer needs and satisfaction, better complaints procedures which not only process the complaint but seek to amend procedures in the light of the complaint, and improved staff development programmes, including customer care training. Thus, for example, Wrekin Council has attempted to create a corporate culture based upon 'Quality, Caring and Fairness' (Hancox *et al.*, 1989), (see Local Government Training Board 1989, pp. 43–5 for case studies).

People in the public sector

In the previous chapter we indicated that organisational change can be imposed from outside or be generated from within. Similarly there are two ways of changing the people dimension of organisations – bringing in new people from outside or developing the existing staff. The Fulton Report (1968) on the civil service recommended both, but as far as the civil service is concerned little of either appears to have been done until the 1980s. Outside consultants have been brought in providing, as previously mentioned, the work of the Rayner scrutinies on the civil service and the various Griffiths' reports on the National Health Service. The civil service encourages secondments into and out of industry and commerce but it remains a drop in the ocean. In 1985, for example, there were 229 secondments *out* of government departments and 157 *into* government departments, making a total of 386 (Cabinet Office, 1987). This hardly represents evidence of interchange between government and outside bodies and does not give civil servants exposure to new ideas. In the National Health Service many of the chairmen of district health authorities are drawn from the business world, often with no health service experience.

The other approach is to change and develop existing staff through organisational development programmes. Thereby increased emphasis is placed upon training and the pursuit of professional qualifications. Paradoxically, the recognition of the importance of people has taken place against a background of staff cuts within the civil service and tighter budgets in other areas of the public sector. Mrs Thatcher's first administration (1979–83) pledged itself to reducing the size of the civil service by 100,000 during the lifetime of one Parliament. This implied a fixation with numbers rather than an examination of their effective utilisation and development. There will thus be a tension between what is required of good management and what is seen as good politics. However, in September 1989, David Mellor, the Minister of State at the Department of Health, announced that £2 million would be made available for the development of managers in social service departments in England (Bell, 1990). Training is a feature of all public sector organisations and is undertaken on a national scale as well as in-house training:

- in the National Health Service the NHS Training Authority was created in 1983–84 and its aims are to develop skills for managing a multi-professional service within a framework of clear values such as concern for the quality of care;
- the Local Government Training Board provide a wealth of material and short courses for officers and councillors in local government;
- the Civil Service College offers courses for all staff and in particular offers courses for senior management which cover managing staff, managing resources, becoming more effective, managing stress, managing time and managing changes in technology.

The issues that we identified in our previous chapter concerning human resource development seem to have been taken on board throughout the public sector. Some sectors are responding more enthusiastically than others. Thus the Employment Department Group has produced a human resource development strategy which defines three key undertakings:

1. To make the development of people one of the group's corporate objectives.
2. To include human resource development in operational planning at all levels.
3. To give everyone the opportunity to agree personal development objectives.

The Group will:

- be clear about its aims and objectives and communicate these to staff;
- have a strategy for developing its staff in the light of these objectives;
- recognise the importance of developing its staff to be adaptable and able to manage change;
- be fully committed to giving human resource development proper priority and making available the necessary time and resources;
- have a range of easily accessible opportunities for individuals to develop, both in their own interests and in those of the organisation;
- promote equality of opportunity for all, irrespective of race or sex; identify and remove barriers to the development of individuals and give particular regard to the needs of the disabled;
- create a climate in which individuals are encouraged to seek out development opportunities;

- seek to provide staff with incentives and rewards for performance and development;
- manage the succession to key identified posts. (Department of Employment Group, p. 3.)

However, commentators on other parts of the public sector are sceptical as to how far, in practice, the development of people has gone. Fitzgerald suggests that: 'It would be fair to describe the state of management development in the NHS as embryonic' (1990, p. 34).

Despite the patchy development of management training, the people element within public sector organisations has been the focus of performance appraisal systems. As we saw in Chapter 8, increasingly such systems are being linked to pay and we have doubts about this aspect of it. However, it does signal a concern with the performance of individuals within organisations. In the National Health Service, for example, individual performance appraisal was introduced in 1986, as was performance-related pay. It is linked to the achievement of individual and organisational objectives. In education the appraisal of teachers has been approved:

Staff appraisal involves qualitative judgements about performance and although it may start as self-appraisal by the teacher, it will normally involve judgements by other persons responsible for that teacher's work – a head of department or year, the head teacher, a member of the senior management team or an officer of the LEA. (Quoted in Department of Education and Science, 1989, p. 3.)

Its stated purposes are to improve the quality of pupil experience, of teaching and learning, staff development, to meet the needs of teachers and to improve the management of the school and its courses. The HMI study argued that it led to more cohesive year teams, tensions were brought out into the open and resolved, work was planned together and it led to a modification of teaching styles. The claims being made for staff appraisal are that it can be linked to staff development and may have positive benefits for the organisation as a whole.

Within the civil service, appraisal consists of an annual interview which assesses performance, promotion and potential. A band system, similar to that used in the National Health Service is used. Thus:

1. Outstanding.
2. Performance significantly above requirements.
3. Performance fully meets requirements of grade.
4. Performance not fully up to requirements of grade, some improvement necessary.
5. Unacceptable.

In a similar fashion a promotability scale is used:

1. Exceptionally fitted.
2. Fitted.
3. Likely to become fitted in the next two years.
4. Not fitted.

Of course, any appraisal system that is based upon qualitative judgements is only as good as those that are doing the assessing and there is always the possibility of subjective judgments based upon personal dislike coming into play. Indeed, the union response to such schemes has been to point out possible problems with such appraisal systems.

Structure

The publication of the 'Next Steps Report' on the civil service has heralded major changes in the structure of the civil service. As the title of the report suggests, the changes so far in the civil service are only a beginning. There is still a long way to go to improve the management within the civil service. The report came up with a number of findings which included:

1. Senior officials respond to the priorities set by politicians and they have skills in policy advice rather than managing people, resources and departments.
2. The civil service is too big and diverse to be managed as a single entity.
3. Too little attention is paid to outcomes.
4. Ministers have too little time to bring about change.
5. Those staff concerned with the delivery of services welcome more clearly defined management.

The report recognised the lack of clear and accountable management responsibility and came up with a number of recommendations, the main one being the creation of agencies carrying out the executive functions of the civil service to be separated from the policy-making core. This proposal is based upon the Swedish system where there are a small number of policy makers at the centre of Swedish central government. The service provides work for autonomous agencies within the public sector; civil servants at the centre prepare budgets, give policy advice and act in a supervisory capacity. Thus, in the Swedish department of education there are approximately 230 civil servants compared to the 2400 in the Department of Education and Science in Britain. In total, there are only approximately 3000 civil servants in Sweden (see Fudge and Gustaffson, 1989). This model must be a very attractive one to a government that wishes to pare down the bureaucracy.

Under the Next Steps model, the minister will set broad guidelines, but the managers of such agencies will have freedom over recruitment, pay, structure, etc. that are involved in the operation of providing the service. The test should be to adopt the structure that best fits the task to be done. In other words, it is a contingency approach to the civil service. The report also recommended that staff must be properly trained to manage the delivery of the services. Thus the picture is of a small core at the centre of the service providing broad guidelines and strategy, and the implementation and detail of such policy carried out in the agencies. By the end of 1989 a number of agencies were already established, which included Companies House employing just over 1000 civil servants, and Her Majesty's Stationery Office employing over 3000 civil servants. Plans were already announced to create agencies for a further 180,000 civil servants including Central Statistical Office, Meteorological Office, Training Agency and Social Security Operations Benefits employing 77,000 civil servants. In principle it would appear that there is no part of the civil service that cannot operate on this core-agency model. (See Management Matters, No. 5, 1990).

Critics argue that this would herald the breakdown of a uniform civil service, but this may be no bad thing if we agree with the contingency approach to organisational theory. More problematical is that the boundary between the core and the agency is not entirely clear and it presupposes that the formulation of policy can be divorced from its implementation. There must be some mechanism for feedback up the system. The most important area of concern is over accountability. It is unlikely that the Treasury will easily relinquish its control over expenditure and yet Treasury control is hardly conducive to agency managers being given the freedom to manage. Similarly, locating responsibility lower down the service means giving power to unelected officials which may undermine the concept of political accountability. Unfortunately, this is a problem that has to be grappled with irrespective of the structure if more decentralised management is introduced.

Whatever the organisational structure adopted, the impetus behind the Next Steps programme is the interrelations between structures, decision making, responsibility, people, etc. The programme recognises that it is no good devolving responsibility for resources, or training staff in new management techniques if the structure does not allow their expression.

The concept of devolved management has permeated all through the public sector:

- clinicians in the National Health Service are encouraged to take responsibility for cost decisions as well as medical decisions;
- in local government devolved management accompanies the decentralisation of service provision;
- in central government the Financial Management Initiative – as we saw in Chapter 10 – encourages devolved management responsibility.

Such developments need to be accompanied by devolved support systems. Changes in the National Health Service as outlined in the White Paper 'Working for Patients' also depends upon the availability of information at all levels to allow clinicians and managers to take resource decisions. The review of the White Paper carried out for the NHS Directorate (Wales) recognised the need for the delegation of operational management and the creation of information processes and skills to accompany such changes at all levels within the National Health Service. (See Health Care Wales, 1989.)

A re-oriented public sector

We have seen how structural changes within the civil service in particular envisage new roles for government departments with policy advice located in a core department and the provision of services by a peripheral agency. In local government the change in roles is becoming more pronounced with a number of developments bringing into question the fundamental role of the local authority as the provider of local services. It has been suggested that a local authority can take on board the role of an 'enabler', working with and through other organisations rather than directly providing the service itself. This would allow the authority to concentrate upon a more strategic approach to the work of the authority, to seek new resources and initiatives and allow the day-to-day running of the service to be provided by others. Those departments that have decentralised already do this to some extent where the centre may give up some of its power over operations and concentrate upon a strategic role. This role fits in very well with the Conservative government's philosophy of reducing the size and scope of elected local government, and in a number of areas central government has sought to limit the functions of local government.

Urban Development Corporations have been created in certain areas to lead the way in encouraging the private sector to take part in urban regeneration. Where such agencies have been created they have taken over the planning function of the local authority. Critics argue that planning permission is now given for schemes that may bring in the most profit rather than those that will fit in with the local environment or be subject to the control of locally elected politicians.

Other examples include the White Paper on Community Care (1989) which proposes that authorities present plans to show how they are fostering the provision of services by other than themselves. The White Paper emphasises the future delivery of care services by private organisations and the voluntary sector. Such proposals seem to fit in with the notion of local authorities acting as enablers rather than the direct providers of services.

Moves towards a greater role for the voluntary sector fit in with the New Right philosophy of reducing the size of the public sector and may be seen as part of the policy shift towards a privatised provision. Similarly, in the provision of health care the Conservative governments throughout the 1980s paved the way for more collaboration between the National Health Service and the private sector. We have already examined the moves towards the privatisation of certain services, such as cleaning and catering, through competitive tendering. The White Paper 'Working for Patients' opened up the possibility of hospitals becoming self-governing trusts. Similarly, in education there is now provision for schools to opt out of local authority control. All of the above illustrates:

1. A change in the way in which the public sector is perceived.
2. A belief in the principles of the marketplace and of competition.
3. An attack upon the monopoly position of local authorities in their role as suppliers of local services.

In these ways we have witnessed a fundamental reassessment of the functions of local government.

All of this can be expressed in terms of a change in values within the public sector. It may be that some have accepted these changes in values more than others;

and it may well be that these new values have been imposed from outside – but changes there have been. In particular, the dominant theme has been to re-orient what is perceived as an inefficient bureaucratic organisation to a public sector that is responsive to the customer, client or patient rather than the officials and professionals who have traditionally run such organisations.

In local government the debate has centred around the concept of the Public Service Orientation argued for by John Stewart and Michael Clarke (1987). The approach is concerned with developing new ways of working which are more responsive to the needs of individual service users and the community as a whole. This approach recognises that:

- a local authority's activities exist to provide service for the public;
- a local authority will be judged by the quality of service provided within the resources available;
- the service provided is only of real value if it is of value to those for whom it is provided;
- those for whom services are provided are customers demanding high quality service;
- quality of service demands closeness to the customer. (1987, p. 161).

Such an approach can be supported by politicians of all political persuasions. From the left the Public Service Orientation may be seen as an attempt to involve citizens in decisions that affect their lives and thus as an extension of democracy. From the right it may be seen as giving individuals choices and taking decisions away from the state. It denotes a belief that authorities exist to provide services for members of the public and that the organisation should be responsive to what the public wants. It thus requires a re-orientation of existing structures, processes and practices towards the customer. In language that we have used earlier, the organisation has to be more open and to look outward rather than inward and upward. Such a re-orientation requires a change in outlook on the part of both officials and politicians.

Conclusion

The response to the new agenda has been, as we have seen, mixed. Supporters suggest that the public sector is changing for the better as it becomes leaner, more efficient and offers a better service. Sceptics argue that many of the new themes have a certain 'flavour-of-the-month' quality about them and offer more in terms of style than substance. We examine the sceptics' case in our concluding chapter. Other critics argue that the obstacles to change, discussed in Chapter 11, are too strong and that the culture of the public sector organisations is too intransigent and will deflect and obstruct change. If change is imposed from above – from politicians – then all the official has to do is sit it out until the next election when a politician of a different political hue will be elected. We can, therefore, wonder if the new agenda is here to stay.

Further reading

On economy, efficiency and effectiveness see Metcalfe and Richards (1987) and the multitude of Local Government Training Board and Audit Commission publications. The measurement of performance is discussed by Jackson and Palmer (1989). On excellence, Peters and Waterman (1982) is essential and on quality see Deming (1986), and Stewart and Walsh (1990) on quality in the public service. Stewart and Clarke (1987) is required reading for an exposition of the Public Service Orientation. Flynn (1990) discusses many of the issues that we have raised in this chapter. The Treasury and Civil Service Committee (1990) examines the Next Steps initiative.

Chapter 13
Conclusion

Introduction

In the previous two chapters we have discussed the changing environment that public sector organisations have been forced to address. We have also examined how they have faced up to this change by focusing on their internal structures, policies and practices. Part of the response has been the emergence of an increasingly diverse public sector. In local government, for example, there are new patterns of service delivery and the all-purpose, self-sufficient authority is being replaced by local authorities characterised by diversity in terms of structure, roles and relations with other bodies. We now find:

- decentralised administration;
- the creation of cost centres;
- management buy-outs;
- direct-service organisations operating as contractors to the council as client;
- private sector firms providing services as a result of competitive tendering;
- locally managed schools.

The key phrases now being used as a way forward for public sector organisations are:

- the learning organisation;
- the innovative organisation;
- the responsive organisation;
- the adaptable organisation.

It is argued that the government of uncertainty is best done by these types of organisation rather than the traditional bureaucratic organisation, (see Stewart, 1986).

The changing environment

Throughout the book we have constantly emphasised that organisations operate within a changing environment and we would expect any changes within society to have an impact upon public sector organisations. Such changes may result from the following:

Demography

The projected decline in the number of young people coming on to the labour market after 1993 and the projected greater share of that market taken by women will mean that employers will have to rethink their employment policies. The civil service, for example, will be competing for increasingly valued groups of people, and its ability to attract them will be dependent upon how its employment packages compare with those in other public sector organisations as well as those in the private sector. As we argued in Chapter 6, the possession of a scarce resource, such as the individual's own labour, may result in increased bargaining power in the marketplace. Similarly, the demand for more professionals with computing skills and financial and management skills may mean a higher cost labour market.

Organisations will have to recruit from those groups that are presently under-represented in the workforce – such as members of ethnic minority groups and the disabled. Organisations will have to rethink their traditional employment practices and come to more flexible arrangements. We would expect to see, therefore:

- increased use of part-time workers;
- rethinking retirement policies;
- increase in job sharing;
- increased use of short-term contracts;
- more working from home;
- improved child care facilities, (see RIPA, 1988).

Social changes – post Fordism

The term 'Fordism' is derived from Henry Ford's mass production approach to the manufacture of standardised motor cars using automation and a semi-skilled workforce. The concept extends well beyond Ford's car factories. It led to the development of a society oriented towards the mass consumption of mass produced goods. Large producers produced goods to a uniform specification, and this was accompanied by mass regulation of the workforce and wage rates. It is argued that we no longer live in such a society. Instead, society has become more fragmented with numerous cleavages. Different groups of people want more customised products and production has changed to reflect this demand. The public sector does not stand in isolation from this trend. The Thatcher governments have actively promoted this by encouraging competition and contracting out of services and thus creating alternatives to what were monopoly suppliers of services. We now have the enabling authority, the customer orientation and the end of the 'captive user'. The idea of a local authority having one meeting a year to hand out contracts does not seem as remote as it did ten years ago.

The political climate

We would anticipate the developments that we examined in Chapters 11 and 12 continuing under a future Conservative government. Indeed Mrs Thatcher instructed her Downing Street Policy Unit to examine ways of curbing the functions and services offered by local authorities. The catalyst for this initiative came after extra cash was given to local authorities to dampen down disquiet following the introduction of the Community Charge in England and Wales in April 1990. The Policy Unit review will examine in detail the individual functions of local authorities and then draw up plans aimed at abolishing one of the tiers of local government. The two services most at risk are education and housing. Further impetus is to be given to local authorities to move away from direct provision and contract out, manage or enable the private sector to do it. Bryan Gould, the Labour Party spokesman, said the review 'spelled the death knell of local democracy'. (*Guardian*, 29 August 1990.)

The Labour Party is also committed to efficiency and quality. Hence, in principle, it supports the Next Steps initiative for the civil service, but the danger of reduced accountability is a worry. Although the Labour Party does not possess a coherent programme for reform of Whitehall it has a general commitment to open government and a Freedom of Information Act (Theakston, 1990).

A change in culture

All of these changes presuppose that there is a culture that can accommodate a dynamic environment. The expectations put on staff to be entrepreneurial, responsive and dynamic will not happen merely by changing the structure. If people are a major organisational resource then their perceptions will also have to change. In local government, for example, the Public Service Orientation requires a change in philosophy and in the core values of the organisation. It will also require a change in the values of both politicians and officials.

The sceptics' response

Critics question the extent to which this new agenda has taken hold and indicate the difficulties that such change brings. Thus, in a reader poll carried out by the *Municipal Review* in conjunction with the Institute of Local Government Studies in 1989, survival was ranked top of the list when asked about the policy priorities for local authorities over the next two years. Sceptical responses may also be expressed concerning the following:

Culture

As indicated above, the Public Services Orientation will have an effect upon both councillors and officers, and we wonder to what extent it will be welcomed by officers who may see their traditional power bases of professionalism and departmentalism being undermined by the increasing power of the consumers. At the same time, councillors may perceive that their authority is being undermined as the electorate have more channels open to them to express their views. Consumers will be able to express their satisfaction or dissatisfaction more directly in terms of consumer forums, customer surveys, tenant participation and so on.

Perhaps the ease of change has been overestimated. Metcalfe and Richards argue that there is a cultural lag before new ideas are put into practice so that:

> . . . the ruling ideas appropriate to an earlier age persist and continue to exert an influence on administrative behaviour and organisational structure long after the conditions in which they developed have disappeared. (1987, p. 16.)

They suggest that there is a 'disbelief' system in Whitehall that refuses to take management ideas seriously and is sceptical of reform. Perhaps also there is a wish to retain elements of the old culture or values. As Tyson argues:

> At the heart of the difficulty of developing public servants as leaders is the question of public policy objectives. The Civil Service is trying to develop managers in different organisational cultures or climates in order to achieve diverse objectives. Most of these objectives are political and change as priorities change. An ideology of managerialism based on efficiency is not enough in motivational terms. There must also be a commitment to the public good, because unless there is a moral purpose to public policy, it has no intrinsic worth. (1990, p. 30.)

From administration to management

Although the *language* of the public sector is now concerned with performance, productivity, rationalisation, efficiency and so on, there may well still be a reluctance to embrace these ideas. Haigh and Morris argue that in large parts of the National Health Service there is a reluctance to speak this new language and that the shift from administration to management has been greeted with less than enthusiasm. They give three reasons for this:

1. There is no consensus on the state of the National Health Service and hence no agreed solution to its problems.
2. The groundwork necessary for the introduction of a new ethos has not been systematically undertaken.
3. The move from administration to management has been lost amongst a host of other changes over funding, technology, government involvement and so on. (Haigh and Morris, 1990).

Changing people

We suggested in Chapter 11 that changing people inside an organisation is one way of bringing about organisational change. However, proponents of management or human resource development may have underestimated the difficulties inherent in this:

- if power is the organisational currency then to expect senior managers to give up power to those lower down or to break up departmental empires into decentralised units is too optimistic;
- according to contingency theory the style of management should be appropriate to the context and hence it may not always be possible, or appropriate, to adopt the participative style of management that human resource development requires;
- an investment in individuals is time consuming and costly and, therefore, organisations may not feel certain that employees will stay with them long enough for the organisation to benefit;
- if efficiency and cost cutting are organisational goals then a people-centred approach may prove too expensive; training budgets are often hit first when resources are scarce;
- the commitment to a common goal is a prerequisite of human resource development, but too often a public sector organisation does not have a mission statement or a clearly defined set of core values.

Round and round again?

In assessing the impact of the so-called public management movement it is important to reflect on the past to examine whether these are new concerns at all. The most important examination of the civil service this century was the Fulton Report. Published in 1968, the Fulton picture of the service was one of an outdated organisation which was in need of major reform. Consider the following quotation relating to the structure of departments and the promotion of efficiency:

> Accountable management means holding individuals and units responsible for performance measured as objectively as possible. Its achievement depends upon identifying or establishing accountable units within government departments – units where output can be measured against costs or other criteria, and where individuals can be held personally responsible for their performance. (Fulton, 1968, p. 51.)

Here, it appears, is much of the public management philosophy: ideas of accountable management, performance measurement, individual responsibility for performance, etc.; also, perhaps, the seeds of the Financial Management Initiative. The Fulton committee considered the option of hiving off – the Next Steps style – and proposed an early and thorough review of the whole question (Fulton, 1968, p. 62). Many of the ideas of the new agenda are not new. Indeed Fulton was followed by attempts to implement rational techniques such as Programme Analysis and Review in the 1970s, but the resurgence of rationalism in the 1980s under the guise of managerialism has seen at least some of Fulton's aspirations realised. (See Greenwood and Wilson, 1989.)

In local government, the Bains Report provided a stimulus for performance review – what happened and why is the Local Government Training Board still encouraging it? Perhaps the answer lies in a shift in values. Under the old value systems, the possibility of the change advocated by, for example, Fulton and Bains, was limited. With a shift towards the values emphasised by, for example, Peters and Waterman, (see Chapter 1), these ideas can be taken on board.

The quality orientation

Despite doubts about the impact of the new managerialism upon organisations it does seem that the concept of quality as we described in Chapter 12 is firmly on the agenda. It is not only private sector organisations that are taking an interest in the quality approach: local government, the National Health Service and central government are also actively considering how they can improve the quality of their services. The stimulus of BS5750 and similar international standards, the requirements of the European Community and more demanding customers serve to place quality firmly on the agenda. The Audit Commission has set up a Quality Exchange which will enable local authorities to exchange ideas on how to improve quality, initially in a limited number of services including refuse collection, waste disposal and street cleaning. The Labour Party has promised to replace the Audit Commission with a Quality Commission to promote the quality of local government services irrespective of who provides them (Labour Party, 1989). The question remains: How can quality be delivered in a consistent and comprehensive way in an austere financial environment?

The impact of 1992

The creation of a single market for goods, services, capital and labour in Europe after 1992 will increase the impact of the European dimension on Britain's public sector organisations. Some authorities already have European liaison and information offices and some services such as the police have close links with their European counterparts. We would expect funds from the European Community to continue to flow into Britain in the form of regional aid and development grants. Within Europe notions of harmonisation, internationalisation and liberalisation are taking hold. According to one commentator :

Changes in perspective and in organisation will be essential for managerial success in the public sector. The worldwide trends of internationalisation, liberalisation and harmonisation will continue to require constant re-appraisal and review of the role, the functions and procedures of public sector organisations. (Phillip, 1989, p. 45.)

Europe will continue to affect the public sector in Britain in terms of:

- legislation: as major employers, public sector organisations will be affected by legislation on health, safety and conditions of work. Trading standards and consumer protection will need to be systemised on a European basis;
- training will have to take account of the European dimension and language training will need to be included in training programmes. A number of polytechnics and universities already have staff and student exchanges with similar institutions in Europe through, for example, Erasmus programmes, and there is a move to 'Europeanise' courses in business studies and public administration;
- public procurement is one area that will have a significant impact upon the public sector. The Public Works Directive, which has been in force since 1973, requires contracts in excess of £5 million to be advertised in the European Community's Official Journal Supplement (OJS), opening up work to competition from the whole Community. Similar directives on utilities (in force since 1990) and on the supply of goods (in force in 1992) involve contracts for smaller amounts. European legislation specifies the procedures that must be followed and time limits, with clauses on contract splitting, lease backs and loan agreements. Public sector purchasing costs could fall dramatically as contracts for public works and supplies are exposed to competition from the Community.

Summary

The agenda will continue to be set, in part, by the wider context within which public sector organisations operate as we have indicated in this final chapter. We cannot predict how public organisations will react to change in the future and to what extent they will be instrumental in setting their own agenda. While prediction is a dangerous business, we venture to suggest that the theme of quality will continue its rise up the public sector agenda as it serves to motivate staff and develop public enthusiasm for the services offered. The challenge of the single market within Europe is one that the public sector has yet to reveal that it is capable of rising to.

Appendix A
Finding out more about public sector organisations

A persistent theme of this book has been change. If we look back to the mid-1970s, we find a public sector which had never heard of compulsory competitive tendering, contracting out, internal markets, customer orientation and so on. This book has described and analysed these developments which dominated the debate of the 1980s. No doubt the public sector of the 1990s will develop its own vocabulary reflecting the directions that it heads.

The student of public sector organisations studies in interesting and challenging times, where the pace of change is seemingly unrelenting. The first problem the student faces is trying to find out what is happening. This section points the reader in the direction of potential sources of information.

Each chapter of the book concludes with a guide to further reading on the topics examined in that chapter. This, together with the references included in the text, will enable him or her to explore further any particular issues. This section will assist the reader in researching specific issues which will unfold in the 1990s. Sources of information can be listed under a number of roughly defined headings.

Reference books

Basic statistical information and reference information on many public bodies is contained in *Whitaker's Almanac* (published annually); *The Statesman Yearbook* (annual) performs a similar purpose but is more international in its focus; *Public Domain*, a yearbook for the public sector (annual since 1986), reviews development in the public sector on a sector-by-sector basis; *Great Britain* is a handbook (annual) aimed primarily at giving overseas readers the official line on what Britain is like. Perhaps this is more noteworthy for what is missing rather than what is included.

There are various specialist dictionaries available including: *The Fontana Dictionary of Modern Thought* (1977) which, though dated, is an excellent guide to major topics in modern thinking.

Newspapers

Quality newspapers (*The Daily Telegraph*, *The Guardian*, *The Financial Times*, *The Independent*, and *The Times*) are an essential resource for students of the public sector. All cover major political, governmental and economic affairs in detail and will provide commentaries which reflect the political view of the paper. *The Guardian* is particularly strong on social policy issues and *The Independent* currently carries an informative column on the work of government departments by Peter Hennessy entitled 'Whitehall Watch' (Mondays).

HMSO publications

Despite cutbacks in their statistical output, HMSO publications remain a rich resource for students of the public sector. Good institutional libraries will hold the most important HMSO publications and many will employ specialist staff who can advise on how the collection is organised. Potential sources of information include:

- Annual publications including: *Civil Service Statistics*; *The Civil Service Yearbook*; the *Guide to Official Statistics*; the *Guide to Public Sector Financial Information*; *Public Bodies*;
- Parliamentary debates;
- Select Committee Reports;
- Green and White Papers, Bills and Acts of Parliament;
- Publications by government departments including departmental annual reports (commencing in 1991).

European documents

As the impact of the European Community takes on greater importance, students will have to make increasing reference to European documentation. At present there are 48 European Documentation Centres in the United Kingdom which act as depositories for all documents published by EC institutions. These documents include periodicals, annual reports, monographs, bibliographies and non-published material such as commission documents and the *Official Journal*.

Weekly and monthly publications

Throughout the public sector there is a range of weekly and monthly publications (for example by professional bodies and collaborative organisations such as the local authorities' associations) which are aimed at specialist subject areas. These are useful because they will inform the reader of developments in their area, summarise and discuss legislative proposals, and debate key issues.

Academic journals

Academic journals provide the reader with informed analysis based on the latest research. Because they can be published more quickly than books, they are often a fruitful source of the latest thinking in a given area. Most academic journals will ensure quality by referring articles to suitably qualified experts in the area for comments and approval. Most journals also include book reviews: in this area, the major journals include *Public Administration* (quarterly by the Royal Institute of Public Administration), *Public Policy and Administration* (quarterly by the Public Administration Committee) and Local Government Studies. *Public Money Management* (quarterly) contains short articles by people from academics, practitioners and consultants on many issues that were raised in the later chapters in this book.

Textbooks

At the introduction to most courses of study, the teacher will recommend a textbook. Textbooks aim to introduce the subject area and will normally refer the reader to further reading in particular areas. Normally they do not present any particular view but, because of the very nature of topics in the social and political sciences, the choice about what to include and what to exclude, and how the material is presented will reflect what the authors consider to be the main issues. The major texts relating to public sector organisations are referred to at the end of the relevant chapters in this book.

Readers

Readers can take many forms. For example, they may be collections of essays demonstrating approaches or presenting case studies on a particular subject. Alternatively, they may take the form of a book reflecting the approach of the author.

Research books

The most specialised form of book is the research book. This will be highly specific and located within a particular subject area and an approach to study. Often research books will review the existing literature on the subject and then present the findings of the actual research. Conclusions from the research will be presented and can be constructively criticised by examining how the research was conducted and whether the conclusions are valid ones. It is usually inappropriate to read research books until you are familiar with the general subject area.

In-house documents

Local authorities are required by law to place much information, including annual reports, plans, minutes of meetings and reports, in the public domain. You may be able to get access to other documents, for example organisational charts, if enquiries are made. These can be particularly useful as they will indicate the latest practice.

People

The oft repeated maxim that 'an organisation's most important asset is its people' usually holds true for the inquiring mind. The researcher can consult teachers, librarians and practitioners.

Good teachers will provide detailed reading lists together with advice on how to use them. Such lists can only summarise the available work on a topic: if you require more specific references then ask. If you have specific enquiries about the work of a particular author, you will usually find that details of their employing organisation are mentioned in the work.

Each library will organise its collection in a specific way. Make use of organised tours of libraries with which you are unfamiliar. Many libraries employ subject specialists who are qualified in a subject area as well as librarianship and these people are worth their weight in gold. Get to know them and the services they offer: you may find that they keep indexes on topics of frequent interest and may offer special facilities for those studying on a part-time basis. If you are undertaking a major project, you will need to conduct a literature search. This is a major undertaking on which librarians will advise you.

Inside large organisations there will be people specialising in collecting data, managing, studying the environment, evaluating policies, etc. Usually specialists are more than willing to discuss their work if they are asked politely. Make sure that you prepare properly: read around the subject, prepare a set of questions, and approach your interviewee politely.

As well as public sector organisations, there are other organisations which are among the so-called policy communities that can provide useful information. For example, local authorities belong to local authority associations and regional networks who may assist you by providing information. The Local Government Management Board (formerly the Local Government Training Board) and the Institute of Health Service Management publish management papers, and specialist academic bodies such as the Institute of Local Government Studies (University of Birmingham) and the School for Advanced Urban Studies (University of Bristol) publish influential papers.

Appendix B
Exercises

Decision-making exercise

This exercise is designed to develop an understanding of the different approaches to decision making within society and within organisations.

Read the statements below quickly and register an immediate response. You have a choice of five responses:

(a) I strongly agree with this.
(b) In general I agree with this.
(c) I am unsure.
(d) In general terms I disagree with this.
(e) I strongly disagree with this.

Responses

1	2	3	4	5	6	7	8	9	10	11	12	13	14	15	16

1. At one time decisions are made in one way but at other times in a different way. It all depends upon the issue.
2. In order to understand how decisions are made it is necessary to recognise that the power of the organisation is divided between a number of different groups and individuals.
3. The decision-making process in your organisation is dominated by a small group of individuals with little access to this group for anybody else.
4. Your boss consults you on all decisions.
5. Your boss never consults you on any decision.
6. You feel like a small cog in a large machine.
7. Civil service mandarins really run the country.
8. In local government chief officers have all the power.
9. Power in Britain is in the hands of the people.
10. Those with positions of authority within organisations should make all the decisions.

11. Decision making in your organisation is made by a few cronies behind closed doors.
12. The decisions made in your organisation are the result of careful deliberation of all the issues and involvement of all the people that have an interest in the issue.
13. Central government always decides.
14. The elected representatives of the people should make decisions.
15. It should be experts that make all the decisions in public sector organisations in Britain.
16. There should be more discretion in your organisation.

What to do now

Take the statements and group them according to your responses to them. Ask yourself the following questions:

1. What is it that the statements I agree with have in common?
2. What is it that makes the statements I agree with similar and yet different from those that I disagree with?
3. Are the explanations offered by the pluralists or the elitists any use here?

Bureaucracy exercise

Consider each of the following scales. Indicate on the scale (where 1 = very closely and 5 = not at all closely) how closely your organisation approximates to the end of each scale.

formal rules	1	2	3	4	5	informal rules
job descriptions	1	2	3	4	5	unspecified duties
written communication	1	2	3	4	5	oral communication
specialised functions	1	2	3	4	5	workers are generalists
clear hierarchy	1	2	3	4	5	fluid organisational form
criteria for promotion	1	2	3	4	5	no criteria for promotion
permanent appointments	1	2	3	4	5	temporary appointments

Low scores indicate that the organisation approximates closely to the bureaucratic form: high scores indicate the lack of bureaucratic structures. Compare and contrast your answers with someone from a different organisation and establish what differences there are and what you have found in common.

Bureaucracy may be a suitable form of organisation for the completion of many tasks: however it may be inappropriate for the completion of others. Ask yourself the following questions in relation to your organisation:

1. Are clear rules which are not open to ambiguity good for the organisation, or would greater flexibility and discretion assist effectiveness?
2. Do explicit job descriptions assist the organisation in setting out who is responsible for what, or do they hamper efficiency by requiring specific tasks to be done by specific people, thus slowing the process down?
3. Does written communication and record keeping lead to precision and accuracy, or does it just generate huge amounts of paper that is never read?
4. Would the organisation benefit from specialists, for example in housing, lettings officers, repairs clerks, etc., or would it benefit from staff having training in a wide range of tasks and could answer public queries more quickly?
5. Is it beneficial for the organisation to have clear chains of command so that decisions can be referred up the hierarchy to the appropriate person, or would it benefit from a more flexible form where structures are based on the particular task in hand?
6. Would the organisation benefit from having clearly established criteria for promotion, such as having attained certain qualifications or having performed certain tasks, or would this mean that young and talented people cannot get promotion because experienced but less able staff are above them in the queue?
7. Is a system of appointments on a permanent basis good for the organisation in that it assists in the provision of a permanent expertise, or would short-term appointment motivate staff and see a continuing flow of ideas into the organisation?

The answers that you give will depend upon a number of factors, including the type of organisation that you work in, the culture of the organisation, the perspective from which you view the organisation – you may find that colleagues in similar positions give different answers. It is important to remember that different *forms* of organisation may be appropriate to different *types* of organisation.

Economy, efficiency and effectiveness exercise

This exercise will assist you to understand how your organisation is using the three E's: economy, efficiency and effectiveness. Before you do the exercise you should have read Chapter 12. As most public sector organisations undertake a large number of complex tasks, it is important that you select one activity for your study.

Task 1

By referring to published documents, for example policy plans or annual reports, establish the aims and objectives of the activity that you have chosen. Summarise these in Box 4 in Figure B.1 with a number of statements which indicate what the organisation intends to achieve.

Task 2

Using the systems approach that we discussed in Chapter 4, consider the inputs to the process, the process whereby inputs are transformed into outputs, and the outputs from the process. Prepare these in the form of simple lists of inputs, activities and outputs and note these in Boxes 1, 2 and 3 respectively in Figure B.1.

Task 3

You now need to collect information on performance measurement. Prepare a list of activities that are measured. Identify which of the following categories each of the measures falls into:

1. Measures of inputs.
2. Measures of inputs in relation to outputs.

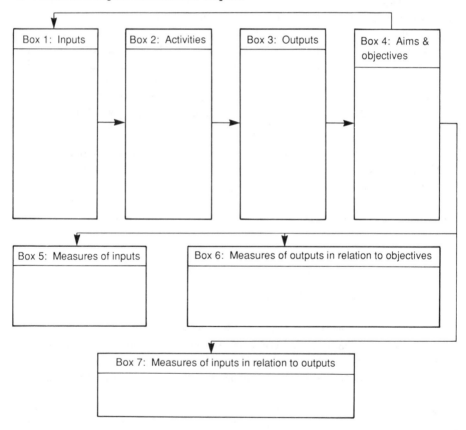

Figure B.1 A method for considering improvement.

3. Measures of outputs in relation to objectives.

Enter these into the appropriate boxes.

Task 4

You now have a picture of how your organisation measures its performance of the task that you have chosen. Examine Figure B.1below and consider whether it emphasises the pursuit of economy, efficiency or effectiveness. You will need to consider *who* uses the information and *how* they use it. All such information should be used to improve performance. Some questions you might ask are:

- are the opinions of employees and customers solicited?
- is the information used to compare performance over time or with other organisations?
- does your organisation formulate action plans to set targets for improved performance?

Task 5

Consider how your organisation could improve its performance measurement. How could it improve its effectiveness? How could it improve the quality of the service?

Leadership exercise

Below are a number of statements for you to consider. Your response should be from 1–5 where:

1 = agree strongly
5 = disagree strongly

When you have made your choice, circle the appropriate number

Questions

	Agree strongly				Disagree strongly
1. Managers should manage and not delegate responsibility.	1	2	3	4	5
2. The participative style of leadership is not appropriate for your organisation.	1	2	3	4	5
3. Most employees are at work only for the money.	1	2	3	4	5
4. The manager should set a good example.	1	2	3	4	5
5. The manager should provide a vision for the organisation.	1	2	3	4	5
6. It is the role of the politician to provide the goals of the organisation.	1	2	3	4	5

7.	The manager should always consult her staff.	1	2	3	4	5
8.	Junior staff should be encouraged to use their own judgement.	1	2	3	4	5
9.	Anyone not pulling their own weight should be sacked immediately.	1	2	3	4	5
10.	Any personal differences between staff should be sorted out between themselves.	1	2	3	4	5
11.	The manager should defend his staff to his colleagues.	1	2	3	4	5
12.	Those with knowledge should be deferred to whatever their position within the organisation.	1	2	3	4	5
13.	The manager should try out new ideas with staff.	1	2	3	4	5
14.	Poor work should be criticised.	1	2	3	4	5
15.	All members of the department should be treated as equals.	1	2	3	4	5

Once you have responded to the statements, give your boss a copy and ask him or her to respond to them. Then compare the two sets of responses and answer the following questions:

1. Are your perceptions of the manager's role the same as your managers? If not, why not?
2. What is your preferred style of leadership, judging by your responses? Is it autocratic or participative? Is it the same as your manager's perception?
3. Would the modern theory of leadership discussed in Chapter 7 work in your organisation? If not, why not?

Bibliography

Aberach, J.D. and Rockman, B.A. (1988). 'Image IV Revisited: Executive and Political Roles', *Governance*, Vol.1 No. 1, pp. 1–25.

Aberach, J.D., Putman, R.D. and Rockman, B.A. (1981). *Bureaucrats and Politicians in Western Democracies*, Cambridge, Mass.: Harvard University Press.

Ackerman, L. (1985). 'Leadership vs. Management', *Leadership and Organization Development Journal*, Vol. 6, No. 2, pp. 17–19.

Adams, J.S. (1965). 'Injustice in Social Exchange', in Berkowitz, L. (ed). *Advances in Experimental Social Psychology*, London: Academic Press.

Adler, M. and Asquith, S. (eds) (1981). *Discretion and Welfare*, London: Heinemann Educational Books.

Albrow, M. (1970). *Bureaucracy*, London: Macmillan.

Armstrong, R. (1985). 'Ministers, Politicians and Public Servants', *Public Money*, September, pp. 39–43.

Argyris, C. (1957). *Personality and Organization*, New York: Harper and Row.

Audit Commission (1985). *Good Management in Local Government: successful practice and action*, London: Audit Commission.

Audit Commision (1988). *Administrative Support for Operational Police Officers*, Policy Papers No. 1, May. London: Audit Commission.

Audit Commission (1989a). *Managing Services Effectively – Performance Review*, London: HMSO.

Audit Commission (1989b). *Management Paper No. 3: Better Financial Management*, London: Audit Commission.

Bacharach, S.B. and Lawler, E.J. (1980). *Power and Politics in Organizations: The Social Psychology of Conflict, Coalitions and Bargaining*, San Fransisco: Josey Bass.

Bachrach, P. and Baratz, M.S. (1962). 'Two Faces of Power', *American Political Science Review*, Vol. 56(4), pp. 942–52.

Bains Committee, (1972). *The New Local Authorities: Management and Structure*, London: Department of the Environment.

Banner, D.K. and Blasingame, J.W. (1988). 'Towards a Developmental Paradigm of Leadership', *Leadership and Organization Development Journal*, Vol. 9, No. 4, pp. 7–16.

Barratt, J. and Downs, J. (1988). *Organising for Local Government – a local political responsibility*, London: Longman.

Barrett, S. and Fudge, C. (1981). *Policy and Action*, London: Methuen.

Beetham, D. (1987). *Bureaucracy*, Milton Keynes: Open University Press.

Behrens, R. (1989). 'Equality of Opportunity in the Civil Service', *Public Money & Management*, Winter, pp. 43–8.

Bell, L. (1990). 'Social Service Departments: preparing for the 1990s', *Public Money & Management*, Spring, pp. 23–5.

Benn, T. (1980). 'Manifestos and Mandarins', *Policy and Practice: the experience of government*, London: Royal Institute of Public Administration.

Bennis, W. (1966). *Beyond Bureaucracy: Essays in the development and evaluation of human organisations*, New York: McGraw-Hill.

Birkinshaw, P. (1988). 'Open Government – Local Government Style', *Public Policy and Administration*, Vol. 3, No. 1, pp. 46–55.

Blake, R.B. and Mouton, J.S. (1964). *The Managerial Grid*, Houston, Texas: Gulf Publishing.

Blau, P.M. (1963). *The Dynamics of Bureaucracy: a study of interpersonal relations in two government agencies*, Chicago: The University of Chicago Press.

Blau, P.M. and Scott, R.W. (1963). *Formal Organisations: A Comparative Approach*, London: Routledge and Kegan Paul.

Bone, D. and Griggs, R. (1989). *Quality at Work*, London: Kogan Page.

Bradford, D.L. and Cohen, A.R. (1984). *Managing for Excellence: the guide to developing high performance in contemporary organisations*, London, New York: J.Wiley and Sons.

Braverman, H. (1974). *Labor and Monopoly Capital: the degradation of work in the 20th century*, Monthly Review Press.

Bridges, Sir E. (1950). *Portrait of a Profession*, Cambridge: Cambridge University Press.

Brimelow, E. (1981). 'Women in the Civil Service', *Public Administration*, Vol. 59, Autumn, pp. 313–35.

Brown R.G.S. and Steel D.R. (1979). *The Administrative Process in Britain*, London: Methuen.

Bruce-Gardayne, J. (1986). *Ministers and Mandarins: Inside the Whitehall Village*, Sidgwick and Jackson Ltd.

Burch, M. and Wood, B. (1990). *Public Policy in Britain*, Oxford: Martin Robertson.

Burns, T. and Stalker, G.M. (1961). *The Management of Innovation*, London: Tavistock.

Butcher, T. (1984). 'Public Administration and Policy Studies', in Englefield, D. and Drewry, G. (eds) *Information Sources in Politics and Political Science: a survey worldwide*, London: Butterworth.

Cabinet Office (1987). 'The Challenge of Change in the Civil Service', *A report on the work of the Management and Personnel Office*, London: HMSO.

Cabinet Office: Office of the Minister for the Civil Service (1988). 'Service to the Public', Occasional Paper, London: HMSO.

Campbell, C. and Guy Peters, B.G. (1988). 'The Politics/Administration Dichotomy: Death or Merely Change', *Governance*, Vol. 1, No. 1, pp. 79–99.

Carvel, J. (1984). *Citizen Ken*, London: Chatto and Windus.

Cassels, J.S. (1983). 'Civil Servants and Management', *Management in Government*, No. 1, pp. 2–19.

Central Transport Consultative Committee (1990). *Annual Report 1989/90*, London: Central Transport Consultative Committee.

Chandler, J.A. (1986). *Public Policy-Making for Local Government*, London: Croom Helm.

Chapman, L. (1979). *Your Disobedient Servant: The continuing story of Whitehall's overspending*, Harmondsworth: Penguin.

Chapman, R.A. (1984). *Leadership in the British Civil Service*, Beckenham: Croom Helm.

Chapman, R.A. (1988). 'The Next Steps: A Review', *Public Policy and Administration*, Vol.3, No. 3, pp. 3–10.

Chapman, R.A. and Greenaway, J.R. (1980). *The Dynamics of Administrative Reform*, London: Croom Helm.

Chapman, R.A. and Hunt, M. (eds) (1987). *Open Government*, London, New York, Sydney: Croom Helm.

Chell, E. (1987). *The Psychology of Behaviour in Organisations*, London: Macmillan.

Child, J. (1977). *Organisation: A Guide to Problems and Practice*, London, New York: Harper and Row.

Clarke, M. and Stewart, J. (1988). *Managing Tomorrow*, Luton: Local Government Training Board.

Connolly, W.E. (1974). *The Terms of Political Discourse*, Heath and Co.

Cousins, C. (1987). *Controlling Social Welfare*, Brighton: Wheatsheaf.

Cox, A., Furlong, P. and Page, E. (1985). *Power in Capitalist Society: Theory, Explanations and Cases*, Brighton: Wheatsheaf.

Crosby, P. (1984). *Quality without Tears: The art of hassle free management*, New York: McGraw Hill.

Crossman, R. (1979). *The Crossman Diaries: Selections from the Diaries of a Cabinet Minister 1964–1970*, London: Magnum.

Crozier, M. (1964). *The Bureaucratic Phenomena*, London: Tavistock.

Curwen, P. (1986). *Public Enterprise: A modern approach*, Brighton: Wheatsheaf.

Dahl, R.A. (1961). *Who Governs? Democracy and Power in an American City*, New Haven, Conn.: Yale University Press.

Davies, M.R. (1988). 'Promoting Organisational Change: Organisational Development as an Approach to Training', *Teaching Public Administration*, Vol. VIII, No. 1, pp. 29–42.

Davis, K.C. (1969). *Discretionary Justice*, Louisiana State University Press.

Dawson, S. (1988). *Analysing Organisations*, London: Macmillan.

Day, P. and Klein, R. (1987). *Accountabilities: five public services*, London: Tavistock.

Dearlove, J. (1979). *The Reorganisation of British Local Government: Old orthodoxies and a political perspective*, Cambridge: Cambridge University Press.

Deming, W. E. (1986). *Out of Crisis: Quality, Productivity and Competitive Position*, Cambridge: Cambridge University Press.

Department of Education and Science (1989). *Developments in the Appraisal of Teachers*, Report by HM Inspectorate, London: HMSO.

Department of Employment Group *Developing People in the Employment Department Group: A Human Resource Development Strategy*, London: HMSO.

Department of Social Security (1988). *The Business of Service*, Report of the Regional Organisation Scrutiny, London: HMSO.

Department of Transport (1983). *Railway Finances*, Report of a Committee chaired by Sir David Serpell, London: HMSO.

Doig, A. (1985). 'Corruption in the Public Service: The Case of the Property Services Agency', *Public Money*, March, pp. 43–47.

Dopson, S. and Stewart, R. (1990). 'Public and Private Sector Management: The case for a wider debate', *Public Money & Management*, Spring, pp. 37–40.

Downs, A. (1967). *Inside Bureaucracy*, Boston: Little, Brown and Company.

Downs, J. (1983). 'Organisational Development: Making Change Happen', *RIPA Report*, Spring, Vol. 4, No. 1.

Dunleavy, P. (1985). 'Bureaucrats, Budgets and the Growth of the State; Reconstructing an Instrumental Model', *British Journal of Political Science*, Vol. 15, pp. 299–328.

Dunleavy, P. (1990). 'Introduction: prospects for British politics in the 1990s', in Dunleavy, P., Gamble, A. and Peele, G. (eds), *Developments in British Politics 3*, London: Macmillan, pp. 1–14.

Dunleavy, P. and Rhodes, R.A.W. (1988). 'Government beyond Whitehall', in *Developments in British Politics 2*, (revised edition), London: Macmillan.

Efficiency Unit (1988). *Improving Management in Government: The next steps*, London: HMSO.

Elcock, H. (1986). *Local Government: Politicians, professionals and the public in local authorities*, London: Methuen.

Elcock, H. and Jordan, G. (eds) (1987). *Learning from Local Authority Budgeting*, Aldershot: Avebury.

Elcock, H., Jordan, G. and Midwinter, A. with Boyne, G. (1989). *Budgeting in Local Government: Managing the margins*, Harlow: Longman.

Englefield, D. and Drewry, G. (eds) (1984). *Information Sources in Politics and Political Science: A survey worldwide*, London: Butterworth.

English, G. (1990). 'Total Quality in the Public Services', *Total Quality Management*, June.

Etzioni-Halevy, E. (1985). *Bureaucracy and Democracy: A political dimension*, London: Routledge and Kegan Paul.

Falcon, D. (1989). 'Reflections', *RIPA Report*, Winter, p. 2.

Fayol, H. (1949). *General and Industrial Management*, London: Pitman.

Ferguson, K. and Lapsley, I. (1989). 'Resource Management in the NHS: The information requirements of hospital doctors', *Public Money & Management*, Winter, pp. 21–5.

Fiedler, F.E.A. (1967). *A Theory of Leadership Effectiveness*, New York: McGraw-Hill.

Fitzgerald, L. (1990). 'Management Development in the NHS: Crossing professional boundaries', *Public Money & Management*, Spring, pp. 31–5.

Flynn, N. (1990). *Public Sector Management*, London: Harvester Wheatsheaf.

Forster, D. and Hadley, R. (1989). 'The NHS Reforms: Conditions for Successful Change', *Health Services Management*, October, pp. 215–18.

Fowler, A. (1988a). *Human Resource Management in Local Government*, Harlow: Longman.

Fowler, A. (1988b). 'New Directions in Performance Pay', *Personnel Management*, November, pp. 30–4.

Fraser, D. (1973). *The Evolution of the British Welfare State: A history of social policy since the industrial revolution*, London: Macmillan.

Fry, G., Flynn, A., Gray, A., Jenkins, W. and Rutherford, B. (1988). 'Symposium on Improving Management in Government', *Public Administration*, Vol. 66, No. 4, pp. 429–45.

Fudge, C. and Gustafsson, L. (1989). 'Administrative Reform and Public Management in Sweden and the United Kingdom', *Public Money & Management*, Summer, pp. 29–34.

Fulton, Lord (1968). *The Civil Service*, Vol. 1, Report of the Committee, London: HMSO #Cmnd. 3638.

Gamble, A. (1988). *The Free Economy and the Strong State: The politics of Thatcherism*, London: Macmillan

Garratt, B. (1987). *The Learning Organisation: and the need for directors who think*, Aldershot: Gower.

Garrett, J. (1972). *The Management of Government*, Harmondsworth: Penguin.

Geeson, T. and Haward, J. (1990). 'Devolved Management – The Berkshire Experience', *Local Government Studies*, January/February, pp. 1–9.

Goldsmith, M. and Newton, K. (1986). 'Local Government Abroad' in Widdecombe, D. *Committee of Inquiry into the Conduct of Local Authority Business*, Research Volume IV, London; HMSO #Cmnd. 9797.

Golembiewski, R.T. (1977). *Public Administration as a Developing Discipline*, New York, Basel: Marcel Dekker.

Gouldner, A.W. (1954). *Patterns of Industrial Bureaucracy*, New York: The Free Press.

Graham, A. (1989). 'Management Development in the Public Sector', *Public Money & Management*, Autumn, pp. 25–33.

Gray, A. and Jenkins, W.I. (1985). *Administrative Politics in British Government*, Brighton: Wheatsheaf.

Greenwood, J. and Wilson, D. (1989). *Public Administration in Britain Today*, London: Unwin Hyman.

Greenwood, R. and Stewart, J. (1985). 'The Key to Excellence? An introduction to Local Government Training Board', *Excellence and Local Government*, Luton: Local Government Training Board.

Greenwood, R. and Stewart, J.D. (1986). 'The Institutional and Organisational Capabilities of Local Government', *Public Administration*, Vol. 64, No. 1, pp. 35–50.

Grey, A. (1983). 'Public Service Ethics', *RIPA Report*, Vol. 4, No. 4, pp. 8–9.

Griffiths, P. (1987). 'Mid-Glamorgan County Council', in Elcock, H. and Jordan, G. (eds.) (1987). *Learning from Local Authority Budgeting*, Aldershot: Avebury.

Griffiths, Sir R. (1983). *NHS Management Inquiry*, London: Department of Health and Social Security.

Griffiths, Sir R. (1988). *Community Care: Agenda for Action*, London: HMSO.

Gunn, L. (1987). 'Perspectives on Public Management' in Kooiman, J. and Eliassen, K.A. (eds), *Managing Public Organisations: Lessons from Contemporary European Experience*, London: Sage.

Haigh, R.H. and Morris, D.S. (1990). 'The NHS: The Administration-Management Interface, A Test to Destruction?', *Teaching Public Administration*, Vol. X, No. 1, pp. 47–53.

Hall, R.H. (1972). *Organizations: Structure and Process*, Englewood Cliffs, New Jersey: Prentice-Hall.

Hall, R. and Quinn, R.E. (eds) (1983). *Organisational Theory and Public Policy*, Beverly Hills and London: Sage.

Ham, C. and Hill, M. (1984). *The Policy Process in the Modern Capitalist State*, Brighton: Wheatsheaf.

Hambleton, R. (1986). *Rethinking Policy Planning: a study of planning systems linking central and local government*, Bristol: School for Advanced Urban Studies.

Hambleton, R. and Hoggett, P. (eds) (1984). *The Politics of Decentralisation: Theory and Practice of a Radical Local Government Initiative*, Bristol: School for Advanced Urban Studies.

Hancox, A., Worrall, L. and Pay, J. (1989). 'Developing a Customer Orientated Approach to Service Delivery: The Wrekin Approach', *Local Government Studies*, Vol. 15, No. 1, pp. 16–25.

Handy, C. (1985). *Understanding Organisations*, Harmondsworth: Penguin.

Harrison, A. and Gretton, J. (eds) (1987). *Reshaping Central Government*, Berkshire: Policy Journals (Hermitage).

Harrison, S. (1988). *Managing the NHS*, London: Chapman Hall.

Haynes, R.J. (1980). *Organisation Theory and Local Government*, London: Allen and Unwin.

Haywood, S. and Day, C. *Introduction to Health Services Management*, Birmingham: University of Birmingham Health Services Management Centre.

Heald, D. (1983). *Public Expenditure*, Oxford: Martin Robertson.

Health Care Wales (1989). Issue 5 December.

Heclo, H. and Wildavsky, A. (1981). *The Private Government of Public Money*, London: Macmillan.

Heffron, F. (1989). *Organisation Theory and Public Organisations*, New Jersey: Prentice-Hall.

Henley, Sir D., Holtham, C., Likierman, A. and Perrin, J. (1983). *Public Sector Accounting and Financial Control*, Wokingham: Van Nostrand Reinhold.

Hennessy, P. (1989a). *Whitehall*, London: Martin Secker and Warburg.

Hennessy, P. (1989b). 'The Ethic of the Profession', *FDA GCHQ Lecture*, London: Royal Commonwealth Society.

Herzberg, F. (1966). *Work and the Nature of Man*, Cleveland and New York: World Publishing Co.

Hinings, C. R., Greenwood, R. and Ransom, S. (1975). 'Contingency Theory and the Organisation of Local Authorities: Part II Contingencies and Structure', *Public Administration*, Vol. 53, pp. 169–90.

Hoggett, P. and Vince, R. (1988). 'Organising for a Change', *Local Government Studies*, Vol. 14, No. 2, pp. 11–17.

Hogwood, B.W. (1987). *From Crisis to Complacency? Shaping Public Policy in Britain*, Oxford: Oxford University Press.

Hogwood, B.W. and Gunn, L. (1984). *Policy Analysis for the Real World*, Oxford: Oxford University Press.

Homans, G.C. (1950). *The Human Group*, New York: Harcourt, Brace and World.

Home Office (1989a). *Magistrates' Courts: Report of a Scrutiny 1989*, Volume 1: The Management and Funding of the Magistrates' Courts, London: HMSO.

Home Office (1989b). Report on the Work of the Prison Service, London: HMSO Cm 835.

Hood, C. (1976). *The Limits of Administration*, London: John Wiley and Sons.

Hood, C. (1986). *Administrative Analysis: An introduction to rules, enforcement and organisations*, Brighton: Wheatsheaf.

Hood, C. and Jones, G. (1990). 'Progress in the Government's Next Steps Initiative', in Treasury and Civil Service Committee (1990). Eighth Report: Progress in the Next Steps Initiative, London: HMSO Appendix 6, pp. 78–83.

Hoskyns, Sir J. (1984). 'Conservatism is not enough', *Political Studies* Vol. 55, No. 1, pp. 3–16.

Howells, D. (1981). 'Marks and Spencer and the Civil Service: A Comparison of Culture and Methods', *Public Administration*, Vol. 59, Autumn, pp. 337–52.

Humphris, P. (1990). 'Developing a Management Structure', in Fielding, P. and Berman, P.C. (eds), *Surviving in General Management: A Resource for Health Professionals*, Basingstoke: Macmillan.

Institute of Health Services Management (1988). *Report on Alternative Delivery and Funding of Health Services*, London: IHSM

Isaac-Henry, K. (1987). 'Information Technology: A Case Study of a Local Authority – the City of Birmingham', *Teaching Public Administration*, Vol. VII, No. 2, pp. 10–26.

Jackson, P. (1982). *The Political Economy of Bureaucracy*, Oxford: Philip Allen.

Jackson, P. and Palmer, B. (1989). *First Steps in Measuring Performance in the Public Sector: A management guide*, London: Public Finance Foundation.

Jenkins, W.I. (1978). *Policy Analysis*, London: Martin Robertson.

Jenkins, W.I. and Gray, A. (1983). 'Bureaucratic Politics and Power: Developments in the Study of Bureaucracy', *Political Studies*, Vol. XXXI, pp. 177–93.

Joint NHS Privatisation Research Unit (1990). *The NHS Privatisation Experience: Competitive tendering for NHS services*, London: NHSPRU.

Jones, K., Millard, F. and Twigg, L. (1990). 'The "right to know": government and information', in Savage, S.P. and Robins, L. (eds) *Public Policy under Thatcher*, London: Macmillan.

Jones, P.D. (1982). 'Public Services Management – An Elusive Concept', *Management in Government*, No. 3, pp. 154–62.

Kakabadse, A. (ed.) (1982). *People and Organisations*, Aldershot: Gower.

Kast, F.E. and Rosenzweig, J.E. (1985). *Organization and Management: A Systems and Contingency Approach*, New York: McGraw-Hill.

Keeling, D. (1972). *Management in Government*, London: Allen and Unwin.

King's Fund Institute (1988). *Health Finance: assessing options*, London: King's Fund Institute.

Klein, R. (1989). *The Politics of the NHS* (2nd edition), Harlow: Longman.

Kleiner, B.H. and Corrigan, W.A. (1989). 'Understanding Organisational Change', *Leadership and Organization Development Journal*, Vol. 10, No. 3, pp. 25–31.

Körner, E. (1984). *A Report on the Collection and Use of Financial Information in the NHS* (Sixth report of the Steering Group on Health Services Information), London: DHSS.

Kooiman, J. and Eliassen, K.A. (eds) (1987). *Managing Public Organisations: Lessons from Contemporary European Experience*, London: Sage.

Kossen, S. (1983). *The Human Side of Organisations*, New York: Harper and Row.

Kristensen, O.P. (1987). 'Privatisation', in Kooiman, J. and Eliassen, K.A. (eds), *Managing Public Organisations: Lessons from Contemporary European Experience*, London: Sage.

Labour Party (1989). *Quality Streets*, London: Labour Party.

LAMSAC 86 (1986). *Managing to Compete*, Conference Proceedings.

Lawrence, P. and Santry, L. (1989). 'Motivating Staff and Raising Productivity in a DTI Division', *RIPA Report*, Summer, pp. 7–9.

Lawrence, P.R. and Lorsch, J.W. (1987). *Organization and Environment*, Harvard: Harvard University Press.

Layfield, Sir F. (1976). *Local Government Finance: Report of the Committee*, London: HMSO Cmnd 6453.

Leach, S. and Stewart, J. (eds.) (1982). *Approaches in Public Policy*, London: Allen and Unwin.

Lee, R. and Lawrence, P. (1985). *Organisational Behaviour: Politics at Work*, London: Hutchinson and Co.

Likierman, A. (1983). 'Applying Private Sector Techniques to the Public Sector', *London Business School Journal*, Winter, pp. 27–30.

Likierman, A. (1988). *Public Expenditure: Who really controls it and how*, London: Penguin.

Lindblom, C. E. (1959). 'The science of muddling through' *Public Administration Review*, Spring, pp. 79–88.

Lipsky, M. (1979). *Street Level Bureaucracy*, New York: Russell Sage Foundation.

Litterer, J.A. (ed.) (1969). *Organisations: Structure and Behaviour*, Vol. 1, New York: J.Wiley and Sons.

Livingstone, H. and Wilkie, R. (1981). 'Motivation and Performance among Civil Service Managers', *Public Administration*, Vol. 59, Summer, pp. 151–72.

Local Government Training Board (1984). *Ethics in Local Government*, Luton: Local Government Training Board.

Local Government Training Board (1985). *Good Management in Local Government: Successful Practice and Action*, Luton: Local Government Training Board.

Local Government Training Board (1987a). *Politicians and Professionals: The Changing Management of Local Government*, Luton: Local Government Training Board.

Local Government Training Board (1987b). *The Leadership Audit*, Luton: Local Government Training Board.

Local Government Training Board (1988a). *Competition and Local Authorities: Organising for Competition*, Luton: Local Government Training Board.

Local Government Training Board (1988b). *Managing Tomorrow*, Luton: Local Government Training Board.

Local Government Training Board (1989). *New Management Trends*, Luton: Local Government Training Board.

Lukes, S. (1974). *Power: A Radical View*, London: Macmillan.

Malpass, P. and Murie, A. (1987). *Housing Policy and Practice*, London: Macmillan.

Management Matters (1990). *Next Steps Celebration*, No. 5, London: HMSO.

Manning, T. (1984). 'Management in the Civil Service: A Trainer's Views and Some Research Findings', *Management in Government*, No. 1, pp. 59–68.

Mansfield, R. (1986). *Company Strategy and Organisational Design*, London: Croom Helm.

March, J.G. and Simon, H.A. (1971). 'The Dysfunctions of Bureaucracy', in Pugh D.S. (ed.), *Organisation Theory: Selected Readings*, Harmondsworth: Penguin.

Maslow, A.H. (1943). 'A Theory of Human Motivation', *Psychological Review*, Vol. 50, pp. 370–96.

Mayo, E. (1971). 'Hawthorne and the Western Electric Company', in Pugh, D.S. (ed.), *Organisation Theory*, Harmondsworth: Penguin.

McCann, J. and Galbraith, J.R. (1981). 'Interdepartmental Relations', in Nystrom, P.C. and Starbuck, W.H. (eds), *Handbook of Organizational Design*, Vol. 2, Oxford: Oxford University Press.

McGregor D. (1960). *The Human Side of Enterprise*, New York: McGraw-Hill.

Merton, R.K. (1940). 'Bureaucratic Structure and Personality', *Social Forces*, No. 18, pp. 560–68.

Metcalfe, L. and Richards, S. (1987). *Improving Management in Government*, London: Sage.

Michael, J. (1984/85). 'Confidentiality and the Civil Service', *Policy Studies*, Vol. 5, pp. 66–79.

Miller, W.L. (1986). 'Local Electoral Behaviour' in Widdicombe, *The Conduct of Local Authority Business*, Research Volume 3: The Local Government Elector, London: HMSO, pp. 101–72.

Mills, Wright C. (1956). *The Power Elite*, Oxford: Oxford University Press.

Mintzberg, H. (1983). *Structure in Fives: Designing Effective Organisations*, New Jersey: Prentice-Hall Inc.

Moore, S.T. (1987). 'The Theory of Street-Level Bureaucracy: A Positive Critique', *Administration and Society*, Vol. 19, No. 1, pp. 74–94.

Morgan, G. (1986). *Images of Organisations*, Beverly Hills: Sage.

Morphet, J.(1990). 'Women in Local Government: A case study', *Public Money & Management*, Spring, pp. 57–9.

Murlis, H. (1987). 'Performance-Related Pay in the Public Sector', *Public Money*, March, pp. 29–33.

Muskett, H. (1989). '1992 – The Impact on County Councils', *European Access*, August, pp. 17–19.

Mullins, L.J. (1989). *Management and Organisational Behaviour*, London: Pitman.

Nairne, Sir P. (1982). 'Some Reflections on Change', *Management in Government*, No. 2, pp. 71–82.

National Audit Office (1986). *The Financial Management Initiative*, London: HMSO.

Newton, K. (1976). *Second City Politics*, Oxford: Clarendon Press.

Niskanen, W.A. (1971). *Bureaucracy and Representative Government*, New York: Aldine-Atherton.

Niskanen, W.A. (1973). *Bureaucracy: Servant or Master*, London: The Institute of Economic Affairs.

Northcote-Trevelyan (1854). Report on the Organisation of the Permanent Civil Service, reprinted in Vol. 1, Appendix B to the Fulton Report (1968), Report of the Committee on the Civil Service, Cmnd 3638.

Norton, P. (1985). *Parliament in the 1980s*, Oxford: Blackwell.

Page, E.C. (1985). *Political Authority and Bureaucratic Power: A Comparative Analysis*, Brighton: Wheatsheaf.

Painter, C. (1989). 'Leadership in the British Civil Service Revisited', *Teaching Public Administration*, Vol. IX, No. 1, pp. 1–9.

Parker, R.A., Rose, A.G. and Taylor, J.A. (1986). *The Administration of Standards of Conduct in Local Government*, London: Charles Knight.

Parsons, H.M. (1978). 'What Caused the Hawthorne Effect? A Scientific Detective Story', *Administration and Society*, Vol. 10, No. 3, pp. 259–83.

Perrin, J. (1988). *Resource Management in the NHS*, Wokingham: Van Nostrand Reinhold.

Perrow, C. (1967). *Organizational Analysis: A Sociological View*, London: Tavistock.

Perry, J. and Kraemer, K.L. (eds) (1983). *Public Management: Public and Private Perspectives*, California: Mayfield.

Peters, A.R. (1990). 'West Germany', in Kingdom, J.E. (ed.), *The Civil Service in Liberal Democracies: An Introductory Survey*, London: Routledge.

Peters, T. and Austin, N. (1986). *A Passion for Excellence: The Leadership Difference*, London: Fontana/Collins

Peters, T.J. and Waterman, R.H. (1982). *In Search of Excellence*, New York: Harper and Row.

Pfeffer, J. (1981). *Power in Organisations*, Marshfield, Mass.: Pitman.

Philip, A.B. (1989). 'The Public Sector and European Integration', *Public Money & Management*, Summer, pp. 41–5.

Pitt, D.C. and Smith, B.C. (1981). *Government Departments*, London: Routledge and Kegan Paul.

Pitt, D.C. and Smith, B.C. (eds) (1984). *The Computer Revolution in Public Administration: The impact of information technology on government*, Brighton: Wheatsheaf.

Pliatzky, Sir L. (1982). *Getting and Spending: Public Expenditure Employment and Inflation*, Oxford: Basil Blackwell.

Pliatzky, Sir L. (1988). 'Optimising the role of the Public Sector: Constraints and Remedial Policies', *Public Policy and Administration*, Vol. 3, No. 1, pp. 35–45.

Plowden (1961). *The Control of Expenditure*, London: HMSO.

Pollitt, C. (1985). 'Measuring Performance', *Policy and Politics*, Vol. 13, No. 1, pp. 1–15.

Ponting, C. (1985). *The Right to Know*, London and Sydney: Sphere.

Ponting, C. (1986). *Whitehall: Tragedy and Farce*, Hamish Hamilton Ltd.

Porter, L.W. and Lawler, E.E. (1968). *Managerial Attitudes and Performance*, Homewood, Illinois: Irwin Dorsey.

Potter, C. (1989). 'What Is Culture: And Can It Be Useful for Organisational Change Agents?', *Leadership and Organization Development Journal*, Vol. 10, No. 3, pp. 17–24.

Public Accounts Committee (1989). *The Next Steps Initiative*, London: HMSO.

Pugh, D.S. (ed.) (1984). *Organisation Theory: Selected Readings*, Harmondsworth: Penguin.

Rainey, H.G. (1983). 'Public Agencies and Private Firms', *Administration and Society*, Vol. 15, No. 2, pp. 207–42.

Redcliffe-Maud (1974). Prime Minister's Committee on Local Government Rules of Conduct: *Report of the Committee*, London: HMSO Cmnd 5636.

Rhodes, R.A.W. (1981). *Control and Power in Central-Local Relations*, Farnborough: Gower.

Rhodes, R.A.W. (1988). *Beyond Westminster and Whitehall: The Sub-Central Government of Britain*, London: Allen and Unwin.

Rhodes, R.A.W. and Midwinter, A.F. (1980). *Corporate Management: The New Conventional Wisdom in British Local Government*, Glasgow: University of Strathclyde – Studies in Public Policy No. 59.

Richards, S. (1989). 'Managing People in the Civil Service', *Public Money & Management*, Autumn, pp. 29–33.

Ridley, F.F. (1983). 'Career Service: A Comparative Perspective on Civil Service Promotion', *Public Administration*, Vol. 62(2), pp. 179–96.

RIPA (1985). 'The Search for Excellence in the Public Sector', *RIPA Report*, Vol. 6, No. 4, pp. 4–5.

RIPA (1988). 'New Approaches to Public Sector Staffing', *RIPA Report*, Vol. 9, No. 3, pp. 8–9.

Roberts, G. (1989). 'Impact of 1992 Starts to Bite', *Municipal Journal*, 3rd February, p. 14.

Roeber, R.J.C. (1973). *The Organisation in a Changing Environment*, Reading, Mass.: Addison-Wesley.

Roethlisberger, F.J. and Dickson, W.J. (1939). *Management and the Worker*, Cambridge, Mass: Harvard University Press.

Rose, R. (1987). *Ministers and Ministries: A Functional Approach*, Oxford: Clarendon Press.

Salmon (1976). Royal Commission on Standards of Conduct in Public Life: *Report*, London: HMSO Cmnd 6524.

Savage, S.P. and Robins, L. (eds) (1990). *Public Policy under Thatcher*, London: Macmillan.

Schein, E.H. (1987). *Organisational Culture and Leadership*, San Francisco: Josey-Bass.

Schmidt, M.G. (1983). 'The growth of the tax state: industrial democracies, 1950-1978', in Taylor, C.L. (ed.), *Why Governments Grow: Measuring public sector size*, London: Sage.

Schmitter, P.S. (1979). 'Modes of interest intermediation and models of societal change in Western Europe', *Comparative Political Studies*, Vol. 10(1), pp. 61–90.

Schumpeter, J. (1976). *Capitalism, Socialism and Democracy*, London: Allen and Unwin.

Sedgemore, B. (1980). *The Secret Constitution*, London: Hodder and Stoughton.

Seebohm, F. (1967). *Report of the Committee on Local Authority and Allied Personal Social Services*, London: HMSO Cmnd 3703.

Self, P. (1975). *Econocrats and the Policy Process: The politics and philosophy of cost-benefit analysis*, London: Macmillan.

Self, P. (1977). *Administrative Theories and Politics: An enquiry into the structure and processes of modern government*, London: Allen and Unwin.

Selznick, P. (1957). *Leadership in Administration*, New York: Harper and Row.

Sharplin, A. (1985). *Strategic Management*, New York: McGraw Hill.

Silverman, D. (1970). *The Theory of Organisations*, London: Heinemann.

Simon, H.A. (1976). *Administrative Behaviour: A Study of Decision-Making Processes in Administrative Organisation*, London: Collier Macmillan.

Simon, H.A., Smithburg D.W. and Thompson V.A. (1950). *Public Administration*, New York: Alfred A. Knopf.

Sisson, C.H. (1959). *The Spirit of Administration*, London: Faber and Faber.

Skeffington, A.M. (1969). *People and Planning: Report of the Committee on Public Participation in Planning*, London: HMSO.

Smith, B.C. (1988). *Bureaucracy and Political Power*, Brighton: Wheatsheaf.

Smith, G. (1981). 'Discretionary Decision-Making in Social Work', in Adler, M. and Asquith, S. (eds), *Discretion and Welfare*, London: Heinemann Educational Books.

Stanyer, J. and Smith, B. (1976). *Administering Britain*, London: Fontana.

Steers, R.M. and Porter, L.W. (1979). *Motivation and Work Behaviour*, New York: McGraw Hill.

Stephenson, T. (1985). *Management: A Political Activity*, London: Macmillan.

Stewart, D.W. and Carson, G.D. (1983). *Organizational Behaviour and Public Management*, New York and Basel: Marcel Dekker.

Stewart, J.D. (1980). 'From growth to standstill', in Wright, M. (ed.) *Public Spending Decisions*, London: Allen and Unwin.

Stewart, J.D. (1986). *The New Management of Local Government*, London: Allen and Unwin.

Stewart, J.D and Clarke, M. (1987). 'The Public Service Orientation: Issues and Dilemmas', *Public Administration*, Vol. 65, No. 2, pp. 161–77.

Stewart, J.D. and Walsh, K. (1990). *The Search for Quality*, Luton: Local Government Training Board.

Stewart, R. (1985). *The Reality of Organisations*, London: Macmillan.

Stewart, R. (1989). *Leading in the NHS: A Practical Guide*, London: Macmillan.

Stoker, G. (1988). *The Politics of Local Government*, London: Macmillan.

Stoker, G. (1989a). 'Urban Development Corporations: A review', *Regional Studies*, Vol. 23, No. 2, pp. 159–73.

Stoker, G. (1989b). 'Creating a Local Government for a Post-Fordist Society: The Thatcher Project', in Stoker, G. and Stewart, J. (eds), *The Future of Local Government*, London: Macmillan.

Stoker, G. and Wilson, D. (1986). 'Intra-Organisational Politics in Local Authorities: Towards a New Approach', *Public Administration*, Vol. 64, No. 3, pp. 285–302.

Stoker, G., Wedgewood-Oppenheim, F. and Davies, M. (1988). *The Challenge of Change in Local Government: A Study of Organisational and Management Innovation in the 1980s*, Birmingham: INLOGOV.

Storey, J. (1989). 'Human Resource Management in the Public Sector', *Public Money & Management*, Autumn, pp. 19–24.

Storey, J. and Sisson, K. (1990). 'Making Managers in Britain: A progress report', *Public Money & Management*, Spring, pp. 9–15.

Stringer, J. and Richardson, J. (1980). 'Making the Political Agenda', *Parliamentary Affairs*, Vol. 33, pp. 23–39.

Taylor, C.L. (1983). 'Introduction: multiple approaches to measurement and explanation', in Taylor, C.L. (ed.), *Why Governments Grow: Measuring public sector size*, London: Sage.

Taylor, F.W. (1967). *Principles of Scientific Management*, New York and London: W.W. Norton.

Taylor, J. and Rose, A. (1985). 'Debating Ethics in Government', *RIPA Report*, Vol. 6, No. 1, pp. 4–5.

Theakston, K. (1990). 'Labour, Thatcher and the Future of the Civil Service', *Public Policy and Administration*, Vol. 5, No. 1, pp. 44–57.

Thompson, D. (1986). *Coalition and Decision-Making within Health Districts*, University of Birmingham Health Services Management Centre: Research Report 23.

Thompson, D.F. (1983). 'Bureaucracy and Democracy', in Duncan, G. (ed.), *Democratic Theory and Practice*, Cambridge: Cambridge University Press.

Toffler, A. (1970). *Future Shock*, London: Bodley Head.

Tomkins, C. and Colville, I. (1989). 'Managing for Greater Innovation in the Civil Service: Customs & Excise', *Public Money & Management*, Winter, pp. 15–20.

Travers, T. (1986). *The Politics of Local Government Finance*, London: Allen and Unwin.

Travers, T. (1989). 'The Threat to the Autonomy of Elected Local Government', *The Political Quarterly*, pp. 3–20.

Treasury and Civil Service Committee (1982). Third Report: *Efficiency and Effectiveness in the Civil Service*, London: HMSO HC 236-I.

Treasury and Civil Service Committee (1990). Eighth Report: *Progress in the Next Steps Initiative*, London: HMSO HC 481.

Tyson, S. (1990). 'Turning Civil Servants into Managers', *Public Money & Management*, Spring, pp. 27–30.

Vickers, Sir G. (1965). *The Art of Judgement: A Study of Policy-Making*, London: Chapman and Hall.

Vroom, V.H. (1964). *Work and Motivation*, New York: John Wiley.

Vroom, V.H. and Deci, E.L. (eds) (1970). *Management and Motivation*, Harmondsworth: Penguin.

Warmington, A. (1983). 'Organisation Theory and Health Service Administration', in Allen, D. and Hughes, J.A. (eds), *Management for Health Service Administrators*, London: Pitman.

Wass, Sir D. (1983). 'The Public Service in Modern Society', *Public Administration*, Vol. 61, No. 1. pp. 7–20.

Watson, T.J. (1987). *Work, Sociology and Industry*, London: Routledge and Kegan Paul.

Weber, M. (1971). 'Legitimate Authority and Bureaucracy', in Pugh D.S. (ed.), *Organisation Theory: Selected Readings*, Harmondsworth: Penguin.

Wedgewood-Oppenheim, F. (1982). 'Monitoring and the planning cycle', in Leach, S. and Stewart, J. (eds.), *Approaches in Public Policy*, London: Allen and Unwin.

Widdecombe, D. (1986). *Committee of Inquiry into the Conduct of Local Authority Business*, London: HMSO, Cmnd 9797.

Wigley, D. (1989). 'Performance Review, Motivation and Organisational Culture', *Health Services Management*, December, pp. 252–5.

Wilding, R.W.L. (1979). 'The Professional Ethic of the Administrator', *Management Services in Government*, Vol. 34, No. 4, pp. 181–6.

Wilmott, P. (ed.) (1987). *Local Government Decentralisation and Community*, London: Policy Studies Institute.

Woodward, J. (1958). *Management and Technology*, London: HMSO.

Wright, P. (1987). *Spycatcher: The candid autobiography of a senior intelligence officer*, New York: Viking.

Wright, P.L. and Taylor, D.S. (1984). *Improving Leadership Performance*, London: Prentice-Hall.

Young, H. and Sloman, A. (1984). *But, Chancellor: An inquiry into the Treasury*, London: BBC.

Index

Public Sector Accounting
Rowan Jones and Maurice Pendlebury

Public Sector Accounting provides a comprehensive examination of the special issues concerning the public sector of the economy. A fully integrated approach is adopted, while giving a cohesive and structured exposition of the accounting and the auditing problems in public sector organisations. The book discusses why public sector accounting is different from accounting for business organisations and examines management accounting, financial accounting and auditing from a public sector perspective.

Examples from the whole range of public sector activities are integrated into the text to illustrate and clarify the issues involved. At the end of each chapter there are exercises which include questions from professional papers.

Written primarily for students of professional accountancy examinations and specialist degree courses, it is also relevant to anyone involved in the management of public sector organisations.

'. . . can be thoroughly recommended. . .' ACCA Students' Newsletter.

320pp   Paper   0 273 02930 4

Management and Organisational Behaviour
2nd edition
Laurie Mullins

This book is concerned with the structure and processes of organisations and the ways in which they interact with people who work in them. This is a managerial, as opposed to a sociological approach to organisational behaviour and it is designed to indicate ways in which organisational performance and effectiveness may be improved by the better use of human resources.

Management and Organisational Behaviour is essential reading for students of business or management at degree, postgraduate and post-experience level and for those on professional management courses. Practising managers and supervisors will also find this book useful.

A Lecturers' Guide is also available.

586pp   Paper   0 273 02985 1

M & E Handbook

Public Administration
Michael P Barber Revised by Roger Stacey

Recommended by the Institute of Purchasing and Supply this book is suitable for public administration students studying for the examinations of the Local Government Examinations Board, the Diploma of Public Administration from the University of London or relevant BTEC courses.

256pp   Paper   0 7121 1754 7